Identifying Citizens

D0905958

This book celebrates the lives of four small but special people, Hannah, Molly, Fin and Ezra. May their identities never be overshadowed by their identifications.

Identifying Citizens

ID Cards as Surveillance

DAVID LYON

polity

Copyright © David Lyon 2009

The right of David Lyon to be identified as Author of this Work has been asserted
in accordance with the UK Copyright Designs and Patents Act 1988.

First published in 2009 by Polity Press

Polity Press
65 Bridge Street
Cambridge CB2 1UR, UK

Polity Press
350 Main Street
Malden, MA 02148, USA

All rights reserved. Except for the quotation of short passages for the purpose
of criticism and review, no part of this publication may be reproduced, stored
in a retrieval system, or transmitted, in any form or by any means, electronic,
mechanical, photocopying, recording or otherwise, without the prior permission
of the publisher.

ISBN-13: 978-0-7456-4155-3
ISBN-13: 978-0-7456-4156-0 (pb)

A catalogue record for this book is available from the British Library.

Typeset in 11 on 13 pt Bembo by
Servis Filmsetting Limited, Stockport, Cheshire.
Printed and bound in the United States by Maple-Vale Books

The publisher has used its best endeavours to ensure that the URLs for external
websites referred to in this book are correct and active at the time of going to
press. However, the publisher has no responsibility for the websites and can make
no guarantee that a site will remain live or that the content is or will remain
appropriate.

Every effort has been made to trace all copyright holders, but if any have been
inadvertently overlooked the publisher will be pleased to include any necessary
credits in any subsequent reprint or edition.

For further information on Polity, visit our website: www.politybooks.com

Contents

Acknowledgements   vi

Introduction   1

1   Demanding Documents   19
2   Sorting Systems   39
3   Card Cartel   63
4   Stretched Screens   84
5   Body Badges   110
6   Cyber-Citizens   131

Notes   156
Bibliography   186
Index   202

Acknowledgements

For some time I have wanted to research and write in a focused way about identification systems, and so I am grateful for several opportunities that have helped me devote attention to this. Working with the Surveillance Project at Queen's University has provided both context and colleagues for studying ID systems, within groupings under the rubric of 'Globalization of Personal Data' (GPD) and, more recently, 'The New Transparency: Surveillance and Social Sorting' (affectionately known as 'NewT'). Each is funded by the Social Sciences and Humanities Research Council of Canada, to which I am indebted. A further boost came in the shape of a Killam Research Fellowship (2008-2010) that allows me to concentrate on questions of identification and of which this book is the first fruit.

A previous product of this research interest was the book *Playing the Identity Card: Surveillance, Security and Identification in Global Perspective* (Routledge, 2008), co-edited with my long-time research colleague Colin Bennett, under the GPD aegis. This contains a number of illuminating chapters from many countries around the world, some of which I have drawn upon in this present book, making it in some ways a companion volume. I also continue to work on this theme, partly in conjunction with another network of researchers, known as IdentiNet, funded by the Leverhulme Trust (UK) and led by Jane Caplan and Eddy Higgs.

The chapters of this present book have each seen the light of day in some prior context or format, at conferences and workshops, but also in earlier published versions from which these have been revised and expanded. Chapter 1 was originally prepared for a conference on 'Technologies of InSecurity' at the University of Oslo in 2007 and the version made for that occasion appears in a book of that title (Routledge, 2008) edited by Katja Franko Aas, Helene Oppen Grundhus and Heidi Mork Lomell. Chapter 2 has a pre-life in *TechnoCrime* (Willan, 2008) edited by Stéphane Leman-Langlois. The idea of the 'card cartel' was tested at the British Sociological Association meetings at the University of East London in 2007 and again at the International Sociological Association Forum in Barcelona in 2008. Much of chapter 5 appeared in an earlier form as an article entitled 'Biometrics, identification and surveillance' in *Bioethics*, 22:9, 499–508 (2008). I am grateful to that journal, the International Association of Bioethics and Blackwell Publishing for the use of this article. Finally, ideas for chapter 6 had their first public airing at a symposium on 'Technology and Democracy' arranged by Darin Barney at McGill University in 2006 and in another form at a conference on 'Surveillance and Democracy' organized by Kevin Haggerty and Minas Samatas at the University of Crete in 2008; proceedings of this latter conference, including my own contribution, are available in a book of the same name co-edited by the organizers (Routledge, 2009).

As well as thanking the thoughtful listeners and readers in those contexts, I must mention my gratitude to several others who have shown interest in this project and who have kindly read part or the whole of the text. These are Katja Franko Aas, Colin Bennett, Krista Boa, Ayse Ceyhan, Andrew Clement, Catarina Frois, Alex Galloway, Kevin Haggerty, Bob Pike, Charles Raab, Mark Salter, Nick Spencer, Irma van der Ploeg, Dean Wilson and Elia Zureik. Add to this Andrea Drugan, my unfailingly patient and positive editor at Polity Press, and the anonymous reader she engaged. Emily Smith, Research Associate at the Surveillance Project, has given generously as a researcher, reader and organizer. Of course, whatever blemishes and blunders remain are mine.

Family members are the most long-suffering of supporters, and I simply do not know where I would be without them. My mother, Jean, in her ninetieth year, takes a keen interest in my work, as do each of our children. Sue, my life-partner, is a constant source of succour and wisdom, without whom I could not do what I do, but who also helps me know when to stop doing it. The book itself, though born in the struggles of this generation, is dedicated lovingly to four members of the next.

Introduction

'Identities' float in the air, some of one's own choice but others
inflated and launched by those around, and one needs to be constantly
on the alert to defend the first against the second . . . .

Zygmunt Bauman[1]

'May I see some ID?' We hear this every day. It is so commonplace
that we take it for granted. But much hangs on what we produce.
Being able to enter some workplaces, or join the fast-track line
at the airport, or simply withdraw cash from an ATM – each of
these depends on having ID. Equally, without the right ID you
may be refused emergency medical attention, denied access to
a secure website, or turned away at the border. In this book I
offer an overview, a general guide to issues raised by the current
trend towards the production of 'new' ID systems and especially
national IDs. As the title suggests, the crucial connections are
between 'identification' processes and 'citizenship' and between
'ID cards' and 'surveillance'.

Citizens have always been identified, and in modern times this
has been rationalized with records of personal details such as birth
and residence, and sometimes with identification documents.
Today, however, ID cards containing microchips, biometrics and

other machine-readable features are being proposed and promoted, sometimes as 'national ID' systems. This involves connections to databases, enabling vastly expanded organizational access to personal data and, hence more surveillance. Not only are identification practices changing, innovations like machine-readable IDs and automated citizen access to government information help to alter the nature of citizenship itself.

The book explores the theme of 'identifying citizens' from a number of angles, historical, technical, political and sociological, with a view to showing why new ID systems raise urgent new questions for analysis, ethics and policy. We have made a world of global trade and consumption that depends heavily upon computer and communication technologies to organize and coordinate everyday life, and ID systems often contribute to its greater efficiency and convenience. But the same systems often replicate and sometimes exacerbate the inequalities and injustices of that world, and they do so in ways that are subtle and that may not be intended by their promoters. These are not the IDs of 'one's own choice' so much as those 'inflated and launched' by others, in Zygmunt Bauman's opening words above. So as well as investigating the rise of the ubiquitous ID, this book also offers critical tools for being 'constantly on the alert to defend the first against the second'.

Today's New IDs

Although I have never held a national ID card, I am asked from time to time for some proof of citizenship. I must include my Citizenship Card in the package when applying for a new passport, for instance. For crossing the border from Canada to the USA, my driver's licence used to suffice, but for most 'citizenship' purposes I would now have to produce a passport. The most obvious moment for citizenship checks is in airports, both on departing from and on arriving in a country. As well, one is often required to show a passport in foreign hotels. In Lebanon recently my passport was demanded at numerous internal military checkpoints, as it had been decades ago when I visited the old 'iron curtain' countries of Eastern Europe. So where and when might I need a 'national ID card'?

If I were a citizen of several dozen countries around the world[2] I would have to carry an ID as a matter of course. French citizens, for instance, assume that they must have their *papiers* with them, as they have since 1940. Although they differ internationally, identification documents would also be needed in countries as far apart as Argentina, South Africa or Taiwan. The list is a long one. The differences are important, however. An ID card may be carried with pride, indifference, reluctance or even fear, depending on the political conditions and the history of using such documents in the country in question. Whether they are compulsory or voluntary, required to be carried at all times or not, or valid for non-government purposes such as banking, also depends on local circumstance. In some countries, IDs are vital for upholding human rights.

But something new is happening. In many countries around the world, plans are afoot to create new national ID card systems either to replace existing non-electronic cards or to introduce a digital ID system from scratch. Such systems are developed in addition to passports, an issue that has proved contentious in some cases. In countries that have had no previous national ID, or at least have only had them at certain times, such as during war, attempts to develop such systems often experience a more bumpy ride than those for whom ID cards are more familiar. The bumpy ride has been felt in the UK and Australia, but also in Japan and Korea, for example. Of course, the variety of historical and cultural backgrounds must be borne in mind. In Japan, for example, establishing a national registry database preceded the issuing of cards. However, in Japan, as in China but unlike the situation in the UK or Australia, the development of national identification represents a shift away from traditional *household* forms of registration. Each factor makes a difference to the outcomes.

Even in countries like Canada or the USA, where there is comparatively high resistance to the idea of a 'national ID',[3] close correlates based on drivers' licences are under development. The US 'Real ID' programme, launched in 2005, is a case in point, but parallel programmes – literally, in the sense that they may well be interoperable with the US systems – are emerging in Canadian provinces such as Quebec, Ontario and British Columbia, where 'enhanced drivers' licences' (EDLs) are under discussion. They contain vital citizenship information, similar to some of the data that would appear in a national ID, and may be used as passport substitutes for crossing the US–Canada border.

Neither drivers' licences nor passports are used by everyone, however. In the USA, holding a drivers' licence is so commonplace that they often serve as a *de facto* ID.[4] But non–drivers exist. The passport is another important modern form of identification also connected directly to increasing rates of mobility in the twentieth century (though their antecedents appeared in the nineteenth century and even earlier) and also to the modern emphasis on nation-state territories.[5] While 80 per cent of British people carry passports, only about 40 per cent of Canadians carry them and less than 30 per cent of Americans do, for example. Now, drivers' licences and passports are tremendously significant forms of identification, but the intended purpose of 'national' ID systems, to identify complete populations of given nation-states, makes these systems more comprehensive and correspondingly consequential.

Identification is the starting point of surveillance. This is true of all forms of surveillance, whether consumers, workers, travellers, offenders or citizens. But as far as the latter are concerned, counting, monitoring and documenting citizens is a fundamental form of state power and technologies for achieving this – from papyrus through print to today's searchable databases – make quite a difference to the reach and effectiveness of that power. The identification systems emerging in the present, enabled by biometrics and radio frequency identification (RFID), offer some distinct advantages in terms of efficiency and accuracy in some contexts, but they also raise questions that go beyond those asked of the bureaucratic and paper file systems, and of passports, that preceded them.

At the same time, identifying citizens is a key theme of twenty-first-century life. It is crucial to keep this broad context in mind. In order to make transactions, to communicate or to travel, ID documents are usually required. You need a driver's licence to drive, a credit card to purchase goods and services, a health card for medical treatment and a passport to cross borders. In most social spheres – touching education, employment, government, entertainment, commerce, and so on – personal identifiable information is routinely registered. It is on the record. A general social process that Nikolas Rose calls the 'securitizing of identity' requires all of us to prove legitimate identity in order to exercise freedom.[6] New kinds of identification systems – including national ID cards – may turn out to be the single most significant development of information systems for governance across the globe.

Of course, the very advent of modern forms of citizenship assumes identification.[7] In modern times, bureaucratic administration demands that all individuals be identified to ensure that they are entitled to call themselves citizens. Without identification one can neither take on the responsibilities of citizenship, such as voting, nor enjoy the benefits, such as protection from external or internal threats to well-being. Most inhabitants of contemporary liberal democracies assume both that the state will tax them, using some unique identification device to ensure that records match their income and circumstances, and that proof of citizenship will count for access to education or legal assistance.

In the twenty-first century, and especially since the massive jolt felt by the USA and others on 9/11, identification and surveillance are in an increasingly close alliance. As Ayse Ceyhan indicates, this is largely due to the fact not only that 'security technologies' are deployed to 'identify' people from their actions, relationships, tastes and preferences, but also that surveillance entails such identification (based on habits, behaviours and movements).[8] However, as we shall see, this connection is at the same time administrative and commercial. 'Security technologies' are perhaps the most publicly prevalent manifestation of a trend that also encompasses more mundane processes of internet use, government service provision and consumer advertising.

All these factors help to make clearer the identification–surveillance connection. At its simplest, surveillance happens when organizations pay close attention, in routine and systematic ways, to personal data. In the case of national ID cards, the organizations in question are government departments, whose purposes, variously, are to enhance administrative efficiency, ensure that benefits and services go to the right people, facilitate law enforcement and national security, and so on. While national ID systems have always had an important surveillance dimension, the surveillance capacities of new digital systems represent a quantum leap compared with older paper-based file techniques. To understand this, we must ask exactly what comprises the emerging systems.

What are ID Cards?

Basically, ID cards serve to associate data with a particular person. They enable access to data held in files (the registry) and they are modified by new data coming in from transactions and interactions. The cards themselves facilitate interactions between the organization – employer, bank, government department or whatever – and the individual. Normally, this also involves the person concerned by checking their knowledge, for instance with a PIN (personal identification number), and some bodily feature, usually a fingerprint but possibly other biometrics.[9] A 'national' ID card system associates citizenship data with a specific person to verify, say, that he or she has residency rights, or is eligible for welfare benefits, or may vote in a general election.

Technically, ID cards come in many types and carry a range of data. Needless to say, the technologies are constantly changing and so card systems are deliberately built as 'platforms'. Platforms offer a base on which to construct a variety of applications and services, and while these often refer to the hardware and software, they are inextricably bound up as well with what users – in the case of national IDs this usually means government departments – expect of the system. As we shall see, ID card systems have certain common features, but they also vary considerably in terms of technological sophistication and style. Finland has a smart ID card, for instance, using identifiers – 'Citizen Certificates' – issued by the Population Register Centre, that may be used for various kinds of commercial transactions as well as for filing taxes or voting in elections. Unlike some other systems, however, the Citizen Certificate may be attached to a mobile device SIM card or a Visa Electron (bank) card.

Perhaps the biggest cause of confusion about ID card systems today arises around the term 'citizenship data'. Policy statements, media coverage and thus public focus tend to be on the cards themselves – What is on them? Are they secure? When must they be produced? But the real issues lie in the card components that are hardest to visualize, because they are 'virtual': the databases. Although the term 'ID cards' is used as a shorthand in this book, it must never be forgotten that today's 'new' ID cards are ID *systems* based on the use of networked, searchable databases. These are what make them 'work' and these are what supply their stretched surveillance power. National registry databases and their equivalents are used both to ensure that facts about citizens are correctly recorded and updated (which may be reassuring) and that treatment accorded to those in the databases is appropriate to the categories in which they fall (which may be risky, at least for some).

How far ID cards are 'reassuring or risky' is one of the main questions that this book explores. In the twenty-first century, identification processes are changing shape in radical ways that take them far beyond what might have been experienced even a couple of decades ago. It is not just a matter of changing technologies, although the changes are unthinkable without searchable databases and networked communications. Nor is it merely that in the political-economic restructuring of the last three decades nation-states are more attuned to security than to welfare and that outsourcing has made technology companies very significant players in the security and surveillance field, though these factors are tremendously important too. And neither can such changes be put down only to today's accelerating processes of globalization, where higher rates of mobility create new challenges for the identification of citizens, consumers and workers within and across national borders.

Each of these factors is complex and the threads have to be unravelled. The technologies do not have 'effects' on their own, for example, but once deployed their use starts to shape everyday behaviours and outlooks. New forms of accountability emerge with digital transactions, and people in different age groups respond differently to electronic communications.[10] Moreover, while political-economic restructuring and the shift from 'welfare' to 'security' priorities among governments does make technology companies more significant players than previously, there is also a persistent underlying cultural belief in the power of technology to solve problems that must also be recognized. Globalization, too, is far from simple. Growing mobility does raise identification issues, but it does so very unevenly, with quite different 'solutions' proposed in different places and for different groups.

All these factors and others are prompting new developments in identification that appear in administrative, law-enforcement and commercial forms and each of them may be located along a 'risk-to-reassurance' continuum. Even this oversimplifies things, however, as the 'continuum' itself is read differently by different people, and something as complex as an ID card may prompt several different responses simultaneously. One key reason for this is confusion about concepts and processes of identity and identification, especially in relation to 'citizens' and 'the state'. Terms are bandied about, often carelessly, when the nuances of meaning are actually profound. Even 'ID card' is often read as 'identity card', when it would be much more accurate and clear – though not more concise – to call it an 'identification card'.

Identity and Identification

When a young-looking person goes into a bar, she may well be 'asked for ID' and everyone knows that in fact some 'proof of age' is all that is required. Has this person reached the legal age for ordering drinks? A card, most likely a drivers' licence, with a photo and date of birth will do the trick. The 'ID' here is 'identification'. However, suppose that the same person is attending a meeting in the bar, at which introductions are called for. 'My name is Amanda, but everyone calls me Mandy,' she begins. 'My family name is Tarasios, which is actually a Ukrainian name with Greek and Russian connections. I think of myself as Ukrainian, even though I've lived here for a long time. And I identify as an Orthodox believer.' This *self*-identification is all about identity and is deeply relational in character.

The name, the personal story, the commitments to place and to persons, these are the stuff of identity. Overlapping these but for different purposes are the instruments of identification, now including digital ID systems. In Portugal, to take one case, while new parents give their baby a name – as is common from time immemorial – at the same time the state now issues a number to be used when the child obtains a first citizenship document at age six. This grants access to things like health and welfare benefits, but also means that an electronic record of medical and other data is initiated. While the parents bestow the name, it soon becomes part of the baby's identity. The identification done by the state, however, is more remote, involving people, organizations and systems that the baby will never know. It is formal, abstract and may even be in tension with 'identity'.

These are seemingly commonsense distinctions, but failure to make them causes many difficulties in discussions of ID cards. More significantly, failure to uphold the importance of each item – identity and identification – and to note the necessary interactions between them has personal and social consequences that may be distressing or worse. There is no way of proving this, but part of the difficulty lies in the fact that the English word 'identification' is a six-syllable abstract noun and 'identity' is easier to say. Why else would computer scientists – and now, as we shall see, others as well – talk of 'identity management' to refer to ways of managing user credentials for logging in to online systems? What is called 'identity' here has to do with user IDs, passwords and codes, and, when embedded in e-Government public service provision, with internet protocol (IP) numbers, caller IDs, email addresses, motor vehicle registrations, and the like. These are 'identifiers' used for 'identification' and are at best proxies for 'identity'.[11]

If one starts with the views of Erving Goffman, then the self – the core identity, so to speak – is forever being 'presented' in everyday life. But from hairstyle to nickname there may be ways of controlling or at least influencing the impressions given to others.[12] So self-expression contributes to identity. Goffman was writing in a pre-popular computer era, however, and although some 'identity management' schemes (such as those proposed in the UK Crosby Report in 2008,[13] which uses the language of 'identity assurance' rather than 'identity management') are directed towards permitting a degree of control over how one's personal data are used, the strong trend, described in this book, is in the opposite direction. Organizational identification is a crucial means of governance in many spheres of life, not least using ID card systems.

This is why it is really imperative that clear distinctions be made – particularly between identity and identification – so that the high stakes may be seen for what they are. But even here, matters are far from simple. Public ire has been hot in the UK over the 2006 Identity Cards Act, among other things because of its association with 'anti-terror' measures. The Belgian e-ID Card, on the other hand, introduced both as an 'e-Government' application and enabler, and as a means of participating in online transactions, seems to have evaded much public criticism, even though it is vulnerable to many of the same objections as the UK ID Card.[14] So what makes the difference? In the end, no doubt, the cards will come to resemble each other more in routine daily use, even though public perceptions of their advent differ.

Gary Marx suggests that how the official use of personal data (as in an ID card) is viewed depends heavily on what sorts of data are in question. The worst case, he says, is when 'core identity [names and the like], a locatable person, and information that is personal, private, intimate, sensitive, stigmatizing, strategically valuable, extensive, biological, naturalistic, and predictive and reveals deception, is attached to the person, and involves an enduring and unalterable documentary record'.[15] He proposes that information about a person be seen as a series of concentric circles, with 'core identity' at the centre, moving outwards through 'unique identification', 'sensitive or intimate information' and 'private information', and with 'individual information' on the outer rim.

No wonder identity, or 'personal identity', is such a notoriously difficult concept to define, especially in relation to computer systems. As Charles Raab points out, data protection law often assumes, in a somewhat circular manner, that 'personal data' refer to 'an identified or identifiable natural person'.[16] So identity would seem to be a composite and malleable entity, with some elements derived from the corporeal person and others from categories or collectivities in which they fit. The concept of 'identity' in the UK Identity Cards Act, observes Raab, intensifies the problem by hanging identity on certain 'registrable facts' or 'personal information' as distinct from

'identifying information' such as a photograph, signature, fingerprint or other biometric. So the state, through legal language and
by authoritatively choosing the descriptive categories, says 'you are
who we say you are'.[17] Not surprisingly, this may raise eyebrows,
if not hackles.

That said, while the distinction between identity and identification is important, it is just that, a distinction. The two ideas also
must be seen in relation to each other. The difference between how
I identify myself and how I am identified by others – or, today, how
a machine system might identify me – is worth maintaining, but it
can never be an absolute distinction. The one depends on the other.
If all the emphasis is on 'identities' as modes of self-expression and
as ways of saying who we're related to and 'identify with', it will
be easy to forget the massive effects of identification as *categorization*
in the modern world. But if this latter dimension is dominant, then
the subtle significance of stories about one's self, one's origins and
aspirations may well be lost.[18]

Identities, Identification and the Other

In this book, identification practices and 'Others' are closely connected. The interaction and indeed mutual dependence of identity
and identification is actually a reminder of the profoundly social
character of human beings. Who we are cannot be spliced out
from our relationships with many other people, whether parents,
priests or publishers; teachers, TV stars or tennis players. Identity
is forged from molten metals of many kinds that flow into who
we become and how we think of ourselves. Even that metaphor
is limited, however, because identity is dynamic and malleable, in
part through its encounter with identifications. Which is a segue
into giving some clues about the underlying perspective of this
work.

The main message of the book is to show how identifying
citizens entails surveillance, especially where new electronic ID
cards are introduced. Surveillance is seen as soon as we are made
aware that massive population registries are required to make an ID

card system function and that this involves networked, searchable databases. As in all such networks, connection and disconnection happen all the time. But this has crucial consequences for some population groups – 'Others' – especially at times when normal rules have been suspended in the name of national security.[19] So who gets connected and who disconnected, or who is included as a 'citizen' and who is excluded from citizenship in fact or in practice, is an urgent question for those trying to understand ID card systems.

The question of 'core identity', discussed in the previous section, is from a personal point of view most likely to be defended by those who feel that national ID cards – and some other IDs as well – carry risks from which they would like to be protected. That sense of 'who we are' relates to family ties, to community bonds, to special places, and even, of course, to how we relate to animals, or to God.[20] No wonder it sometimes collides with the attempts of others – not to mention organizations or machines – to 'identify' us. Stepping back from the surveillance question for a moment, let me make a few basic observations about identity.

At its heart, identity is a relational concept. This book attempts to avoid the sterile debates between 'constructed' and 'imposed' identities (even though elements of 'construction' and 'imposition' are unavoidable) and between the supposedly 'stable' identities of modern times and the 'fluid' identities of the postmodern. Whatever constitutes a 'core identity', it can never be an isolated human operating alone. And however it appears today, it may have altered by tomorrow. Identities always involve others, and never remain the same. They are negotiated and evolve in ongoing ways through interaction with others. Identities cannot be reduced to rules; they are too dynamic to be defined in a permanent way. As I shall suggest, following Miroslav Volf, identities appear on a wider canvas of relationships. They are bound to be affected, for better or for worse, by identifications, but what frames them is the quality of relationships. In the world of ID cards, as in the world of ethnic conflict analysed socio-theologically by Volf, the real choices are between exclusion and embrace.[21]

The fact that I start from a critical point of view does not mean that this book is unmitigated in its critique of ID cards. Indeed, as with so much surveillance,[22] ID card systems are ambiguous. They are the product of a world of modernity, now 'liquid' and 'light' according to Zygmunt Bauman,[23] that appears to 'need' IDs to function effectively. In order to use the internet or to engage in banking or even education today, some identification system is essential. The difficulty is that ID systems are built on a bureaucratic base that already distances itself from the ordinary lives of real people, and this distancing process is compounded by electronic networks that are invisible and little understood by those ordinary people (I include my readers and myself here). In the process we lose sight of each other's faces and can no longer hear each other's voices. I should stress that I do not for a moment discount the possibility of creating ID systems that are both efficient and secure as well as strictly limited in scope and that actually protect those whose data reside in the databases.[24]

Why should they need 'protection'? Well, all technological systems, in my view, should meet the social-ethical requirement of at least doing no harm and at best fostering fulfilled and flourishing human life. As Ayse Ceyhan reminds us, no technology may be reduced to a mere technical, scientific or symbolic device.[25] All technologies are human activities, and so, as Heidegger proposed, we have to explore both the kinds of activities technologies reveal and the character of the ends to which they are means. But we also have to explore the contexts in which they appear. Ceyhan is right again: ID cards in particular should be seen in the context of the uncertainties and anxieties of liquid modern times, in global risk societies and the transformations of violence epitomized by the 9/11 attacks.[26] This means that particular vulnerable groups should indeed be protected.

These vulnerable groups may be considered as 'Others'. The concept of the 'Other' (capital O) is taken from the work of Emmanuel Levinas,[27] where he distinguishes between other people in general, in the mass (other = *autre*), and those whose otherness is radical, who are quite distinctively different (Other = *autrui*). This is the kind of usage adopted here. As a philosopher of ethics, Levinas goes on to argue that human beings only discover who they are by seeing the Other and by putting the Other first (which echoes both ancient Jewish and Christian ethics). He argues that western thought tends to absorb or subsume the Other into others-in-general and resists this by focusing on the 'face' of the Other as a means of getting to know, rather than merely to know about, the other person.

Indeed, according to Alfred Schütz, all too often we only know others as types or categories,[28] which is exactly how ID systems work too. This is why, as Charles Taylor would say, the 'politics of difference' is so important. The post-Second World War generation was raised on the modern 'politics of equal dignity', which is fine as far as it goes. In a more globalized world, Taylor would say, recognizing *unique* identities of groups and individuals is important to avoid assimilation, where someone – say, a guestworker (*Gastarbeiter*) from Turkey in Germany – may be caught in what he calls a 'false, distorted, and reduced mode of being'.[29] The relationships in which such identities are caught are skewed, unjust.

Whatever the specific rationale given for introducing ID cards – entitlement to state benefits, ease of travel or transaction, safeguard against 'identity theft' or crime control – it is those based in regulating immigration or anti-terrorism that present most acutely the risks to Others. The idea of 'national' ID cards, resting on some notion of 'national' identity, may be traced back to nineteenth-century efforts to create a popular fiction that would unite people within the territories where states ruled. Being born somewhere came to be equated with membership of a community for which the state would take responsibility, and also 'define, classify, segregate, separate and select'.[30] In other words, as Giorgio Agamben insists, the sovereign state drew, tightened and policed the boundary between 'us' and 'them'.[31]

The considerable complication to this today, with the world's liquid, global and mobile features, is that people flow across old borders, sometimes in trickles, sometimes in tides, but always seeping into or swamping over ingrained ideas of the 'national'. Those who for whatever reason do not fit find themselves exposed, precarious. This is where the ethic of the Other meets ID systems. It asks that the faces and the stories of Others not be hidden and unheard in the struggle to rationalize and regulate those global currents, eddies and swirls. It hints, hopefully, that the disingenuous 'embrace' of the state be replaced with a risky, self-giving 'embrace' of the Other.[32] It is a tough call, especially when governments play the cards of fear and suspicion and companies sell their cards as the means of consumption and convenience. But if we discover our very humanity in being there for the Other, then the alternatives are less than human, or dehumanizing. Later chapters will show more of what I mean.

Identifying Citizens

Here is a road map to help you on your fairly brief journey through this book. I start by tracing some historical background. In a short book this is necessarily suggestive rather than exhaustive. I show how identification systems have been associated especially with nation-state administration in general ways – for taxation, to take an obvious example – but frequently also for colonial, conscription and crime-control purposes. This in turn suggests some key continuities between earlier systems and contemporary ones, continuities that deserve not to be overlooked in the haste to see today's high-tech ID card systems as predominantly 'new'.

The nature of the 'newness' of digital IDs is explored in chapter 2. Here, one of the key characteristics of 'ID cards as surveillance' – social sorting – is teased out. A few moments ago I observed that surveillance, including that based on ID card systems, enables discrimination between different groups and categories of citizen. Now, searchable databases and software protocols deepen this dimension of IDs. Much surveillance-power hangs on the growing computer-assisted capacity of 'social sorting'.[33] Its clear benefits include greater sophistication in placing citizens in appropriate categories, such that they can indeed take full advantage of their rights and privileges, so that prized values such as fairness or equality before the law may be maintained. At the same time, it is precisely such social sorting that can produce opposite results from those desired by most citizens: to discriminate unfairly or according to opaque criteria, in ways that are likely to disadvantage in particular those who are already socially marginalized.

The consequences for citizens of new IDs certainly cannot be read off the new technologies, vital though their influence is. So chapter 3 introduces a new theory for understanding identification practices today – the 'card cartel' More cumbersomely, this translates as the 'oligopolization of the means of identification'. As we have already seen, the national registry database is the crucial – but often ignored – factor in new IDs. Such databases are created not only by government departments but also by other agencies. In many cases, they are multi-purpose cards, which means that more than one government department and even corporate and other entities are pulled into the picture.

In Finland, for example, citizenship data and health information are on the same card. Despite technical and legal limits on information exchange, the increased capacity for data sharing is itself significant. One implication is that questions arising cannot be reduced to some notion of 'state-and-citizen'. Both categories are mutating and being both diminished and augmented in significant ways. For instance, the 'state' relies increasingly on companies and softwares that code the data in particular ways, often relating to the demands of 'risk management', and this produces categories of 'citizen' and 'non-citizen' that are ambiguously framed.[34]

Another way that the notion of state-and-citizen must be rethought relates to the global context of new IDs. While the impression may be given by the production of 'national' IDs that single nation-states are involved with identification, in fact their production is also being globalized. The language of 'interoperability' is often heard (authorities want enhanced drivers' licences to work across North America, for example, or for national IDs to be checkable throughout the European Union). To help us explore this, we meet the metaphor of 'stretched screens' in chapter 4, which expresses this expansion of identification between as well as within countries. Both elements of the metaphor have double meanings here: firstly, in that screens are 'stretched' both widely (their geographical reach) and deeply (in terms of plumbing the depths of personal data); and, secondly, because the computer 'screens' stand for the enhanced technologies and also for the more granular 'screening' that they enable.

The idea that personal data go deeper and deeper today is pursued further in chapter 5, where we examine what I call 'body badges'. At a very intimate level, the means of identification is sought in unique body characteristics. Biometrics is increasingly providing the tools for what is claimed to be accurate identification and verification, including in new IDs.[35] It was the UK EU presidency that proposed a fingerprint biometric in 2005 that would be standard throughout the EU and would involve the creation of a very large database.[36] The iris scan machines used for airport passenger security checks are another obvious example of verification using bodily features, but even DNA data are being sought for some purposes, for example in terrorist or criminal cases involving an EU country and the USA.[37] This means that the line between technology and the body is blurring; identities are defined in terms of bodily features – a fingerprint or a facial image – captured in an algorithm. The implications of this are manifold. For instance, the body itself becomes a text or at least a code. And the objectified body is assumed to offer superior information than that which might be presented in a verbal dialogue such as an interview.

Finally, the book wraps up in chapter 6 by returning to the basic question of what new IDs mean for citizenship. As we have argued, new IDs have everything to do with surveillance and thus also with power, governance and democracy. They are products of, but also agents of, changing conceptions of what it means to be a citizen. In contrast with the situation obtaining in North America and much of Europe in the middle of the twentieth century, when citizenship struggles were for social equality, today they are about cultural identity and the recognition of group difference. Indeed, as Selya Benhabib observes, this strains the edges of the 'national citizenship' envelope, as new ways are needed for 'incorporating aliens and strangers, immigrants and newcomers, refugees and asylum seekers, into existing polities'.[38]

Earlier forms of what might be termed 'welfare state' citizenship aimed at *inclusion*, legally, politically and economically. And although by definition any attempt to say who is included assumes that some are excluded, today's modes of citizenship, as represented by ID card regimes, are aimed at the *exclusion* of certain proscribed groups. These are the 'usual suspects' of illegal immigrants, welfare cheats, criminals and would-be terrorists. Deciding exactly who these 'others' are and how to identify, categorize and ban them or limit their movements is a key task within new ID schemes. The consequential means may be technically novel, but do the ends not seem strikingly similar to those of historical ID practices – colonialism, crime control and war measures? We shall see.

1

Demanding Documents

The close association of citizenship and identity papers that we take for granted today was not enforced until the early twentieth century.

Valentin Groebner[1]

To demand production of the card from all and sundry is wholly unreasonable.

Acting Lord Chief Justice Goddard[2]

Among the more offbeat items appearing on the American Public Broadcasting Service's *Antiques Roadshow* are slave tags. The little tin badges, which slaves were once obliged to wear, have become collectors' items. They indicate the year the tag was made, the occupation of the slave, such as 'house servant', and an ID number corresponding to one stored at the local treasurer's office. In South Carolina, where many may be found, black slaves often escaped from their white masters. A suspect could be asked to display his or her tag to distinguish local slaves from runaways. A misshapen disc, rather than a document, was demanded.

Now, collecting such slave tags as antiques is not uncontroversial. Some object that this amounts to further exploitation of past pain. Collectors defend the practices, however, claiming them as 'an inspiring testimony to the strength of human spirit in the face of seemingly overwhelming adversity',[3] To preserve these artefacts is to learn from the past and to help prevent such atrocities happening again, they say. Without entering this particular debate, it is worth observing that contemporary controversies over identification are frequently marked by their lack of historical sense. The purpose of knowing about past identification practices and of seeing reminders of their demeaning, destructive and dignity-destroying possibilities is not to tar today's initiatives with the same brush so much as to strive to ensure that such egregious errors are not repeated.

Today's ID cards have genealogies that can be traced back to several historical sources. As well as the evolution of general state administration, especially for taxation purposes, identification is historically important for colonialism, conscription and crime control. Genealogies, as understood by Michel Foucault, are both successful and failed schemes, on the one hand, and local knowledge and experiences, on the other, that may throw light on present-day developments.[4] Much may be learned from the history of the quest for stable IDs in the modern world that applies to the continuing story in the present.

National identification systems, based on some kind of card or booklet, have existed for a long time, though they were limited initiatives at first. The origins of the modern state system in Europe between 1400 and 1600 signalled the start of administrative schemes for authenticating and identifying individuals.[5] Couriers, for instance, were obliged to indicate that they were legitimate carriers of messages by wearing special insignia or badges. Certain people, such as Gypsies, were assumed to be carrying false identities in the mid-1500s because illegitimate persons could not have legitimate ID. (This particular example has not gone away, yet. In 2008 a highly contentious plan to fingerprint Italian Gypsies – 'Roma' – camping on the edges of cities was extensively modified when the government decided to add fingerprints for everyone to the national ID card.[6])

Pilgrims and diplomats also had to wear insignia or carry passes, which tended to be largely graphic so that authorities could recognize signs with ease. In sixteenth-century Cologne and Freiburg, beggars were required to change the dates and serial numbers on their badges in order to control copying. Increasingly, weight was placed on the written descriptions of physical characteristics ('permanent distinguishing marks' of today's passports) such that names and faces could be linked at least loosely.

After the French Revolution, citizenship came to be associated with registration and eventually with *les papiers*, and by the twentieth century – as Caplan and Torpey's *Documenting Individual Identity*[7] shows – a number of schemes for national identity cards had been discussed in places as far apart as Argentina[8] and the UK. In the latter, registries were set up and cards issued as early as 1915 and, more successfully, in 1939.[9] Meanwhile, of course, passports for international travel became commonplace. But passports, by definition, are for travellers who wish to cross national borders. The intent of most national ID schemes today is eventually to cover entire populations.

It is important to note that many identification systems were at first partial, designed to control specific segments of the population defined as 'suspect' and potentially beyond the reach of the state. Curiously, the cases of crime control and colonialism are closely linked, as we shall see. The early use of fingerprinting in British India was used in the solution of murders, but also to reduce risks of violence in the 'indigo disturbances' of the 1860s, in which peasants revolted at the British monopoly of dye production for use in English textiles. (Mahatma Gandhi would champion this cause in 1917.) Limited uses in colonial control or in the police tracking of recidivists marked early uses of fingerprints, but, once established, fingerprinting for identification was to expand steadily.[10]

What links early and later efforts to provide stable identification systems is the demand for documents, to discover some reliable means of distinguishing the one from the many and of sorting the alien from the citizen or the imposter from the genuine. This is prompted partly by new travel possibilities, which produce visitors not known through routine face-to-face contact. It was clearly the case that in early modern Europe the mobility of both messengers and migrant groups created problems for which identification documents were the official response, but the demand for ID documents went well beyond this. It is the official demand for documents of personal identity, for a range of related reasons, that links today's quest for new IDs with earlier practices. Without an historical perspective, ID systems may appear as a novel development, whereas in fact the continuities are quite striking.

Travel is one important factor. Modern modes of transport and communication permit travel of many kinds and for many purposes, but the proportion of populations that can travel and the processes of travel themselves have multiplied immensely since early modern days when transport and communication were still vitally linked. Formerly, communication depended on transport – the horse or ship that enabled the message to be transmitted – but the invention of the telegraph split these two apart.[11] Communication could occur without transport. However, there is a sense in which the relation has not disappeared so much as reversed. In a world of new technologies, transport now depends on communication. One cannot travel far without having to produce some marker or message that identifies and situates the traveller. Today, the information communicated often comes directly from the body of the traveller.

In what follows, I trace some identification efforts aimed at making citizens more 'legible'[12] within the 'embrace'[13] of the state and show how these have historically had to do with colonial administration, crime control and the exigencies of war.[14] They have to do with both travel and transactions. The quest for security and certainty of identification has had ambiguous results. While administrative efficiency is sometimes enhanced, new kinds of insecurities and uncertainties may also appear that have on occasion placed bloody blights on human history. The certainties sought often involve clear categorization – the imposition of classifications – that has facilitated the sorting of actual populations, not merely for determining entitlements, but for inclusion and exclusion, and even for mass murder and genocide.

Identification and the Legibility of Citizens

One process that distinguishes the modern nation-state as such is the official attention accorded to individual details as part of the embrace of the individual by the state. John Torpey uses embrace in the sense of 'grasping' or 'registering' citizens in ways that both include and exclude particular persons.[15] In the telling trope used by James Scott, such an embrace – to mix metaphors – made citizens more legible to the state and this in turn depended on both rising literacy and the growth of official records.[16] However, it should also be noted that although the embrace of the state or the greater legibility of citizens may have deleterious effects, for example, on levels of public trust, identifying citizens may also be the means of ensuring their entitlements and their rights.

Improving citizens' legibility may be undertaken for all kinds of reasons. In 1666 a detailed census was taken in New France, the first such census in North America. Undertaken by French colonial authorities in part of what was to become Canada, it was largely for taxation purposes, but also to initiate an incentive scheme to encourage families to have more children.[17] Making citizens legible would increase not only revenue but also reproduction, it seems. John Torpey, in his work on the passport,[18] insightfully shows how identification could help to create a monopoly on the means of movement. However, nation-states also document identities in order to mobilize economic resources through taxation, to redistribute resources to citizens in need through welfare programmes and also through health and education, and finally to maintain peace and order.[19] The latter refers both to external threats from other powers and to internal ones from rebellion, violence or crime. It is important to note that each initiative has a stake in adequate documentary identification and the parallel monitoring of populations. Identification has several interlinked purposes.

One of the most ancient reasons for registration and identification was to facilitate the taxing of citizens by the state and, conversely, to ensure that those eligible for state benefits received that to which they were entitled. Worlds touched by Christianity have no difficulty recalling that Jesus' own birth coincided with a major tax-related registration under Roman rule. The Romans also used *tesserae* (marked bone or ivory rods) to identify slaves, soldiers and citizens in relation to financial transactions. In ancient China, 656-221 BC, tax and registration occurred in relation to war-making,[20] and similar systems existed in Greece and, even earlier, around 2500 BC, in Sumer. In Crete, perhaps 4,000 years ago, cylinder seals were used to create personal identification devices worn as a stamp or a button in necklaces or bracelets and generally formed from clay.[21] While these were used to distinguish their bearers, for example by ensuring they were worn in burial chambers at death, it is not clear if they had official status.

Historians have little to say about identification processes in the ancient world, presumably because it was assumed in relatively fixed, local settings with little travel opportunity that by and large people were known to each other for most practical purposes. In early modern times things started to change, although even then such change was very slow and limited. As Edward Higgs has shown,[22] identification systems appeared as part of a long-term, uneven process of rationalizing state activities in more modern times, and these were generally expanded as needs arose and new techniques were produced that could make them more administratively efficient. Births, marriages and deaths, once locally registered in European or North American parishes, gradually became a state function. Such data would eventually become basic 'breeder' documents from which to create others.

Part of the problem was that in some cases surnames (or 'family' names), the basic ingredient of any identification system, were not always stable. Many nineteenth-century immigrants to the USA and Canada, for instance, had no permanent surnames on arrival.[23] Earlier cases of identification marks related not so much to immigration as to indigent people whose impoverished circumstances obliged them to move in search of sustenance. Though, for example, there were early cases of internal passports in sixteenth-century England, where the poor or vagabonds had to wear badges, this system did not last or develop.[24]

By the mid-twentieth century, citizenship – which involved registration but not necessarily a card carried on the person – had, as T.H. Marshall argued,[25] expanded to include not only legal and political rights but economic and social ones as well. Marshall's studies of citizenship offer some important insights that still have a bearing on today's world, globalization and neo-conservative restructuring notwithstanding.[26] One may query Marshall's account of citizenship in its details, criticize it for paying insufficient attention to the role of possessive individualism,[27] or acknowledge its need for updating for twenty-first-century situations. But, importantly, he showed that the ways in which citizenship operated in Western Europe and North America were broadly beneficial. It incorporated populations within inclusive societies that institutionalized a variety of rights and duties. At the same time, while such processes appeared congenial to majority populations, the growth of citizenship was not in all ways even and fair, and indeed was contested periodically. And, of course, documentary identification is required for each kind of citizenship right to be exercised effectively.

Gérard Noiriel writes about the *révolution identificatoire*[28] that produced various cards and codes for state identification purposes in the nineteenth century. These may have had a positive effect on those qualifying straightforwardly as citizens of France, but the use of such markers is also bound to cut both ways: the embrace of the state includes some but excludes others. Noiriel's analysis of the rise of the identity card in France and the treatment of foreigners based on certain methods of identification shows how social context and technology both play a role in producing a need for national identification. That such identification was at times used for discriminatory practices[29] already rings warning bells about today's enhanced power – from biotechnology in particular – that could much more readily and profoundly produce discrimination, based on genetic and biological factors over which the individual has no control.

Such processes could be taken far further than they were in France. In the mid-twentieth century, infamous systems of internal passport were developed under the Nazi regime in Germany, in South Africa under apartheid, and in the Soviet Bloc. In Germany, where, as Zygmunt Bauman has poignantly shown, the administration of the Holocaust represents the apogee of modernist rationality,[30] International Business Machines (IBM) was recruited to provide the technical infrastructure for genocidal identification.[31] In South Africa, pass laws formed a kind of internal passport system that restricted the mobility and the life-chances of black Africans. Interestingly, IBM, along with the UK firm ICL, also had a role in supplying the pass-book computer infrastructure from 1953. The hated pass-books featured in protests and demonstrations against apartheid (although the ANC, perhaps ironically, proposed another ID card system, HANIS, in 1996).[32] And in the former German Democratic Republic, internal passports were used to keep tabs on citizens. Their related Stasi (secret police) files, seen in Florian Henckel von Donnersmarck's poignant film *The Lives of Others*, or Timothy Garton Ash's book *The File*,[33] contributed to control by fear.

Internal passports were used, earlier, in Stalinist Russia, and these, too, distinguished between desirable and undesirable populations. The Stalinist state sought to engineer society through either inclusion or exclusion, but the most detailed and comprehensive aspect of this identification, categorization and monitoring was the internal passport and domicile registration system.[34] As well as documenting individual details, the passport was administratively linked to places of residence and work. It could thus be used to create a hierarchy of need for food and commodities in the times of scarcity that characterized the 1930s. Beyond this, it was also used for policing, state building and the larger state project of making socialism work. Categorization by passport enabled the state to distinguish between 'threatening or alien (*chuzhie*) populations' and loyal ones, or ones 'close (*blizko*)' to the regime.[35] Shearer notes that the passport system could be read as a 'demographic and geographic map, literally, of Stalinist-style socialism'.[36]

The internal passport functioned in some ways analogously to the more familiar external passport system, only within the physical borders of the nation-state. The passport gave the state an instrument for discriminating among its subjects in terms of rights and privileges. It regulated the movements of certain groups, restricted their entry into certain areas and denied them the liberty to move away from their residential areas.[37] As Marc Garcelon points out, this amounted to a form of 'internal colonialism' entailing 'administrative differentiation' between citizens and subjects.[38] But it also set up a tension. In order to survive, the authorities had to incorporate a variety of culturally distinct groups. However, knowing that their inclusion was on unequal terms, those subaltern groups were likely to resist such incorporation.

Not only did the internal passport form the centrepiece of the Soviet surveillance and control system, its repercussions are also felt in the successor states that emerged after 1989 and the fall of communism. In 1995, for example, the mayor of Moscow was ordered to clear the city of unregistered persons from the Caucasus and Central Asia, using passport designations. Nearly one million Chechens – their passports stamped 'enemy of the people' – had been deported by Stalin in the 1940s, and it was their children who fought for Chechnya in the mid-1990s. As Garcelon observes ironically, the internal passport maintained particular national identities rather than ever creating an internationalist and unified 'new Soviet man'.[39]

These examples of bureaucratic population control through the use of state identification systems differ from each other in important ways. Each one reflects the political priorities of its time and place. Given these priorities, the identification system was an ideal means of distinguishing between different sectors of the population and meting out quite different – not to mention highly unjust – treatment. Furthermore, bureaucratic and, even more so today, electronic identification systems facilitate the potential of negatively discriminating practices due to the ways that individual officials – or whole departments – may distance themselves from those whose life details are thus administered. Knowledge of history should give pause to any who believe that contemporary systems are somehow immune from the temptations of control or privilege.

Identification and Colonial Administration

Many early modern countries were involved in colonial rule, both internally with indigenous peoples or slaves, and externally with overseas territories. In the American Old South, for instance, while slaves were officially denied their *identities* – they were treated as sub-human non-persons – their supposed capacity for theft, arson or escape made them prime targets for *identification*.[40] The slave surveillance system on the plantations was based on what Christian Parenti calls three 'information technologies: the written slave pass, organized slave patrols, and wanted posters for runaways'.[41] In fact in Virginia the earliest pass laws (1642)

were directed against poor whites such as Irish indentured serv-
ants, but by 1687 South Carolina made such laws apply to black
slaves. Literate slaves had an advantage (which is why slave owners
usually tried to prevent slave access to education), as did those
whose mothers had given them distinctive names so that they
could keep track of their whereabouts. Black resistance heightened
white resolve, however, and pass systems spread.

By 1793, South Carolina, as noted at the start of this chapter, was
using brass or tin tags – 'slave hire badges' – containing the name,
date, occupation and number of the slave. Later ones have also been
found in Virginia; one such carries on one side the words 'Aunt
Jemima Johnston, born 1799, the Nicholas Plantation, Warrenton,
Virginia' and on the other a crude depiction of the 'big house' and
its 'slave quarters'.[42] Names and numbers were used to connect
the slave to city records at the treasurer's office of payment of the
annual slave tax.[43] Such cross-linkage with official records was
extended with manumission, as the papers – still including written
personal descriptions – distinguished between free and unfree subjects. A slave pass from Charleston, South Carolina, later found in a
prayer book, reads, 'My boy Mack has my permission to sleep in a
house in Bedon's Alley, hired by his mother this ticket is good for
two months from this date. Sarah H. Savage, Sep_ber 19 1843.'[44]
The sorts of written description available in the passes and papers
were replicated in the wanted posters, which, as Parenti observes,
indicated both the nature of control and its limits; the slaves had
already escaped. Some of the descriptive styles outlived the slave
passes after the outlawing of the system, reappearing in early passports and in the control of immigrant labour.

A quite different situation of colonial administration existed
in nineteenth-century India, where British rule included important experiments in identification. In 1858 Sir William Herschel,
working with the East India Company in Bengal, initiated the first
successful scientific forensic identification technique. As a member
of the Indian Civil Service, he wished to draw up a contract with
a road construction materials supplier and asked him, a Mr Konai,
to supply a handprint. He proposed that fingerprints be used more
generally for legal documents, but the idea did not fly. As magis-
trate of Hooghly, however, he instituted the taking of pensioners'

fingerprints to obviate fraud, and those of prisoners, so that they could not hire someone to substitute for them.[45]

This was not the end of the story, for Edward Henry and Azizul Haque of the Bengal Police perfected and systematized fingerprinting for forensic identification in 1893. While criminal groups and allegedly deviant populations were affected by these, the colonial state also kept detailed records of political intelligence on 'subversive activities' that extended to most domains of life. According to Sengupta, informers were cultivated in the 'criminal underground, the postal department, amongst railwaymen, soldiers, political activists, trade union members, lawyers, prostitutes, clerks, thieves, teachers, workers and students'.[46] The Indian Telegraph Act (1885) also permitted many kinds of state scrutiny of information.

Another example of colonial administration, one that is very poignant in the light of subsequent events, is that of the Belgian system of ethnic classification in Rwanda. It began with anthropometric measurements and ended with the issuance of obligatory identity papers stating one's ethnicity.[47] These papers became the means of genocide in 1994, based on fixed group identities, arranged hierarchically, and the fostering of distrust and hatred between the groups.[48] Similar systems were developed throughout colonized countries of Africa, such as in the Portuguese colonies of Mozambique and Angola. As in the American South, pass laws existed in the Cape Colony from the 1700s, and Britain maintained these after their takeover in 1806. Mainly to regulate cheap and slave labour, such passes were common throughout British colonies in Africa and the practice was perpetuated within Belgian, French and Portuguese rule as well, although only in the former two cases did indirect rule using local indigenous leaders prevail.[49]

The original terms *Hutu*, *Tutsi* and *Twa* existed in pre-colonial Rwanda and Burundi and referred to either occupational or status distinctions that were flexible and could be changed. Europeans arriving in the late nineteenth century fitted these groups into new taxonomies that privileged Tutsis due to their supposed similarity to Europeans (and thus their assumed superiority). Racial stereotypes, which assumed distinctiveness and mutual antagonism, were also developed for the other groups. However, when the Belgian authorities issued ID cards in the 1930s, it appears that the main aim was simply to regulate Belgian subjects and not to implement indirect rule through Tutsis.[50] Nevertheless, in practice, the newly fixed identities served to deny Hutus crucial opportunities for education and employment, which in turn spawned the ethno-nationalist movements of the 1950s that denounced this subordination.

When the tables had turned in the 1990s, and Hutu military and political power was ascendant, the ID cards played a fatal role in determining who would live and who would die in the genocidal bloodbath. The compulsorily carried cards had to be shown at barricades and many Tutsis were killed on the spot when the documents were demanded. But some Hutus were also slaughtered because of their appearance, under suspicion of having false cards. Longman concludes, tellingly, that Rwandans had come to accept the principle behind the cards, 'that identities were fixed and unchanging, that everyone in the country could be clearly classified into one of three categories based on their parentage. It is this ethnicization of Rwandan society that ultimately made genocide possible.'[51]

Identification and Crime Control

From earliest historical times, means have been found of marking lawbreakers. During the early modern era, within the New World, this took the form of a physical mark on the skin: in the East Jersey codes of 1668 and 1675 burglars received a 'T' on the right hand and a forehead 'R' for a second offence, whereas adulterers in Puritan New England received the scarlet letter 'A'[52] (hence Nathaniel Hawthorne's 1850 novel). By and large, markers were unnecessary in relatively immobile situations of local communities where most people were known to others. But with urbanization and industrialization came what Georg Simmel called the 'society of strangers',[53] and this, along with the emerging machinery of municipal, state and national bureaucracies, offered the rationale and the means of marking populations singled out as lawless or troublesome. As nation-states developed general systems of citizen registration, so specific kinds of identification were also sought for maintaining social order.

Adequate means of criminal identification were sought constantly and ever more urgently during the nineteenth century, on both sides of the Atlantic. A good guide to this is the work of Simon Cole.[54] The reason was not simply the desire to identify correctly in relatively rare cases of imposture or mistaken identity, but to find ways of coping with rising crime rates. It was widely believed that recidivism was a real problem, but without adequate identification it could not be proven that the same person had committed crimes repeatedly.[55] Descriptions and photographs were circulated, and in the UK an *Alphabetical Register of Habitual Criminals* was established in 1877. Increasingly, photos were sought as superior to written descriptions. With the emergence of the (no doubt hyped) 'confidence man' in the USA, the forger who could even deal in changed identities became the catalyst for better identification,[56] especially that which focused on the face. Add to this physiological differences emphasized by what came to be known as the Italian school and the time-consuming quest for 'distinctive marks' used in Britain, and one sees how the search for stable identities was considered urgent.

In the end, fingerprinting was to become the most widespread mode of criminal identification, despite great efforts to use Bertillonage – a system, named after its inventor, Alphonse Bertillon, of body-measurements, photos and a detailed description (*portrait parlé*)[57] – anthropometry and other modes of fixing identities. Problems of classification, to which Francis Galton made the chief contributions, were first worked out in colonial India, as noted earlier, and by the 1920s the superiority of fingerprinting over other modes was generally acknowledged. However, parallel developments in the USA and in Argentina – the former in contexts where the 'society of strangers' was more pronounced than in Europe – gave some fingerprinting a somewhat different cast. The connections between 'immigrants' and criminality were sometimes carefully traced in North America, for example with the influx of Chinese workers relating to the 1848 gold rush and transcontinental railway building boom.[58] The 1882 Chinese Exclusion Act in the USA aimed at restricting the immigrant flow except in the case of workers who returned to China temporarily. But how to identify them? Once again, fingerprinting was soon preferred to physical descriptions because, as in India, officials viewed the problem as being compounded by the difficulties of recognizing one individual from another

In Argentina, towards the end of the nineteenth century, Juan Vucetich, in charge of the statistical bureau of the La Plata police, developed further fingerprinting classification techniques that were also used in the categorizing of immigrants. He produced his system of 'dactyloscopy' to simplify an earlier attempt to classify fingerprints on 101 variables. Vucetich added identification cards to the mix, thus indexing a large criminal identification file. But his work also furthered the cause of whitening Argentina, which had already succeeded in exterminating much of the Native American and severely reducing the African American population. What was once applied to blacks, whites and Indians was also applied to different European groups, some of whom were deemed preferable immigrants to others. Crime statistics had become confused with immigration issues and selective law enforcement strengthened the view that immigrants were primarily to blame for crime.[59] These 'racial others' helped hasten the development and success of Vucetich's dactyloscopic scheme.

Interestingly, observes Cole, early dactyloscopy was thought of less as a forensic technique and more as a classificatory one for linking bodies in custody to their criminal records. And this also helps to explain the quest for a universal system that could eventually depend on remote records and that would, with the development of electronic storage systems, be used in conjunction with central-ized identification bureaux. Moreover, it gives the backdrop to more than one proposal for universal fingerprint identification systems in the USA, for instance the 1943 Citizen Identification Act, which called for ID cards with fingerprints.[60] By this date, in fact, automation was already significantly underway, with IBM supplying card-sorters and punch-card systems for US fingerprint files. Three decades later, Automated Fingerprint Identification Systems (AFIS) were being used in the USA and elsewhere.

The practice of fingerprinting addressed a basic issue in all kinds of identification, not only criminal identification. While a surname is a prerequisite, and carrying an ID document may help the state authority to associate reliably a name with an individual person, that individual still must cooperate for the system to work. To achieve cooperation, states often make entitlement depend on the production of clear identification, and in harsher regimes they will punish individuals who fail to produce them. In situations of defiance, however, people will refuse or fail to identify or will dissemble and identify falsely. Fingerprinting has the advantage from a state perspective of being a universal bodily mark, which at the same time acknowledges the uniqueness of each person. Today, this is extended to other biometrics, from facial topography and iris scans to DNA samples.[61]

As far as identification for crime control was concerned, the systems were intended to identify and demarcate racial difference and criminality, to isolate and exclude. As we shall see, although some methods have been updated, it has sometimes proved difficult for law enforcement organizations to forsake some of these discriminatory features that characterized the earliest attempts at identification for crime control.

Identification for War

War has offered opportunities for creating identification systems in several modern societies. Both the need to discover who is fit, willing and available for military service and the need to distinguish effectively between loyal citizens and potentially hostile resident aliens have been behind mass identification programmes. More broadly, however, war and surveillance are connected in other ways that also help to contextualize specific dimensions of surveillance such as personal identification.

In general, it should be noted that the relationship between the military sector and surveillance has been underplayed. It deserves further historical and sociological investigation. As Christopher Dandeker has shown, the industrial and democratic revolutions in Europe and America catalysed the bureaucratization of military power and therefore an expansion of their surveillance capacities.[62] But not only did the modern state control military power, the imperatives of modern war also helped to extend the bureaucratic surveillance that had developed in the military *back into* the wider society.[63] The desiderata for a 'security state' spell increasing ties between the state and the military sphere, some of which work themselves out in the veil of secrecy regarding some specific operations and organizations and in the erosion of civil liberties relating to assembly, movement and the provision of information, areas in which the quest for new ID systems has been paramount.[64]

Edward Higgs shows how the 'information state' in England was pushed forward significantly after 1914 both by military threats to Britain and the empire and by the deepening and widening of the welfare state.[65] Until this time the connection between military service and citizenship was not strong and no internal passports were used, as they often were in continental states. With the First World War, however, the population was brought into closer connection with the central state and personal data collection and analysis expanded accordingly. Yet liberal traditions, modest aims and limited technologies meant that this expansion was not yet dramatic. The General Register Office (GRO) oversaw military recruitment data gathering and this was also linked with data on potential munitions, mining, railway and agricultural workers. A register of war refugees was also maintained to protect against fifth columnists and the GRO sent information on enemy aliens to the intelligence services, MI5.

In Britain, the first national ID card appeared as the result of a fierce debate between supporters of conscription and those who wished to continue the voluntary method of obtaining recruits for the armed forces.[66] There had been a systematic official registering of births, deaths and stillbirths in Britain since the mid-nineteenth century, with a central repository of certificates held in London.[67] Registers were also maintained of marriages, TB sufferers, voters, the mentally deficient, National Insurance contributors and primary and secondary school pupils. But no list was both universal and had up-to-date addresses. Beatrice Webb had campaigned for some time for a national ID card system, believing that progressive social reform would be served by such an innovation, but in the end it was the interests of 'industrial purposes', on the one hand, and 'military and naval purposes', on the other, that catalysed the National Registry into being.

By July 1915 the efforts under the National Registration Bill produced the results urgently sought by the War Cabinet, that almost 1.5 million men were still available for national service, but any broader aspirations associated with it remained unfulfilled.[68] Not until September 1939 was the idea revived, now for 'national service, national security, and the administration of rationing'.[69] A central National Register Office held records (near Southport) and ID cards were required for renewing ration books. They were also used for routine policing, and this was the context in which they were eventually rejected for peacetime use. In 1950, Mr Willock, a speeding motorist, refused to show his ID card and his right was upheld in court on the grounds that the card was a war measure (see second epigraph above). The rationing registration system was transferred to the new National Health Service, but now without the ID card.

Continuity and Change in Large-Scale Identification

Whereas mobility partly explains the impetus behind nascent ID systems and internal passports, it is not the whole story. When registration systems are connected with brands, badges or paper or plastic documents, this certainly seems to facilitate the regulation of movement. However, the very act of identification and the growing requirement to produce proof have several profound social meanings, whether to indicate obligation or entitlement, to offer evidence of previous criminal records or none, or, even more importantly, to distinguish between those who are legitimate citizens, subjects or residents of a nation-state and those who are not. The latter distinction is one that invariably rests on judgements about ethnicity and race, many of which are deeply prejudicial, divisive and exclusionary.

An aspect of the formation of modern nation-states, especially by the nineteenth century, was the determination of what it meant to be French or British as distinct from other groupings. The 'essential nationhood' of one group was threatened by the possible invasion by non-national groups. In the British case, says Linda Colley, Catholics were suspect, as were peoples from colonies in India or Africa.[70] Dangerous classes were associated through literature and the imagination with alien and non-inbred races, in contrast to good middle-class empire-supporting identities. Thus the colonial experience and the codes of race together helped to constitute governable subjects.[71] In this light, markers of identity and internal passports could be viewed as reinforcing the nation-state as such by providing contrasts between legitimate and illegitimate identities. Workplaces and residential areas could thus be regulated, as could the territorial borders of the nation-state.

Various kinds of identity document appeared in the course of the twentieth century, from drivers' licences in the 1920s through social insurance cards and eventually health cards and credit cards.[72] While the *carte d'identité* existed in France, the *Personalauweis* in Germany or the *Bilhete de Identidade* in Portugal, other documents – such as the drivers' licence or the social security card in the USA – have been used as if they were ID cards. The Social Insurance Card, introduced in Canada in 1964, has served in this way, despite 'privacy' protests about function creep. The point is both that ordinary citizens have become increasingly accustomed to producing ID when documents are demanded, and that institutions have deepened their dependence on such cards, along with the corresponding registries and records.

It is important to observe that the categories used help to produce the citizens as such.[73] Modern states, dependent on rational bureaucratic administration, are more or less bound by that fact to treat people according to their schemata. As Scott notes, schemes that started life as the inventions of census-takers, judges or police officers 'end by being the categories that organize people's daily experience precisely because they are embedded in state-created institutions that structure that experience'.[74] He goes on to say that pass-books, ID cards, and the like, 'acquire their force from the fact that these synoptic data are the points of departure for reality as the state officials apprehend and shape it'.[75] If one needs a standing before the law, or to acquire entitlements, the classificatory documents provided by the state must be produced for the state.

Conclusion

The demand for documents, encountered only occasionally in the ancient world, is a commonplace feature of the modern one. As this chapter shows, internal identification documents have developed sporadically and patchily in modern times, paralleled by the passport as an external ID.[76] Specific perceived needs have generated a quest for such documents, such that many systems for crime control, colonial administration or conscription have been partial and limited to specific population groups, at least at first. The role of racialization within ID documents runs right through several of the narratives discussed here, as does the search for rational ways of systematizing the task of classification that identification inevitably entails. The picture has been painted with a broad brush in order to outline some key characteristics. Many details are missing, for which readers are referred to the sources.

During the twentieth century those 'racial and rational' features of identification systems were magnified, and, in many of the cases mentioned here, with tragic results. Unfortunately, merely knowing about them did not prevent their being perpetuated, sometimes (in the case of post-Holocaust Israeli classification of Palestinians, for instance) by the very people who had suffered from the brutal effects of classification by others.[77] In less dramatic cases, the attempt to create stable national identification systems simply glossed over some of the problems of ethnic categories and pressed ahead to find the most technologically effective ways of establishing and maintaining them. Specific political economies, cultural currents and geo-political forces do make a difference, but these threads are still discernible, even though history may never be reduced to a single logic.

Newer ID systems combine several functions that have been found historically in discrete markers and registers, relating to military service and taxation, on the one hand, and social insurance, permanent residence and associated benefits, on the other. Insofar as these may also be denied to some groups, however, it is worth noting the connections between excluded or suspect groups, especially where the boundaries are blurred between 'dangerous classes' and 'immigrants'. As we shall see, a key question from the point of view of citizenship rights and responsibilities is whether new ID card systems will be able to escape the negative histories that have dogged such documents in the past.

This question will be answered in part by looking at the ways in which population groups are classified, but also by examining the new means of classification. Those rudimentary efforts to apply machine technologies to identification, such as the work of IBM in Nazi Germany, have today become the taken-for-granted, assumed approach. As we shall see in chapter 2, today's ID systems are profoundly technological and utilize the full range of advanced computing and communication know-how, including that *sine qua non* of classification, the searchable database. Just as one cannot generalize from one case of 'racial' discrimination to argue that all ID systems are hopelessly compromised, so it is misleading to suggest that the new technologies are in themselves the cause of problems in identification. On the other hand, today's attempts to create systems for national identification cannot properly be understood without first examining their capacity to function as sorting systems.

2
Sorting Systems

In the process of making people and categories converge, there can be tremendous torque of individual biographies. The advantaged are those whose place in a set of classification systems is a powerful one and for whom powerful sets of classifications can appear natural . . .

Geoffrey Bowker and Susan Leigh Star[1]

In Canada in 1940, during the Second World War, national registration was introduced that required all citizens to be registered and to carry ID cards. The idea was to make a basic distinction between those 'needed' for industry and government and those who could be enlisted in the armed services. For this, data were collected and compiled on all Canadians regarding their occupation, craft training, employment, country of birth, immigration status, languages spoken and health. But as Scott Thompson has shown,[2] because the card was needed for obtaining employment or access to government services, this created great hardship for First Nations people who did not want to be registered and immigrants living in Canada who were not citizens. It also sparked further identification and surveillance procedures for other alien national groups – and 'communists' – in Canada that led in turn to imprisonments.

To introduce a national ID system is to employ a triage, a sorting system that puts citizens into categories to be better 'seen' and thus differently treated by the state. I deliberately chose an example from the 'pre-computer' era to show that sorting is part and parcel of identification systems regardless of technology. However, it is precisely the sorting capacity of ID systems that is vastly amplified by the use of new technologies. Take the case of the developing UK ID card system. Personal data on the ID cards include name, address, date of birth, gender, nationality and biometrics. Although the card system has various stated purposes, such as curbing illegal immigration and employment or combating organized crime and terrorism, these problems affect only a minority of the UK population. Necessarily, each of these purposes depends on the setting up of categories of terrorist/non-terrorist, fraudulent/non-fraudulent claimants and legal/illegal immigrants. In each area, highly sensitive matters are at stake in the determination of the categories and of course the software codes by which they will be recognized.

As well, the social categories in question are all ones in which there is a high degree of vulnerability. Those suspected of terrorist activities or proclivities are by definition likely to be members of minority groups; claimants to government benefits and services are likely to be already disadvantaged; and immigrants, whether legal or not, are also in positions of relative powerlessness. Extensive literatures exist on each area, and since 9/11 especially, the risks of new identification schemes to minorities, particularly to Muslims, have become all too well known.

Not only this, but surveillance categories are sometimes elastic, as recent reports of the Pentagon's checking on student emails show. The Department of Defense database known as Talon (set up in 2003) monitors emails to keep track of potential terrorist threats. But it includes students protesting the war in Iraq and even some engaging in a 'critical mass bike ride in solidarity with Earth Day'.[3] The social sorting of new IDs touches some unexpected groups as well as the lives of the weakest and most marginalized members of the population, including those who have been disadvantaged through racial profiling.

This chapter confronts directly the question of 'ID cards as surveillance'. It shows what comprises today's 'national ID cards' and shows how the database has become central to the processes of identification. But because the database is so significant to identification practices, surveillance capacities associated with identification are also expanding rapidly. The surveillance involved in ID card systems has some distinctive characteristics compared with earlier forms, especially that it makes the crucial classification process far easier than was the case in file-and-paper systems. Overall, and through several related mechanisms, new ID card systems often seem to favour more exclusionary and less inclusive notions of citizenship, by sorting 'desirable' and 'undesirable' populations, based on the criteria of 'identity management'. These are amplified by the use of biometrics.

None of this means, of course, that older registries and identification document systems did not aim to discriminate between different groups so that they could be treated differently. Also, both discretion and stereotyping existed within such systems, as common characteristics of bureaucratic organization. Discretion allows some flexibility, for example through the use of interviews, and stereotyping results from the simplification required to facilitate judgements.[4] However, opportunities for discretion become more limited with automation, and stereotyping, for better *and* for worse, tends to be built more decisively into new ID systems. Indeed, one can say that the prejudices of system designers may become embedded in the softwares, such that stereotypes, with which such systems work routinely, may be negative ones for some groups or individuals.[5]

New ID card systems are a species of surveillance, then, but they also share a key characteristic of much contemporary surveillance in that they facilitate forms of 'social sorting'.[6] This is a large-scale and far-reaching trend, enabled in fine-grain form by the use of searchable databases and associated techniques such as data mining,[7] characterized by the classifying and profiling of groups in order to provide different levels of treatment, conditions or service to groups that have thus been distinguished from one another. New ID cards are intended to include those designated as eligible members of nation-states (citizens and permanent or temporary residents who are not full citizens) and to exclude others (who may not only be ineligible but also in some cases be undesirable).

ID Cards and Registries

In new national ID systems, the card is the visible component but the power of the surveillance lies in the registry database. Older ID documents were just that, cards or papers carrying written information about citizenship in the country in question, along with a unique number, a photograph, fingerprint or other supporting features. Today's new plastic national ID cards still carry a photo and personal details but also an embedded chip. Examples include the *MyKad* from Malaysia, the *Carta d'Identit Elettronica* (or CIE) in Italy and the *Juki-net* card and Alien Registration Card in Japan. Given the range and scope of current developments in many countries it is no exaggeration to speak of a global trend towards the production of new national ID systems. They are hailed, variously, as the means to increased government efficiency, as flagships of national technology policies, as security against identity theft, as new means of law enforcement, and as a key element in the 'war on terror'.

As media accounts in the past few years demonstrate, introducing new IDs is not always uncontroversial. They have been disputed in several countries around the world – the UK, the USA, France, Australia, Japan, South Korea, to name a few. But the controversies seldom get to the heart of the changes occurring, largely because they tend to focus on the cards themselves and on issues such as the likelihood of random police demands for their presentation. While such demands, where they occur, are indeed disturbing from a civil liberties viewpoint, new ID card systems are dependent on electronic infrastructures and in particular on national registries. In all ID card systems, whether 'national' or not, this is where the real surveillance power lies: to discriminate between different categories and groups, for differential treatment.[8]

A closer examination of any ID card will show why this is the case. The main features of an ID card, common across many systems, are the name, number(s), facial image, institutional regalia, machine-readable components (chip, magnetic stripe, optical barcode, etc.). The visible elements on the card are only the tip of the iceberg, however. Each element represents a much fuller techno-organizational apparatus which, like the iceberg, lies out of sight, below the surface. Figure 2.1[9] shows, rather like a sonar probe submerged below the water to chart the size of the iceberg, how much more there is to a national ID card than a piece of plastic in one's pocket. If the berg is big, there may be some grounds for reassurance, say, about climate change, but there may also be some serious risks to shipping. In the end, as Figure 2.1 demonstrates, the card itself is dwarfed by all the other components of the socio-technical system. Is this reassuring or risky?

Interestingly, while governments often appear reticent to explain that there is much more to ID cards than meets the eye, members of the public in many countries become much more cautious about their supposed benefits when the presence of a 'data-berg' beneath the surface is made apparent to them. A nine-country international survey undertaken in 2006 shows this clearly. Even in a country like Hungary, which stands out as a place where respondents are confident (77 per cent 'strongly agree') that national ID cards are necessary, a mere 11 per cent think that government efforts to protect data in a national database are 'very effective'. In all other countries but Japan – Canada, the USA, France, Spain, Mexico, Brazil and China – thinking about a national registry database and how safe those personal data might be in it introduces a note of considerable caution contrasted with the somewhat more sanguine response to the idea of carrying an ID.[10] To varying degrees, people around the globe see magnified risks with ID cards when they realize that they have associated national registry databases.

Computer-based identification systems, which first appeared in the twentieth century, are rapidly becoming universal. Schemes for national identification as such have always displayed a potential for state interference in everyday life, but this has been downplayed in the light of plausible rationales for their introduction. However, the information technologies on which they now depend are becoming more sophisticated and powerful. This spells gains for efficiency and productivity but also accentuates questions about civil liberties and human rights.

This is because administrative identification now involves automated systems for social sorting. What qualitatively alters the character and scope of new ID card systems is precisely what makes

The Italian ID (*Carta d'Identità Elettronica*) is a typical example of today's 'new' national IDs.

ICAQ compatible MRZ: Name of issuing municipality, family name, given name.

Printed personal data and card holder's signature.

Italian insignia

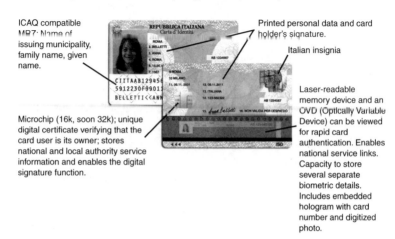

Microchip (16k, soon 32k); unique digital certificate verifying that the card user is its owner; stores national and local authority service information and enables the digital signature function.

Laser-readable memory device and an OVD (Optically Variable Device) can be viewed for rapid card authentication. Enables national service links. Capacity to store several separate biometric details. Includes embedded hologram with card number and digitized photo.

Connected Databases

Ministry of the Interior: Information system for local municipalities; logs, records and updates personal data. Provides unique serial number.

Taxation Code Department

Italian Population Registration Centre: has unique centralized population index.

INA (Italian Central Agency for Data Exchange)

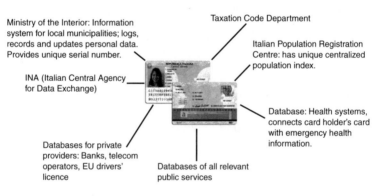

Database: Health systems, connects card holder's card with emergency health information.

Databases for private providers: Banks, telecom operators, EU drivers' licence

Databases of all relevant public services

1. Oversight: CNIPA (formerly AIPA) – The National Agency for Public Administration Innovation
2. Issuing Authority: IPZS – The Italian Mint, a government-owned company that collates technologies and merges them onto the card, along with the Ministry of the Interior serial number
3. Technology Corporations:
    A. Drexler Technology Corporation: Optional memory card
    B. LaserCard Systems Corporation: Developing, marketing, selling optical cards
    C. Laser Memory Card S.R.L. of Italy
    D. L.C. Sistema S.P.A. Manufacturer of optical memory card reader/writer and optical memory cards (i.c.)

Figure 2.1

them 'new' – their reliance on searchable databases and networked communications. What such networked databases do is to enhance the surveillance capacities of ID card systems, thus not only bringing them in line with other such administrative systems but also offering to other systems a means of overall communication and coordination. Within already existing discourses of classification that discriminate between different social groups, relating to policy choices on areas such as immigration, anti-terrorism or identity theft, the decision to use networked, searchable databases does make a decisive difference.[11] Identification systems and especially 'national ID card' systems thus represent a crucial dimension of surveillance societies.

Without supporting technologically determined kinds of arguments, it is also worth observing that the adoption of new technologies does have other kinds of consequences as well. The outlooks of those using such systems as well as specific behaviours may be altered through interaction with the technologies. Various kinds of effects are discussed in this book, including the distancing effect of technologies that mediate between individuals and groups, the growth of beliefs about technological capacities or security (which may be either positive or negative), and the tendency to seek technological 'solutions' when they are apparently available. Each of these affects the spread of identification as surveillance.

New ID cards are surveillance systems, then, and exhibit traits of the kinds of surveillance that have been growing rapidly since the latter part of the twentieth century. Such surveillance is typically centred on data from the human body,[12] is automated, connected with control, especially access control,[13] and aims at universal coverage within specific jurisdictions.[14] In the case of ID systems, biometrics offers the body as a means of authentication; the database–card relation is electronic, often using radio frequency identification (RFID) scanning to facilitate automatic functioning; access control for both travel and transactions is involved; and national ID card systems proper in principle cover the whole, at least adult, population.

The association of ID cards with databases means that these are systems for social sorting, permitting extensive discrimination between different populations through modes of classification that in the case of national IDs often include ethnicity and religion. The older Israeli *Teudat Zehut* ID card, for example, established in 1949, used Yehudi (Jewish), Aravi (Arab), Druzi (Druze) and over 100 other options such as Circassian and Bedouin, and 'non-Jew'. From 2005 ethnicity was omitted from Israel's ID cards, even though whether or not someone is a Jew can still be checked by looking at the date of birth. Hebrew ones are different from others. The pressing policy and political challenge for any country is to establish systems that avoid exclusionary bias and in which accountability for handling personal data is paramount. To explore this further, however, the first step is to consider the relation between 'eligibility' and 'legibility'.

Citizenship: Eligibility and Legibility

A further way of thinking about why new national ID card systems are qualitatively different from older ones is rooted in the relation between eligibility and legibility. Eligibility for various rights and services may be secured or guaranteed by an identification system that indicates who exactly are *bona fide* citizens. So-called e-Government schemes require citizenship authentication for access to a department, such as taxation or health. But the device for proving eligibility is at the same time a means of greater legibility by the state. Citizens may be brought more directly under the eye of government by means of unique identification systems. This is what James Scott means when he talks of this aspect of government administration in general as 'seeing like a state'.[15]

Although taken for granted by many, citizenship is a contested issue, especially for refugees and asylum seekers or for nationals whose children are born out of the country. So how, asks the representative of government, can one distinguish the real thing from the fake, the imposter? The answer is to find a reliable means of verifying identity that connects a record with a person. Modern states are in part constituted by their capacity to name, count and classify citizens, which they do by requiring documentary evidence such as the birth certificate or by mounting the census that enumerates populations according to citizenship, among other things. As well, in the twentieth century, increasing use was made of ID card systems and passports as means of checking on who really is a citizen.[16]

Two hundred years ago, when modern nation-states were being born, much attention was paid to the question of citizenship. Bit by bit, many rights, privileges and responsibilities came with citizenship, each of which was connected with an individual.[17] Being a member of a certain family, clan or class meant less for citizenship than proving that one was a resident, born of specifiable parents in a particular place. What once had mainly religious significance, the details of birth, marriage and death, now took on a new administrative significance in the burgeoning bureaucracies of government. The state sought to distinguish between one individual and another by clear and unambiguous criteria, so that the rights of citizens were extended only to those who were genuinely eligible.

The means of keeping track of these personal details, the surveillance that makes life legible, is thus very ambiguous. On the one hand, tremendous benefits accrue to citizens through being able to vote, be educated or hold health coverage. But on the other, the state can also use those records to limit the activities or movements of citizens, or, worse, to deem certain citizens second-class and consign them to inferior or even brutal treatment. As we saw in the previous chapter, in the 1930s, Nazi Germany used early IBM machines on census materials, registrations and ancestral tracing records to sort undesirable Jewish citizens from desirable ('Aryan') ones, and in Rwanda in the 1990s, the Belgian colonial ID card system was the means of singling out Tutsi targets for Hutu slaughter. In both cases, horrendous genocide was the outcome.[18]

Today, every nation-state from Mexico to Morocco to Mongolia has complex and sophisticated ways of keeping tabs on individual citizens, recorded in large-scale departments such as employment, education, health and taxation. Since the latter part of the twentieth century, most of these records have been computerized. This adds efficiency, at least in theory,[19] because of the hugely increased storage and transmission capacity available and, importantly, the ability to search those databases remotely. But the ambiguities of such state surveillance have never gone away. If anything, they have become more marked. Identification systems, for example, may simplify our interactions with government departments, granting ready access to information or benefits. But equally, they can be used to make dubious and sometimes dangerous distinctions between classes of citizens, advantaging some at the expense of others.

At a fairly mundane level, requests for drivers' licences or for welfare payments undergo subtle but solid change as governments switch over to online contact with citizens. One of the key characteristics of this change is increased layering and sorting of those citizens. In the UK, the use of online services has led to an urgent quest for answers to 'identity management' questions: can the government department be sure who is doing business with them online, and how can government assess the reduced risks of doing business with citizens online?[20] As Taylor, Lips and Organ say, the consequence of the 'search for service improvements, cost reductions and risk-managed service delivery' is that 'government becomes increasingly aware of the profile of the citizen'.[21] That is, citizens become progressively more legible to the state.

In the driver's licence case, the basic details are entered through the 'Government Gateway' to be checked against existing databases to make sure, for example, that the driver has not been disqualified. The data are then sent to Experian, a large, private data-management company, which checks the data against numerous public and private sector databases that eventuate in a 'trust score' for each applicant, who will be higher rated – 'layered' – by customer databases of clearing banks than of mail order companies, for example. Applicants can only proceed to the next stages if the score is at or above the level set for that transaction.

Similar changes occur with 'e-benefits' claimants, though Taylor et al. describe this case as 'vertical sorting' rather than 'layering'. In the UK, only internal databases are used to assign benefit claimants to categories, each associated with risk scores. The aim is to discover levels of trust in relation to claimant error or fraud. After an initial interview where the data are collected, claimants are assigned to social categories of risk. In the case of housing benefits, for example, the lowest on the scale are pensioners and the highest of all are single parents living in private landlord accommodation. Local authorities are assumed to prioritize reviews for those of highest risk categories. The socio-demographic groupings that result are clearly consequential in different ways for different claimants.

Why Social Sorting is Central

The early twenty-first century has seen the development of several new national identification systems. Indeed, some systems, such as those in Malaysia (*MyKad*) and Japan (*Juki-net*), have their roots in administrative and commercial ventures of the later twentieth century, but others, such as those in Italy and the UK (approved in Parliament in March 2006), are in part responses to 9/11 and the 'war on terror'. The USA has yet to develop a national ID system, but the current attempt to rationalize and integrate federally the driver's licensing system (previously on a state-by-state basis) into the Real ID will create a *de facto* national ID system. And in Canada, while there is as yet no clear plan to develop a national ID system, the logic of both administrative and security arrangements points in its direction.[22]

ID cards of various kinds have been used for centuries, and, as noted earlier, in modern times they have been associated both with humdrum administrative efficiency and with colonialism, crime control and war.[23] The focus of these older systems is the production of the card, on demand, to prove identity. New national ID card systems, however, are based on a national registry, a database (or databases in some cases, such as the UK) containing personal information that can be searched and checked independently of any demand to see the card held by the citizen. The unique identifier contained in the card is also the key to unlock the database(s) and thus is itself a source of considerable power for good or for ill.[24] To understand the significance of this we have to step back and see the context in which new, often multi-purpose, national ID systems are being developed.

The microelectronics-based information revolution that began in the 1970s revolutionized the storage, retrieval, processing and transmission of data. In fact, it was as much about communication as about storage and processing. Personal data could be passed with ease from one department to another such that what once required official permission or even legal warrant became routine. From the point of view of bureaucratic efficiency, communicating computers appeared to enhance organization by offering data matching between, say, customs and employment or education and police departments; meanwhile, citizens had less and less say in what happened to their personal records.

Computerization of government administration ushered in the era of what Roger Clarke calls 'dataveillance'. Clarke defines dataveillance as the 'use of personal data systems in the investigation or monitoring of the actions or communications of one or more persons', and he observes that this facilitates 'mass surveillance' as opposed to the more familiar 'personal surveillance'.[25] The latter might be used to track specific suspected criminals, whereas the former is a means of identifying individuals as members of a category of interest to the surveillance organization. The information-intensivity of computing and communication power that expanded rapidly from the 1970s onwards allowed for more fine-grained decision making that contributed further to a 'data imperative' in which more and more data were sought in the name of maximizing knowledge and efficiency.

As Clarke argued two decades ago, reliable identification methods are essential in the quest of what he then described as a 'dossier society'. With a range of data systems in place, gathering data for various purposes, along with some means of connecting them via telecommunication networks, only consistent identification is required for a cost-effective system of dataveillance to develop, without a central or national databank ever being established. This permits data matching (sometimes also called record linkage) that offers new and possibly illuminating combinations of data which may help to enhance physical security and detect or prevent error, abuse or fraud, thus improving tax or welfare schemes in government or financial and insurance services in the private sector. At the same time, dangers are evident, as suspicion may appear where previously no grounds existed, just because of an apparent data match.

I say apparent, because many matching schemes have been exposed as erroneous. Most often, this is where the statistical and computing techniques involved in matching the records of two or more databases (a common practice since the 1970s) produce incorrect 'hits'. At roughly the same time as Clarke discussed dataveillance (in the mid-1980s), Gary Marx and Nancy Reichman showed that half the matches in a New York State program were spurious.[26] Data-input error or the failure to update records was the main cause. Today, more opportunities for error occur as matching has proliferated. One way is through sophisticated computer profiling, where a profile of characteristics of individuals (often suspected of illegal activities such as welfare fraud or terrorism) are matched with databases to single out some for closer scrutiny. And another is 'front-end verification', where databases are matched for specific individuals who are applying, say, for welfare or unemployment benefits.[27]

By the 1990s, then, software had been developed that made searching through a database much easier. As Lawrence Lessig points out, earlier systems of monitoring involved people who typically only noted difference and did not collect searchable records; today's use machines that notice any and every transaction that together become searchable records.[28] This makes profiling possible and enables what Oscar Gandy calls the 'panoptic sort',[29] which discriminates between different classes of person – say, internet users – on the basis of the sites they visit, or frequent flyers, who receive better services in return for their 'loyalty' to the airline. These may influence if not manipulate customers in particular ways that, over time, come to appear as normal. That is, the categories themselves help to make possible certain kinds of actions and also have consequences for how we conceive of ourselves or others.[30]

The searchable database enables discriminatory judgements to be built into systems, affecting different populations differently, and such judgements may as easily work against individuals as for them.[31] Although data protection and privacy laws[32] were developed to limit such activities, these have found it very hard to keep pace with technical change or, dare one say, the ingenuity of those trying to sidestep regulation. In the case of ID card systems, the unique personal identifier makes it possible to obtain access to several kinds of database; the more multi-purpose the system, the more databases are likely to be involved. If the UK ID card system is, as advertised, to guard against 'identity theft', then this suggests that commercial data relating to banks and credit cards will be accessible as well as those relating to government departments such as immigration or health.

The combination of computing with communications capacities in surveillance – and this is clearly true for ID systems – has a further implication which, though indirect, is singularly significant. It introduces a new reliance on those providing expertise, both technologically and commercially. In an era of outsourced services, the role of technologists and businesspersons within organizational bureaucracies has become increasingly significant, such that it is inappropriate to understand surveillance of personal data without considering the technological – usually software – and business practice – information management – priorities that now also inform the handling of personal data. This trend is also made possible, of course, by the economic restructuring that accompanied the technological revolution we have been discussing. It helped to produce what we now call globalization and also stimulated innovations such as outsourcing, now applied to aspects of ID systems.

The interplay of technological and business practices with organizational control occurs in the development of identification card systems. In any computerized system, the key to records retrieval is to have consistent and, if possible, unique identifiers, and in this case for individual citizens. As we saw earlier in the Italian case, LaserCard, a major international company which also supplies similar products for other countries, including India, Saudi Arabia and Canada, works through a local Italian company, Ritel, to design and manufacture the national ID. Such companies have a reputation for quality, reliability and efficiency to protect. What spells efficiency from one point of view, however, spells potential social control, or, more precisely, subtle forms of governance, from another.[33] But from where does this governance originate?

In part, national ID systems may be seen as a means of increased state control, but they are also the products of technical and business expertise. So-called 'smart' cards have been in use for some time in commercial settings, but only more recently have they broken into the market of government administration.[34] LaserCard, to continue with this example, is a Mountain View, California company, started in 1968 and specializing in secure identity documents for business as well as government use. It competes with other global corporations that have similar specialties, including Gemalto, Giesecke & Devrient GmbH, Sharp, Sagem Orga and Oberthur Card Systems. Moreover, these ID systems, along with related biometric passports, rely on techniques of identity management developed in the online internet world. That is, modes of regulating who may or may not have virtual access to websites and other electronic domains are now applied to the offline world of borders and citizenship classification. This is discussed more fully in the next chapter.

Note must also be taken of the growth of biometrics as a means of verification (checking that the individual is who he or she claims to be) and identification (checking that the individual's record matches that in the relevant database). All new ID systems use some kind of biometric, based on a feature of the human body. Fingerprints, iris scans, facial topography and hand scans all count as biometrics, and these enhance both passports and ID card systems today. The idea is that accuracy will be increased and the possibilities of fraud will be reduced by using biometrics. While PINs and passwords may be forgotten or lost, the body is always available and provides a direct link between the record and the person. As I observe in chapter 5, however, some surveillance problems persist with the use of biometrics.

The old bureaucratic logic of government administration now works its way through both biometrics and networked identification systems into a world fraught with subtle nuance – identities and identifications. In this world those with access to resources are highly mobile – international businesspersons, tourists, and the like – and their identification systems (from credit cards to frequent flyer cards) tend to accelerate ease of movement. But for others, who are working (or, worse, unemployed) migrants, refugees or asylum seekers, not to mention those with distinctive 'Muslim' or 'Arab' names, these systems tend to militate against movement both within and between countries. While older, twentieth-century understandings of citizenship stressed the *inclusion* of all eligible persons in systems of health, welfare and legal protection, newer citizenship practices, including ID systems, seem to stress *exclusion* of undesirable elements.

These newer exclusionary modes of governance are dubbed by Didier Bigo the *ban*opticon. If Bentham's *pan*opticon was intended to get all citizens to comply, welfare-state style, then today's methods are more particular. Bigo argues that specific groups such as suspected welfare fraudsters or terror suspects are blamed before they have done anything, 'simply by categorizing them, anticipating profiles of risk from previous trends, and projecting them by generalization upon the potential behaviour of each individual pertaining to the risk category'.[35] This is not general social intervention, but targeted, using information and technology to try to produce a risk-free society through a customized allocation of governmental resources.[36] There is also a wider dimension to this.

As the economic and political disparities between the global south and north have grown, so resistance to the rich north has taken new and, for some, unexpected forms. In particular, the deep-seated humiliations of the Arab world at the hands of western colonial and economic powers has helped to spawn what is now regarded as a key international problem – a sort of permanent crisis – of global terrorism. Key events, starting symbolically (though not historically) with 9/11, have catalysed rapid growth of new surveillance and identification systems once again geared to establishing unambiguously who is a *bona fide* citizen of which country.[37] The difficulty is that in a globalizing world many people are on the move, and ID systems are sought that classify them according not only to citizenship but also to status – temporary, permanent, national, and so on. As we have seen, searchable databases already facilitate social classification and categorization. In this context, they appear as a godsend.

But not only are new ID systems raising questions about the reality of the very citizenship rights that identification was once supposed to guarantee – freedom of movement, freedom from want, equality before the law, and so on – they are themselves subject to globalizing forces. Governments now seek ways of 'harmonizing' their identification procedures both for border crossing and for internal policing and controls, and, once again, this is facilitated by the new technologies. The International Civil Aviation Organization (ICAO) is a prominent player in this process, as it sets standards for biometric passports and, by implication, for new national smart ID programs such as that in the UK. International conventions are held to develop 'globally interoperable systems' for identification in the field of 'MRTDs' (machine-readable travel documents).[38]

This globalizing of surveillance[39] through the regulating of mobility and transactions and through 'interoperable' agreements on technology standards appears to be contributing to what Oscar Gandy calls the 'cumulative disadvantage' associated with social sorting systems that use searchable databases.[40] Although the context in which he discusses this is the discriminatory practices of insurance companies, which frequently have the effect of exacerbating racial disadvantage, the same kinds of sorting mechanisms facilitate cumulative disadvantage on an international level, affecting immigrants, asylum seekers, refugees, and the like, in disproportionate ways. This is the main burden of chapter 4.

Sorting, then, is central to new ID systems. It permits what might be called remote control, especially 'policing at a distance'. It contributes to what Kevin Haggerty and Richard Ericson call the 'surveillant assemblage',[41] that only partially coordinated coming together of many and varied contemporary practices and processes that record, monitor, locate, track, observe and, yes, identify individuals so that they can be profiled and their personal data can be mined for further analysis. Indeed, identification processes are central to this assemblage. This is obvious from post-9/11 international policing and anti-terrorism activities,[42] but also from more mundane matters such as international financial transactions. It is often argued that improved identification practices, and especially the development of national ID systems, could increase the effectiveness of many components of information-based social interactions, or, in other words, the surveillant assemblage.

Directions in Surveillant Sorting

Identification and citizenship belong together in the modern world. Citizenship has increasingly come to be viewed as an individual matter for which a system of personal records is required. While this now appears in the broad swathe of 'dataveillance' that exists across a range of government departments, the common denominator within them is the need for identifiers that will distinguish one individual from another. This facilitates the social sorting that such systems are constructed to achieve. Increasingly, however, such identifiers are also used across different domains.

As James Rule pointed out more than thirty years ago, for example, and as noted in the previous chapter, the US driver's licence is often used in practice as a universal ID in that country.[43] Today, pressure is on to find IDs that work for several purposes – border crossing, fraud control, access to government information and perhaps for commercial (video rental) and semi-commercial (libraries) activities as well – which is shaping the field in fresh ways. As we have seen, the same criteria for identification are now sought across national boundaries too.

The key developments in this story could be read as technological progress, but whatever one's judgement on this, it is the (let us assume) unintended consequences that count. For however much one acknowledges, rightly, the ambiguity of surveillance as seen in areas such as ID card systems, the key problem is that, once established, systems can easily acquire an apparent life of their own which is much easier to initiate than to halt or redirect. When agendas such as the 'war on terror', curbing the migration of undesirable groups and even the quest for solutions for credit card fraud are shaping the development of ID systems, the purportedly abstract and 'impersonal' demands of a classic bureaucracy do seem somewhat undermined.

ID card systems offer unique identifiers and thus are critically significant for all government activity. This can range from anti-terrorism to access to government information. But the chief difficulty always lies in the powers granted to the state (now in alliance with corporate and technical bodies) that has control over the means of identification. In the UK case, the lack of clarity about the primary purpose of the ID system is a key issue for those attempting to evaluate the progress of development.[44]

An additional issue raised in relation to identification regimes as sorting systems is how much information is sought. It is clear that the trend is towards seeking more and more personal data, as different kinds of databases – commercial, administrative, law enforcement – come to be viewed as appropriate sources for 'national security'. Behind this, however, is a subtly shifting rationale for data gathering: the move from 'risk' to 'precaution'. So while the new technologies of personal data processing are important, the fresh imperatives lying behind them are also highly significant. As Lucia Zedner points out, the idea of 'precaution' arose in the field of environmental sciences, indicating that it may be imperative to act even when some – as in the climate change debate – are still insisting that there is insufficient evidence.[45] In crime control or anti-terrorism situations, however, and applied to individuals, the precautionary principle gives powerful licence to pre-emptive action – in this case, garnering personal data 'just in case' – which may have deleterious effects on human rights and civil liberties.

As well, there are other serious difficulties confronting the sorting systems of identification. One is the reliability of the biometric tests on which ID systems rely[46] and another is the increasing remoteness of verification processes with the globalization of such systems. These are discussed in chapters 4 and 5. Another issue is that ID systems often subtly classify populations according to opaque criteria. It is notoriously difficult, for example, to try to discover who is on current 'terror watch-lists' or 'no-fly lists'. People are often surprised to learn, inadvertently, that they have been on official files for decades. Canadian academic, activist and singer Teresa Healy set off a radiation alarm (meant for nuclear bomb detection) and was pulled aside for questioning when crossing the US border in 2007 after a recent nuclear-tracing hospital test. It turned out that the officer had a fingerprint file on her dating from a peace demonstration in the 1980s. And 67-year-old Andrew Felmar was also stopped at the US border in 2007 and told he had a life-time ban for narcotics use – he was a psychotherapist doing experiments with legally obtained LSD between 1967 and 1975.[47]

The Politics of Sorting Systems

How can new ID systems, whose use is so consequential for those citizens identified and classified by them, be made accountable to others beyond political constituents and corporate shareholders? Is there a larger frame than combating fraud or regulating immigration or even national security within which the administration of citizenship via ID systems may be understood? Put another way, can identification processes which inevitably are 'sorting systems' yet be made compatible with the desires of ordinary citizens not merely for national security but also for human security (defined below), which is both more global and more personal?

At present, to take one prominent example, the British case of a multi-purpose national ID system does not offer much promise in this regard. It is far from clear that even national security will necessarily be enhanced by the emerging ID system. Many have suggested that national security would be better served by improving border security and conventional intelligence gathering, an idea that is underscored by the August 2006 Atlantic flight terrorist plot involving more than twenty Britons that led to three convictions for murder (though not for conspiracy to blow up airliners).[48] Although the US Administration claimed that the operation showed the need for more advance passenger data,[49] it is clear that the alleged plot was actually foiled not by the production of more data from travellers but by the use of informers, undercover agents and tip-offs.

Responses to new ID programmes vary considerably, which is hardly surprising given the basic ambiguity of such systems. In some countries, such as Belgium, where the practical benefits for citizens were stressed by policy makers, the electronic ID took the place of earlier systems with relatively little public concern expressed. At the same time, in other countries, anxieties and misgivings may be heard in public debate over new IDs. Municipalities and states in Japan and the USA have objected to the new uses of personal data by refusing to cooperate, and in Britain numerous vocal protests accompanied the passage of the Identity Cards Bill through Parliament.

Objections to the Australian 'Access Card', a proposed multi-purpose identifier that appeared to its opponents as a backdoor national ID card, almost led to its defeat under the John Howard coalition government and to its abandonment by the new Kevin Rudd Labour government that came to power in November

2007.[50] The kinds of objections made should be considered by regulators, from the case against ID systems altogether – that they are superfluous and their objectives can be met by other means – to arguments about testing and improving the technologies *before* they are adopted and bringing the measures in line with at least EU Data Protection requirements.[51]

Assuming, pragmatically, that it is now too late to turn back the ID system tide in the UK, the challenge for regulators – from the Information Commissioner and elsewhere – is to take every opportunity to enforce rigorous safeguards and transparency and accountability of use. Experts argue that the eventual system need not be as negative as its critics fear. Other countries that have yet to adopt or even to debate ID systems would do well to heed the whole debate as it has unfolded in the UK. Even though the Home Affairs Committee of the UK Parliament,[52] concurring in part with a report from the London School of Economics (LSE),[53] concluded that the ID proposals were ineffective, costly and a violation of civil liberties, the proposal has been pushed forward and, to date, has succeeded.

Former Prime Minister Tony Blair assured the British public, against the evidence, that the civil liberties objections no longer carry weight, and this seems to be linked to the often-heard argument of despair that cards are already carried for every purpose anyway. Why not one more? The reason why not, say the civil libertarians and privacy advocates, is that other cards, such as drivers' licences, credit cards and passports, are held voluntarily. The non-obligatory character of the initial ID system should fool no one, they say. The history of 'function creep' suggests strongly that once the card is needed for a range of service-access, it will become *de facto* compulsory. Moreover, the voluntary cards relate to single roles, as drivers, consumers or tourists, whereas the ID card system gives the government powers – and this is the regulatory challenge – to monitor activities across a range of roles that include the three mentioned as well as those more conventionally associated with government administration.

The challenges to would-be regulators of ID systems are thus manifold and urgent. If hard-won human rights are not to be further stripped away in the name of a 'war on terror' or of claims about greater administrative efficiency in service delivery, then ID systems need to be scrutinized very closely. The best possible ID system has civil liberties risks to be faced. Critics argue that the oversight of technical and legal provisions should be made more transparent and workable and public concerns should be heeded much more diligently. It is hard to escape the conclusion that at present the political need to be seen to be doing something and the persistent pressure from high-technology companies seem to be dominant.

If 'national security' is one of the key drivers of ID card development, then it is worth observing that there is an even broader context. The best large frame for considering such matters as the protection of vulnerable populations is the notion of human security. Although it is not in competition with 'national security', it begins at a local community level and with the real everyday concerns of individuals and families. Combating terrorism is not usually high on such priority lists, although freedom from fear and from want are more likely to be. According to Mary Kaldor, such human security concerns may be locally rooted but they are simultaneously based in rights, multilateralism, legitimate government, and have a regional focus.[54]

Might there be a parallel development to the paradoxes of ID implementation in the mushrooming of video surveillance in all the major cities of the world? Similarly to ID card systems, closed-circuit television (CCTV) is an information technology-enabled system that has grown rapidly in response to fears about lack of safety and security, is endorsed or sponsored by governments and is marketed aggressively by technology corporations. Despite the lack of evidence that CCTV works for the purposes stated by its promoters – in May 2008 a senior UK police spokesperson lamented that only 3 per cent of street crimes in London were solved using CCTV images, despite Britain having more cameras than any country in the world[55] – the expansion of CCTV coverage continues. Part of the reason, ironically, is that the British public claims to feel safer with CCTV in operation, and the government and police authorities know that they have their support in expanding CCTV coverage.

It is clear, however, that the new technologies underlying ID systems have yet to be refined to a point where they can be said to have proved their reliability. More seriously, it is also clear that the rationale for most systems includes particular attention to marginalized or vulnerable groups – immigrants, asylum seekers, refugees, welfare claimants, terror suspects, and the like – so the social sorting enabled will likely affect them first. Where we do have evidence, historically, of pre-electronic ID systems, the record is stained with everything from cumulative disadvantage to the proscription of certain groups to genocide.

New national ID systems play a crucial, pivotal role in the development of contemporary surveillance societies. Given the spiralling media-amplified public fears, the making of political mileage out of conspicuous and expensive 'anti-fraud' and 'anti-terror' schemes, and the corporate pressure from persuasive high-tech companies, the struggle for human security and against potentially civil liberties-compromising measures like ID systems is likely to be long and tough. The evidence presented here and the implications of present trends strongly suggest that it is a struggle eminently worth engaging.

Conclusion

Today's national ID initiatives are systems for sorting populations according to a variety of criteria for differential treatment between groups. Although national IDs have always involved social sorting, this dimension is deepened by the use of new technologies that diminish the significance of the card itself, compared with and now dwarfed by the databases of personal information made accessible to relevant authorities through the use of the card. This fact becomes the more significant when we consider the ways in which governments around the world are adopting new ID systems of one kind or another, aided and abetted by technology corporations that are very keen to obtain the lucrative contracts (the theme of the next chapter); and that the driving force behind that adoption is not the relatively limited notion of 'risk' so much as 'precaution', which creates a voracious and apparently insatiable appetite for more data.

Strong government and corporate momentum – and, para-doxically, public desires in some cases – pushes new IDs. Where publics have questioned new IDs, a variety of modes of resistance have appeared. These include civil liberties lobbies and privacy or data protection groups, right through to municipalities or states that refuse to participate in ID schemes that seem to be simply unnecessary or unnecessarily intrusive or coercive. Few, interest-ingly, have really majored on the social sorting arguments in their opposition to ID card systems. Some question the unreliability of the technologies; others, their cost. Yet others, such as the LSE group in the UK, worry about the relatively untested nature of the technologies. Factors such as untried systems, unreliable technolo-gies and unprecedented personal data-garnering operations along with somewhat ominous historical precedents and the potential of new data-mining techniques could pose questions about whether ordinary citizens really have 'nothing to fear' (as they are so often assured, if they have 'nothing to hide').

However, for those who would enter the current debates over ID card systems there is a further problem. Not only are the terms of the debate changing as 'identity and identification' take on new connotations and as the idea of 'identity management' becomes significant, but the very items supposedly connected by ID cards – states and citizens – are themselves undergoing subtle and not-so-subtle alteration. An older vocabulary, which assumed that nation-states are the primary players and that citizens relate to those states in terms of rights and duties, is being eroded by the tides of outsourcing, on the one hand, and consumerism, on the other. Today, technology corporations, not to mention the software protocols themselves, play much larger roles in the production of systems such as ID cards. And the new 'consumer-citizen', oper-ating in a market mode, sees first the convenience offered by ID cards. We can make sense of this emerging situation by considering what I call the 'card cartel' – the focus of the next chapter.

3

Card Cartel

The Malaysian *MyKad* National ID Card project . . . could truly be described as a killer application for smart card technology.

Smart Card Solutions website[1]

You have government on a holy mission to ramp up information gathering and you have an information technology industry desperate for new markets.

Peter Swire[2]

In 2008 new national ID card systems were announced in at least two African countries, Nigeria and Angola. These are expensive schemes for relatively poor countries but the respective governments deem them necessary for overcoming fraud associated with multiple registrations in places like hospitals, banks and embassies (Nigeria) and for 'homeland security' (Angola).[3] The companies providing the systems are well-known global players. Nigeria's National Identity Management Commission appointed two consulting companies to guide the search for a replacement for Sagem, the previous ID supplier, while Angola's equivalent group named LaserCard as the major winners of the bid for an identity management system.

Missing from many accounts of new ID card systems is a political economy perspective that explores the corporate as well as the administrative and governmental aspects of national identification. And yet the facts are clear. Big business works with big government in what is now a booming security industry. In the USA, an industry expert for the business magazine *Intelligent Enterprise* noted that 'Homeland Security will help fuel an IT recovery. IT solution providers may one day look back on the War on Terror and be grateful for the opportunities born out of turmoil.'[4] In September 2001 Oracle CEO Larry Ellison saw the possibilities for national IDs right away, before the dust had settled at Ground Zero. He offered the US Administration free software for a national ID system. Numerous others have followed his lead in seeking to become key providers of identification and other security technologies in the aftermath of 9/11. It is a lively marketplace[5] and has induced the OECD to name a whole new field of enterprise, 'the New Security Economy'.[6] Sociologically, this means that ID card systems cannot properly be understood without a serious political economy of security and surveillance.

That many governments around the world are scrambling to introduce or implement new ID card systems is evident, but the role played by 'world events' such as terrorist attacks or public concerns such as 'identity theft' is only part of the story. The role played by outsourced agencies is considerable, and is influential, given the dependence of relevant government departments on their expertise and advice. The corporations involved in ID card production are large and, because they depend on government procurements, relatively buoyant. They include IBM, Sagem, Oracle, Sun Microsystems, Drexler, Microsoft and others – household names in the communication and information technology field. They range across related fields from smart card applications, to scanners, to biometrics.[7]

In this chapter a theory of citizen identification is outlined. It explores the control of the means of identification using ID card systems, not only by nation-states, but also by corporate interests and software protocols. Going beyond classic sociological treatments of 'monopolies' over the means of production (capitalism) or of violence (the state), a kind of 'oligopolization of the means of identification' is arguably underway. This in turn raises questions about how corporations obtain contracts and what the consequences are in different contexts (for instance, LaserCard in Italy, Canada and, now, Angola) and about the technical protocols (for example of identity management) that affect the scope and operational modes of new IDs. It also challenges conventional understandings of citizenship.

The point of theory is to explain some phenomenon, to place it in a context that throws light on its genesis, its current significance and its likely future. In what follows, I locate national ID card systems in such a context which I hope will help to show what is happening. IDs are very technology-dependent, and the logic of the technology must be taken seriously. At the same time, I want to indicate how – as with all technologies – they are socially shaped by powerful interests. Not only is there a close mutual constitutive process, but also national ID card systems already evince a particular way of seeing the world – indeed, of *being* in the world – and they speak to some specific circumstances and situations in which they appear to 'fit'.[8] The world is already framed, in the twenty-first century, in ways that seem to call for ID cards. For many, they make sense. Their time has come.

Theorizing the Card Cartel

Before I go any further, let me say two things about my theory of the 'card cartel'. One, it is critical of the view that national ID cards have to do merely with a relationship between 'citizen' and 'state'. Indeed, it is just these terms that must be opened up for inspection. What I propose is that ID cards are the product not only of the 'state' but also of firms and protocols, and that what it means to be a 'citizen' is changing as the means of identification help to define and produce citizens in fresh ways. In what follows, the focus is mainly on the former question, about IDs as the 'products of the state'. Two, the theory is meant to be tried out in different situations. I do not imagine that it will fit every case perfectly, although I do think that it helps us to focus on variations within the general theme mentioned in my first point. So with regard to specific countries, the question is: how far does this argument work here? And; which part of the theory is particularly applicable here, and why?

Some of those who applaud the arrival of national ID card systems often downplay their social significance. In this view they are 'merely' a means of rationalizing systems or making certain processes – such as distributing welfare benefits or granting citizenship rights – more efficient. They assert that so far from being about 'identity', that preciously personal sense of who we are, it's a matter of identification or how others see us. Indeed, in a digital era, it is not 'identification' but 'verification', or checking that you are who you say you are, that counts here. Even 'identification' is too elevated a term for such matters. In other words, those who promote the use of ID cards often propose that they are a merely 'technical' matter.

Sociologically this makes no sense. Matters of identity and identification are always social and always interact with each other, however technological the media on which they depend. They are ways of distinguishing certain individuals and groups from other individuals and groups. Identity and identification establish and signify relationships of similarity and difference.[9] Processes of classification and of attachment are always involved, and in the case of national ID cards both the classification and the attachment are in relation to the nation-state. Not *only* the nation-state, perhaps, but *at least* the nation-state, and predominantly so. Perhaps a personal example will help.

In 1976 I was classified as a temporary visitor to Canada when I first taught at a Canadian university. Thus was I distinguished from other groups, such as immigrants or refugees. In the early 1990s I was slotted as a 'landed immigrant' (it would now be 'permanent resident'[10]), but in the mid-1990s, after further bureaucratic process to check my eligibility, I was re-classified as a Canadian citizen. My personal attachment to Canada is incomplete, however, because, having been born in Scotland, I still hold a British passport as well as my Canadian one, and I have good friends and family in the UK, not to mention a fondness for stone terrace houses in Yorkshire, or for the craggy Scottish highlands. I identify as 'Canadian' but also identify *with* some British places and people. I should also say that, as a white male, I'm aware that such identities and transitions are easier to negotiate than if it were otherwise. My relatively smooth mobility is privileged.

National ID card systems are about similarities and differences, and about classification and attachment. They can never be merely technical instruments of efficiency or convenience, even though that may be how they are sold. They have long pre-histories in the modern world, in which citizenship was reinvented as individuated membership of a given political community with certain rights, privileges and responsibilities attached, and from which 'non-citizens' were excluded. In the globalizing world of today, with its affluent mobility across national borders and its impoverished quest for better living conditions among refugees and migrant workers, ID card systems acquire some additional meanings that are sometimes sharply at odds with each other. And these meanings cannot be cut free from broader contexts of social ordering and digital control[11] that constantly seek more accurate data so that precautionary[12] and pre-emptive measures may be taken. They have a past, present and future orientation.

Let me draw attention to some resources available for theorizing ID cards and also suggest ways of going beyond them. Two sources are particularly useful: Nikolas Rose's work on the 'securitizing of identity'[13] and John Torpey's on the 'monopoly of the means of movement'.[14] The former shows how today's world increasingly demands proof of legitimate identity in order to exercise freedom. We all carry numerous cards – from bank cards to drivers' licences – that display our virtual identity as found on a database and give access to various kinds of privileges. Registration becomes routine in numerous everyday contexts. Processing personal identifiable data marks the merger of automated technologies and the bureaucratic administration of persons across a range of roles. National ID cards appear as 'natural' extensions of this; indeed, according to some, they will eliminate the need to carry so many cards.

The latter source, Torpey, suggests that a particular kind of 'securitized' identity is visible in the passport. In this case, he says, the state looms large. Contrasting pre-modern situations in which travel and border crossing were relatively unproblematic (and, for most people, much more rare of course), Torpey shows how passports have become a means whereby modern governments monopolize the 'means of movement'. One cannot now expect to move from one country to another without some documentary identification such as a passport that will permit exit, entry and, of course, re-exit, return and re-entry. The passport is the standard document, but in countries that form a regional bloc, such as the EU, equivalent documents now exist alongside the passport.

Now, unlike Rose, who cautions against seeing in the securitizing of identity the 'tentacles of the state spreading across everyday life' because in fact the process is 'dispersed and disorganized',[15] Torpey sees a strong state role in the invention of the passport. This is not just to utter the obvious: passports are properly provided by the appropriate government department. The state, Torpey avers, 'expropriates' from individuals the legitimate means of movement. The result is to 'deprive people of the freedom to move across certain spaces and to render them dependent on states', not only for access but for an '"identity" from which they can escape only with difficulty and which may shape their access to various spaces'.[16] Clearly, this is a more politically critical view than Rose's, and it is also the direction that this present study takes.

Yet while my thesis about ID cards echoes aspects of Torpey's 'monopoly' view, it acknowledges, with Rose (following Foucault), that 'government' is achieved by multiple forces. I suggest that what is emerging today may best be understood as a kind of 'card cartel' or, more clumsily, an oligopolization of the means of identification. The forces driving national ID card systems are like a combination of firms that get together to keep prices artificially high and to keep out competition. This will differ depending on how strong or weak is the state in question. In one case, oligopoly may well be an unintended consequence of political-economic restructuring, outsourcing and technological dependence. In another, there may be some hint of a deliberate oligopolistic arrangement.[17]

In an oligopoly a small number of competitive firms control the market and are the only actors from whom the particular commodity may be obtained. The 'commodity' is legitimate identification and the 'firms', I suggest, are the nation-state, technology corporations and, less obviously, because they are not actors in the same sense as the others, the softwares governing the identification protocols. So beyond Torpey's singular state I suggest a combination of forces. The economic metaphor is no accident, because beyond Rose's dispersed processes of identity securitization I suggest that some actors are nonetheless more important than others.

Controlling the Means of Identification

Torpey's theory of the passport takes Karl Marx's and Max Weber's work as a springboard. The former argued that the capitalist class expropriates the means of production from the workers, leaving this group with only the cash nexus, wage labour, as the link between them. The capitalist wants to maintain a monopoly on the means of production as a source of profit. Weber parried this with the proposal that modernity bequeathed another sort of monopoly, but this time one owned by the state. Rather than permitting small-scale fiefdoms or duchies to wield weapons or wage war, only the state could control the means of violence. Torpey's contention is that these two leave out another important area, the capacity to travel where one wills. For him, the passport is emblematic of another monopoly: on the means of movement and on sorting out who belongs where.[18]

Torpey deals with national ID cards *en passant* as a documentary 'grey zone' between international passports regulating movement outside and internal passports regulating movement inside the territory of the nation-state. He sees ID cards as enforcing intermittent (rather than constant, as with internal passports) checks on movement and also as offering rights to democratic participation, public services and transfer payments.[19] With the latter trio of rights access, ID cards are seen to have more in common with international passports in that they offer access to benefits of citizenship.

As Torpey rightly says, all three documents – passports, internal passes and ID cards – are used to 'construct and sustain enduring identities for administrative purposes. That is, they enhance states' embrace of individuals' in pursuit of their administrative, economic and political aims.[20] And they assume, Torpey avers, that people cannot be trusted to say truthfully who they are. Put more strongly, states suspect the veracity of all self-identifying statements by putting the burden of proof on the document. ID cards are thus part of what might be called a culture of suspicion. If this appears to be overstating the case, then at the very least one should say that ID systems are a means of increasing the visibility of citizens and non-citizens to the state, of making them more 'legible' (as James Scott says[21]). Either way, the state's identification tends to take precedence.

If this is so, then might it not be equally valid to highlight what the documents have in common, namely their capacity to yield legitimate identifications? In this case another way of seeing national IDs and other citizenship documents would be to view them as generic identifiers, with passports, visas, and the like, fulfilling part but not all of the possible functions of the 'legitimate means of identification'. As well, passports are usually used by a certain proportion of a given population, whereas national ID cards tend to be compulsory for all (even if roll-outs are patchy or 'non-nationals' have different cards or some schemes start out as 'voluntary' ones).

Building on Torpey, then, we can say that ID card systems work for both monitoring movement and for offering access to citizenship privileges. Legal protection, medical care and unemployment benefits would all be good examples of this. Indeed, some multi-purpose cards relate to other functions as well, such as opening bank accounts. Thus ID cards offer a legitimate means of identification for movement *and* for money, for travel *and* transactions. As Torpey says, what such documents achieve is to 'discourage people from choosing identities inconsistent with those validated by the state'.[22]

But is it only the state? In Torpey's view, legitimate 'identity' production is a state monopoly. Without entirely agreeing with Rose's position, I propose that, at least with regard to most current ID card systems, while the state may still validate identity, their production is a joint effort, involving both procurements by corporations and software protocols. Pressures exist, pushing for ID card systems, from all three sources: the state, corporations and software (or, more properly, the logic of identity management protocols, to which we turn in a moment). The latter may become embedded in standards (such as those required by the International Civil Aviation Organization, ICAO, for, say, biometrics in new-generation passports), but here I refer to protocols, the more general instructions or digital tools for implementing projects rather than the rules and requirements that have been agreed upon for a field such as the standards for international passport components.

Politics, Procurements and Protocols

Many nation-states around the world are in the business of discussing, devising or developing advanced ID card systems for national identification. None has anything like a complete system yet, but several, such as Belgium, Italy, Japan, Malaysia and Sweden, have made significant strides in this direction. Governments have chosen or have been presented with various routes, or combinations of routes, to the establishment of ID systems, from e-Government initiatives to post-9/11 security enhancement. Specific spurs, such as tackling identity theft, illegal immigration and welfare or medical care fraud, also play their part.

Equally clearly, as such national ID systems are by definition related to nation-states, both the legal backing for them (such as the US Real ID Act 2005 or the UK Identity Cards Act 2006) and the financial support for them are arranged by government (even if the costs fall at least partly on individual citizens). Any international agreements surrounding their use, such that, for instance, they are interoperable across a select range of other countries' borders, are also agreed at a national level. Lastly, administering them long term is ultimately a government matter as well, however much this, too, can be delegated to others in specific instances.

Now, this is in some ways at odds with the analysis offered by Nikolas Rose. He stresses that in the later twentieth century citizenship came to be realized not primarily in relation to the state or a single public sphere but in a variety of practices from working to shopping.[23] Thus the securitizing of identity may appropriately be thought of as 'securing the obligatory access points for active citizenship',[24] which has both inclusionary and, by the same token, exclusionary consequences. This, too, will differ from country to country. The analysis is an important one, but could be taken to imply that government in the sense of the nation state has somehow moved into the shadows (and for that matter that who exactly the excluded groups are and how they become excluded is not an analytical priority). Clearly, however, in the case of national ID card systems, the state is very important.

Having said that, in what some call an 'information era', other actors play a part too. The 'information era' has some mutually dependent relationships with political-economic restructuring and outsourcing, and is at the same time dependent on a digital infrastructure, so both firms and technologies are involved. It is no secret that global corporations are in the ID business, the most prominent example of which, post-9/11, was Larry Ellison's above-mentioned offer to the US Administration of free software to run a national ID card system as a means of bolstering national security. Less obviously, perhaps, but no less significantly, softwares and codes that underpin the protocols for 'identity management' themselves drive aspects of ID card systems. Indeed, the very concept of 'identity management' arose within online access protocols and has now been transposed into the world of offline controls at 'borders', both physical and virtual.

Procurements, Firms and Identification

Turning to the second of these 'partners' within the 'oligopoly', it is important to note that a number of different kinds of corporate body are involved significantly, including marketing and consulting firms. Some are opportunistic, while others see ID cards as part of a steady-state strategy. An example of the former is Steven Brill, a journalist writing about the post-9/11 world, who in 2003 set up a new company, Verified Identity Card Inc., so that people could voluntarily (and for payment) offer an electronic card at airports indicating that they had no link to terrorist groups or a criminal record. He brought in the Civitas Group as an investor (co-chaired by Samuel R. Berger, a national security adviser to President Clinton, and Charles Black, a former senior adviser to Presidents Reagan and Bush senior). Other partners included Transcore (who make the E-Z pass toll system) and Choicepoint, the Georgia-based consumer data broker.[25] The company later became Verified Identity Pass Inc. (the VIP acronym is no accident) and sells biometric passes for access to public places such as airports, office buildings and sports arenas, often under the name Clear.

It is usually established high-technology corporations that play a major role, however – even if they sport start-ups and spin-offs – and these are the ones discussed here. Of course, businesses have often provided services for government departments in the past, especially where matters of citizenship or national censuses are concerned. There is a long history of state–corporate cooperation. International Business Machines (IBM), for example, began, in a sense, in the glitch-ridden US census of 1880 that a census employee, Herman Hollerith, was detailed to improve. His punch-card system proved a winner for the 1890 census and Hollerith went on to found IBM. More than a century later, in 2007 IBM was keen to sell its 'Secure ID solution' especially to European countries developing national ID card systems.

These connections are no mere coincidence. There's a lot of history in that 'more than a century later' phrase. If one looks at the UK case, for example, the wartime ID card was not the only use made of identifiable personal data. As Louise Amoore indicates, in the 1940s the Board of Trade turned to Price Waterhouse accountants for a means of rationing clothes. To prevent clothing shortages and inflated prices, these accountants produced a number system that could reveal habits and behaviours and reliably verify individual claims.[26] Interestingly, Amoore observes, in 2002 IBM acquired the consulting arm of what had by then become PricewaterhouseCoopers, so that integrated databases and software models could be bundled with risk management and 'future-proofing'. This reveals a subtle shift from war-time exigencies, where identification was simply to *prevent* clothing shortages, to the *pre-emptive* identification characteristic of war-on-terror modes of management.

Indeed, Amoore's work continues the story, by tracing the

connections between IBM and the UK retailer Marks & Spencer (M&S) in their search for algorithmic techniques to build profiles of 'unknown' identities based on trails of transactional data and related consumer behaviour. Targeting 'unknown' identities in prosaic settings such as cinema foyers, which enabled a marketing focus on those who had not actually left traces of their own, was applied by the same IBM personnel – notably, Rakesh Agrawal – to security settings in 2004. And what was happening on one side of the Atlantic often paralleled developments on the other. In the same years, the Defence Advanced Research Projects Agency (DARPA) was working on its Total Information Awareness (TIA) program that built on similar customer relationship management (CRM) models of consumer behaviour to try to discover potential terrorists, currently 'unknown' within given populations.[27]

IBM, PricewaterhouseCoopers and M&S are just three corporations among others whose activities span commercial and security spheres. On the one hand, the stakes are high in such large-scale systems, and, on the other, companies have expertise that no government could hope to match. From a government and an industry viewpoint, both have to be involved. Government departments have to decide exactly what sort of a system they require, and the procurement process enables them to identify which companies might best do the job. This fact has led to some confusion, for example in the case of the UK ID card system. Some companies, unsure of whether or not making critical interventions in the pre-procurement process will affect their chances of obtaining a contract, have kept quiet at just the time when their expertise might have been useful. Jerry Fishenden of Microsoft, an adviser to the UK scheme, complained about this in *The Scotsman* newspaper.[28] As he also pointed out, no corporation would want its name associated with a failed IT project. Corporate reputations are at stake.

At the same time, what sorts of schemes are possible depends on the levels of technology available, the infrastructure to make them work together and the kinds of protocols required to connect individual citizens and government and other agencies using the system. Today, the very idea of a national ID card system has built into it several technological assumptions: that a digital infrastructure exists to support it; that linked databases can handle the volume of personal data traffic required; that those databases are searchable; that biometric technologies are adequate for verifying identities; and so on. A 'national ID card' is unthinkable without these and other components that can be supplied only by high-technology companies.[29]

From an industry viewpoint, the corporation aims to position itself as a potential supplier of hardware, software and expertise. This promises not only to enable the ID system, but also to strengthen the digital infrastructure of the country in question. Corporations have a larger agenda than merely to supply ID systems for 'government purposes', and the platform for this is the trade exhibition. Take, for example, the Indonesia Infrastructure Conference and Exhibition in November 2006 in Jakarta. The event was opened by the Indonesian President, Susilo Bamang Yudhoyono, and was described by interested parties as an attempt to 'kickstart development in the country's infrastructure sector'.[30] The local Hewlett-Packard president stated that 'The National Identity System solution from HP enables the government to develop and apply a complete ICT [information and communication technology] infrastructure.'

As Robert O'Harrow says in a book that carefully details the relationship between high-technology corporations and US security after 9/11, 'The government's turn to surveillance was almost reflexive.'[31] He adds later, 'Law enforcement and intelligence services don't need to design their own surveillance systems from scratch. They only have to reach out to the companies that already track us so well . . . .'[32] The 9/11 Commission's final recommendations underscored this link. Under the heading of 'Border Security', the item 'Standardize Secure Identifications' received a relatively high 'grade' of B- from Commission members. Their judgement was based on evidence that the Real ID Act 'has established by statute standards for state-issued IDs acceptable for federal purposes, though states' compliance needs to be closely monitored'.[33] The report does caution that 'without movement on the birth certificate issue, state-issued IDs are still not secure', which is partly why the grade scored was not higher. The Real ID plan has only staggered, not marched, since 2005, but among those calling on Congress, the Department of Homeland Security and state governments to press forward with it is the Information Technology Association of America.[34] The ITAA's mandate is to 'promote the continued rapid growth of the IT industry'.

Another telling incident, reported by O'Harrow, concerns the way that Hank Asher, the owner of Seisint Corporation, got to demonstrate his identification product, Matrix, in the Roosevelt Room of the White House in January 2003. Having earlier convinced Florida State officials of the power for criminal investigations of his record-searching engine, he was ushered by Florida governor Jeb Bush (President George W. Bush's brother) into the presence of Vice-President Dick Cheney, FBI Chief Robert Muller and Tom Ridge, soon to be head of Homeland Security. The result was that Asher was given $8 million to speed Matrix's further development.[35] Later, Seisint along with Matrix was sold to Lexis-Nexis for $775 million, and, with others, such as Choicepoint, was soon continuing its outsourced personal records business on behalf of customers including Homeland Security's aviation screening program, CAPPS II.

Although this survey is far from systematic, it does indicate clearly the importance of the role of high-technology corporations in providing ID card systems. The systems themselves are by definition technological, and in the present political-economic context it is unthinkable that the hardware and software would be sought elsewhere than in private profit-driven corporations. The companies often present themselves as being concerned about the national interest and about fostering security 'solutions', but whatever the case, they have a broader vision for their products, within an enhanced ICT infrastructure. There is yet another dimension to this, however.

Protocols, Technologies and Identification

Increasingly, the common language[36] linking ID card systems and industry is that of 'identity management', and this leads into a discussion of the third 'partner' in the 'oligopoly on identity'. This 'partner' is not a person or a company but the technologies themselves. That such entities could be partners in an oligopoly follows from the view of technology underpinning this analysis, that technologies are socially shaped and are in part a response to a world that is also culturally shaped by them. Technologies do in a sense have political biases built into them.[37] I have in mind both the general technological orientation of 'identity management' and specific protocols associated with it. If this argument is correct, then it also fits the proposal that ID systems represent concerns with both travel and transactions. Identity management pertains in the first place to online business practices and has (been) migrated over to the physical world of border controls. In both cases it has to do with patrolling thresholds.

Most generally, the technologies involved in identification cannot be isolated from their social contexts. They have no separate moment of existence. As Bruno Latour argues, there are 'actors', entities that do things, and 'networks', which tie together two systems of alliances, people and things.[38] Actors and networks constitute each other. I want to suggest that the protocols embedded in identity management are in this sense actors – they do something. What do they do? Well, they operate through code, and, as Lawrence Lessig explains in *Code and Other Laws of Cyberspace*, software and hardware not only make cyberspace what it is but also regulate cyberspace as it is. Code is the 'law' of cyberspace.[39]

Now, Lessig and Latour are not making exactly the same point, but their work is in a sense complementary.[40] The idea is taken further by Alexander Galloway, who explores what philosopher Gilles Deleuze might mean by 'control society' with specific reference to the internet: 'Protocol is to control societies as the panopticon is to disciplinary societies.'[41] Leaving on one side the question of how appropriate it is to characterize 'societies' in this way,[42] Galloway comments that Foucault's notion of biopower is 'protocological'. It is all about the 'administration of bodies and the management of life'. The internet is the largest information management system, but identity management shares several of its features.

Protocols are the standards governing how specific technologies are implemented. They operate at the level of coding and, for Galloway, are the means whereby control exists after decentralization. While TCP/IP (Transmission Control Protocol/ Internet Protocol) enables computers to talk to each other uni- versally and thus appears to be anything but controlling, DNS (Domain Name System), which matches network addresses to network names, is very hierarchical, and this machine contradic- tion is at the heart of Galloway's argument about control. Protocol is, for Galloway, a 'management style' that permits control when traditional systems of control such as bureaucratic hierarchy or cen- tralization have slipped away.[43] Electronic flows, which Galloway refers to as 'nomadic' because they seem to wander at will, are harnessed by protocol, which guides distributed networks. Despite using words like 'nomadic', these are of course non-human systems, but once in place, they do serve to direct traffic in particular ways which affect outcomes in the human world.

Identity management operates by means of protocols and is seen as crucial to the transitions of the web from 'library' to 'marketplace' – these protocols are required for full possibilities of exchange to be realized. Google provides a perfect example. At its heart, identity management is seen in terms of supporting common identity needs of both government and private transactions.[44] The aim is a 'single sign-on' in both public and private spheres and maximum inter- operability. Customer relationship management system methods are increasingly common to each sector and identity management is seen as a tool to enhance this.[45] As far as e-Government is con- cerned, user IDs are increasingly required for access to public sector web areas. In the private sphere, Microsoft's 'Windows Live ID' is an example of an identity management protocol that offers single sign-on across a range of Windows products and applications.

A key means of securitizing identities for identity manage- ment purposes is the burgeoning field of biometrics,[46] but I shall not explore this further here as it is the topic of chapter 5. Suffice it to say that biometrics reinforces the idea that 'verification' or 'authentication' rather than identity and identification is important here because the question is one of qualification. Which body is qualified, and which disqualified, from access to these resources, privileges, spaces?[47] As Dean Wilson demonstrates in relation to borders and suspects, despite the claims that biometrics contrib- utes to 'neutral' verification techniques, such measures are in fact 'embedded in and constitutive of emerging processes of social classification and discrimination'.[48]

What the Card Cartel Theory Does and Does Not Say

The production of ID card systems may be seen as the outcome of a process between oligopoly members, understood through a triangulation of the three primary partners. This approach to ID card systems helps explain their provenance, their form and their futures. The idea of an oligopoly – or a card cartel – points to the power relations that govern the production of these systems. The term 'identification' is a reminder that ID card systems exist for just that purpose, to regulate the legitimate means of identification.

Theoretical resources discussed here are used in a 'toolbox' fashion. Firstly, the attempt to situate ID card systems in identity management protocols is not an Actor-Network-Theory (ANT) or Social Construction of Technology (SCOT) approach *per se* but benefits from both. However, I stress that not all actors have an equal explanatory role. Corporations and government departments play a significant part. Highlighting the role of corporations, secondly, is not to surrender to the simplistic views that reduce explanation to the operation of some mysterious capitalist impulses, but simply to show how they are a key component in a government arrangement for citizen and consumer identification. Important here, too, are the relationships between politicians and corporations. Increasingly, the latter are invited to display their wares to the former or to act as 'experts' in explaining what the technologies can do in the cause of surveillance. The protocols are meshed with the relations of ruling. Thirdly, the state is seen here variously as embracing citizens or making them more legible, but it is also argued that states are unable to act on their own. They depend on the high-tech corporations for the know-how, on softwares for the means of 'managing' identities and on international standards bodies such as ICAO for achieving interoperability.

I hinted early on that ID card systems appear to be appropriate at this moment; their time has come. This argument most resembles those of philosopher Martin Heidegger,[49] but it depends on the confluence of streams flowing into the ID card river. The logic of providing a card for travel-and-transactions, which ultimately includes all (so that it can exclude some), arises from business-technology sources. National ID card systems do not exist on their own or even as merely part of some concerted 'anti-terror' strategies after 9/11. They fit within a broader framework of already existing ways of doing business, of managing, that have parallels in crime control[50] and other fields. They assume that technological means are essential, and that the components of these are networked communications, searchable databases and, in the ID card case, biometrics. These in turn depend on other items such as scanners and readers. The technology choices provide the 'horizon of intelligibility', the best ways of making sense of the needs of the time.[51] Technological 'solutions' are assumed to be most appropriate, and these in turn assume a certain relation between humans and the world.

Seeking the origins of current ID card proposals merely in the various government initiatives, especially post-9/11, is thoroughly inadequate. For one thing, some origins lie much deeper, in crime control, colonialism[52] and war administration, but for another, part of the logic lies outside government. It is not merely that governments are outsourcing some services, delegating some tasks to external agencies, but that those agencies – corporations and technologies – help to define and constitute the systems themselves. Behind this is the larger framing of the world in which technological approaches are sought first and foremost and, indeed, are treated with reverence sometimes bordering on idolatry. Despite the disastrous 9/11 attacks and the prevailing pessimism that followed, many still view the internet very optimistically,[53] and it is this world of 'cyberspace' that is thought by some to offer hope.

Another thing that the card cartel theory helps to explain is why ID card systems of strikingly similar kinds are introduced despite deep political controversies over the acceptable rationale for them. In the case of the UK, where debate on the reasons for having new ID cards ranged over identity theft (the electronic commerce argument), anti-terrorism (the national security argument), curbs on illegal immigration and employment (the economic stability argument) and ease of access to government services (the e-Government argument), the idea of having a national ID on a smart card with biometric features based in a national registry went ahead anyway. As then Prime Minister Tony Blair declared in a November 2006 press briefing, the real reason for introducing national ID cards is 'modernity' (by which he seemed to mean 'being up-to-date'). This argument does not downplay the debates over the precise type of cards and the most appropriate software and hardware for them, which themselves vary by national context. It simply shows that determining the technical logic of the system does not necessarily depend on the reasons given for having the card in the first place. It is an example of the varying power of the different forces in the oligopoly.

The point of discussing oligopoly, however, is that it is a system of rule. Indeed, it indicates how 'digital rule' has become centrally significant.[54] If this argument is correct, the protocols of identity management are rising to a prominent position within the triangulated forces fostering ID card systems today. The securitized identities are indeed manifold and, yes, citizenship is realized through other means such as consumption and employment. But the state is still involved as an enabler and as a coordinator of planning. Moreover, as we have seen, the role of competing corporations is also vital in providing the means and the model for ID systems. Political economy is still present and must be considered as indispensable to the overall explanation.

If there is a system of rule, however, there are also subjects, but these, too, alter within the oligopoly of identification. New ID schemes tend to create citizens in the image of the leading motifs of the societies that give them birth. In societies dominated by consumption, it is unsurprising to find that citizenship is subtly recreated in terms of consuming. Particularly with e-Government, where citizens are conceived as people gaining access to services and benefits for them, the consumer or client mentality is apparent. Equally, if the leading motifs informing 'citizenship' are ones designed to root out and outlaw certain specified groups, then identification processes will reflect this. Needless to say, if these motifs – consumer-and-outlaw – operate at one and the same time they could well turn out to be mutually supporting. We return to this in chapter 6.

The consequences for citizenship, at least as conceived in ways that are inclusive and based on the extension of rights and obligations, are profound. The nature of the rule is through social sorting; classification for differential treatment based on varying profiles is written into ID card systems. At the very least, analyses of ID card systems should explore the consequences, and thus also policy alternatives, of this for those likely to be most negatively affected by national IDs – visible minorities (often 'Arab', 'Muslim' ones), welfare recipients and refugees and asylum seekers.[55] These are the ones for whom 'cumulative disadvantage'[56] is a reality and who are easily rendered invisible – as persons whose plight should, by right, be noticed – by the same system that states use to *increase* legibility.

Today's card cartel is also mobilized to increase legibility in new ways, especially with a view to that of previously 'un-read' or unknown identities. As we have seen, the 'classification for differential treatment' is, for national security purposes at least, based not so much on 'known' suspects as on profiles constructed on 'possible' suspects. The shift of knowledge is from past and present activities and behaviours to predictions and presumptions about future ones. While such pre-emptive logics may have questionable consequences in commercial spheres, the issue of correct and appropriate identifications becomes acute in cases of 'national security'. In the latter case, not only economic disadvantage but also the risk of detention, incarceration and worse may afflict those whose profiles mistakenly expose them as 'suspects'.

Conclusion

The simultaneous appearance of national ID card systems in many countries around the world cannot be explained merely in terms of post-9/11 panics (though the cultures of fear generated in the wake of 9/11 may well be decisive in giving them their chance). In any case, the 'post-9/11' argument only works in some countries. In others it is a monumental irrelevance. Rather, ID card systems may be seen as an 'oligopoly of identity' or a 'card cartel'. Different pressures, at once governmental, commercial and technological, converge to make the development of ID card systems seem like a 'solution' to several perceived problems at once. If one official rationale will not work, another will. National security fears may clinch a deal in one country while cutting no ice in another. At the same time, the idea of 'interoperability', looked at next, galvanizes attempts to produce compatible card systems in more than one country.

This builds on but goes beyond Rose's work on the securitizing of identity, which shows that citizenship is achieved today through consuming and working as much as through relations with the state and which highlights the importance of being able to demonstrate legitimate identity in order to exercise freedom. It also builds on but goes beyond Torpey's work, acknowledging the power and the 'embrace' of the state. But rather than seeing only 'state control', I add corporations and softwares to the narrative, and rather than focusing on the 'means of movement' that passports regulate, I show that it is identity itself that is regulated by ID cards, for both travel *and* transactions. How this occurs, I propose, is through the protocols of identity management which, it is assumed, are vital to all forms of identity control. This in turn will vary depending on the cultural conditions obtaining in any given nation-state.

As this chapter has noted frequently, national ID cards are under construction in many countries around the world. Indeed, the political economy of these ID systems shows how the card cartel is an international phenomenon. But it does not end there, with simultaneous development or with global corporations providing hardware and software for quite different societies and situations. The quest for 'national' security is at the same time a movement to seek *international* security and especially to find standards for security measures that are acceptable across borders and regions. Thus the kinds of identity verification, profiling, monitoring and tracking enabled by new IDs mean that the screening of travellers may occur anywhere. The technologies are tensile, or, as I say more specifically in the next chapter, are 'stretched screens'.

4

Stretched Screens

We do now need more information flowing internationally about who are potential terrorists and who are potential suspects.

Gordon Brown[1]

Interoperability is a term that has only recently crept into our consciousness . . . .

James Backhouse[2]

During 2007 the head of Interpol, Ronald Noble, attacked the British government for its failure to use available database resources to check up on would-be immigrants. He said that Interpol, the international police cooperation agency, had the passport numbers, fingerprints and photos of 11,000 suspected terrorists in its database but that the UK makes only fifty checks per month, compared with France's 700,000 or Switzerland's 300,000. This puts UK citizens at risk, he said.[3] Many questions could be pursued from this story, such as what might be learned about contrasting treatment of immigrants in different countries or how the association of terrorism with immigrants could affect the latter, or even whether the different 'checks' are commensurate with each other. However, in this chapter, which is about the growing globalization of identification practices, the focus is on the national and international circulation of identifying data with personal names, numbers and images.

Time was when matters of official identification and surveillance occurred primarily within the nation-state. If one thinks of the historical material in chapter 1 or of the 'police states' of the former Soviet Bloc countries, this is evident. Of course, international spying is an ancient art, but for routine purposes identification systems were relatively local in scope. The personal data filed in the labyrinthine archives, ledgers and cabinets of former East Germany, and made more recently (in)famous in the film *The Lives of Others* (2005), are a case in point. The 'lives' in question are local ones, within the state territory. Indeed, that film pivots on the local situation in that the main character, Gerd Wiesler, a Stasi surveillance officer, is drawn into the lives of those he is charged with monitoring and whose personal data he tracks.

The contrast with globalizing identification practices could not be greater. The borders that once contained surveillance data become increasingly porous and the digitized records seep at first and later flow freely courtesy of airline companies that are required to pass on passenger name records (PNRs); of credit card companies handling international business transactions; and of police who cooperate in checking the records mentioned a moment ago, of migrants moving from one country to another. In each case the process has become increasingly automated and is by definition remote. The chances of a Gerd Wiesler appearing as an official who gradually develops empathy with those whose lives are scrutinized slim down to vanishing point. For the processes are handled largely in databases using search engines and sometimes data-mining techniques made visible to officials on computer screens.

Screens have an interesting relationship with identification today. The police officer runs an ID check on the dashboard-mounted screen in the mobile police station once thought of merely as a police cruiser. The shiny surface of the screen belies the depth behind it as first the basic check, and then, if necessary, the fuller search enabled by data-mining software reveal personal details of surprisingly fine-grained quality on the person pulled over. But not only may screens hide unsuspected depth; in certain circumstances they may conceal a breadth, a range and a scope that are correspondingly wide. If the officer is in Canada, the data drawn upon may originate a continent away, on the Atlantic rather than the Pacific coast, or even, under certain circumstances, an ocean away, and from a quite different country, courtesy of an Interpol database.

The 'virtual window'[1] permits very wide vision indeed: a stretched screen that pulls its images and data from distant sources. But the ironic ambiguity of 'screens' is that they may at once permit seeing and being seen. And the verb to 'screen' may be used in both senses. Visual images, such as those of faces, may be screened, this time on a TV screen (although the internet is increasingly used for such screening it is not described as 'screening'), but using a computer, persons may be screened with ease. That is, they may be 'seen' through their data image on the screen. And such screening depends at some point on identification or at least verification procedures. The burden of this chapter is the ways in which such screens are becoming increasingly stretched, with as yet unknown results.

In the twenty-first century, citizens of the so-called 'advanced' societies are governed by identification. That reference to the 'twenty-first century' is no mere flourish. More and more, and more rapidly, identification is now becoming central as never before. As well as the obvious ways in which identification has become a crucial feature of the post-9/11 world, especially for international travel through borders and at airports, we are also identified within cell-phone location-based services, in employment situations, for all sorts of internet transactions, and in what are referred to generically as 'e-services' or, more usually, 'e-Government'.

Is all this some beneficial breakthrough for which we should be grateful, or a sinister conspiracy about which we should be anxious? In my view, neither, necessarily. More helpfully, these developments may be viewed as the complex consequences of ongoing transformations: political economies that developed from the 1970s, involving outsourcing in particular; of the rapidly expanding use of communication and information technologies for organizational efficiency; and of consumer-orientated personalization applied in many and varied contexts. These are historical conditions created by actors of all kinds and are simultaneously not of our choosing. 'Governing by identification' describes a way of analysing current developments, and although the stance taken here is critical – at times very critical – it is critical partly in the way that one might use 'globalization' as a *problématique*: not merely to decry it but rather to probe and assess.

The ways in which identification is required have proliferated, multiplied and metamorphosed into a vast amorphous system with many dimensions. The means of determining who is eligible, who has access, who may claim or who is a suspect is frequently found in a database, a biometric, some profiling software or, more likely, a combination of the above. While all manner of people may be screened for all manner of purposes, the question of identity is always at the forefront. Does this record match that person's details? Can these two apparently similar cases be distinguished? As I have already hinted, the situations of those identified vary considerably, as do the consequences of identification. As we shall see, increasingly, and particularly for some social groups, the 'difference' created by identification is interpreted and experienced as Otherness.[5]

Before going further, however, it must be stressed that the goal of 'interoperability' is just that, a goal. It is easy to fall into the trap of imagining that technical potential is social and political destiny. South Africa's recent experience offers a cautionary tale that may well have parallel lessons for others. The Home Affairs National Identification System (HANIS) had some precedents but officially began life in the mid-1990s. An automated fingerprint system would work with a biometric database that would in turn be integrated with the Population Register and the entire population would receive ID cards. It did not happen; at least it has not yet. Keith Breckenridge's analysis suggests that while single systems, such as healthcare or migration, or having a single corporation oversee the whole system, might work, full interoperability has proved an elusive goal. As he notes, 'the conflict between a tool designed for national security and the demands of the banking and social welfare system have proven, to date, irreconcilable'.[6]

In what follows, the idea of 'stretched screens' is explored through several connected concepts. The first, 'liquidity', reminds us of the fluidity of relationships in a globalizing world and its implications

for identification practices. The second, 'governing by identification', shows how central these identification practices have become
to determining people's life-chances and opportunities. Third,
we consider the importance of 'identification protocols', before
turning, fourthly, to an examination of a key case in the globalization of ID protocols: the role of the International Civil Aviation
Organization (ICAO) in 'interoperable' international ID documents.[7] The impetus for the ICAO role in IDs comes both from
9/11-prompted security measures and from fears about 'identity
theft'. Some contexts and actual cases of interoperability are considered. The fifth concept is 'ubiquitous computing', which also
requires identification protocols. Lastly, we return to the centrality
of identification for mobility and social participation – or lack of
it – in today's world. That the 'screens' are 'stretched' to include
more movements and more processes involving identification does
not mean that they are more inclusionary.

Liquidity and Identification

Today's stretched screens represent a significant shift from earlier
times when a more solid and territorial modernity held sway and
when checking identity was a relatively local and limited affair.
Checks may have been necessary for the bank or the factory, by
the city police or the hospital, but without a lot of population
movement, such screening was relatively static. In today's light or
liquid modernity[8] – as Zygmunt Bauman calls it – however, where
mobility is endemic, screening has been stretched across time and
space in ways hitherto unimaginable. Not only are large-scale
formal systems such as national ID card schemes involved, a host
of other modes of identification – a veritable identity assemblage
– play their part within the world of stretched screening.

The idea of liquidity as applied to contemporary conditions is
discussed in more than one way by Bauman. In several of his writ-
ings he contrasts the earlier modern period dominated by fixed
and hardware 'heavy' centres of power such as the nation-state
with today's mobility and lightness, characteristic of softwares and

the free circulation of technology and capital in a global market. Liquidity also reflects, more soberly, a world, also described by Bauman, of uncertainty, insecurity and risk. It is these features that generate the desire for new ID documents and verification protocols that reflect both differential mobility and the felt need to address the uncertainties and insecurities of the global era.

The liquidity of the new situation has a number of characteristics. One is the way that borders are blurred in a globalizing world. The old idea of territory having edges or defined limits has liquefied. Airports, for example, with their extensive 'border' apparatuses, are not normally located on the geographical lines separating one country from another or from the ocean.[9] New identification documents both shift the border inside the country and shift it beyond the border, as when, for instance in Europe, ID cards from a 'foreign' country may be checked remotely from its borders. The screening process stretches to include citizens of distant countries.

Another characteristic is that there is a certain liquidity, or elasticity, in the limits imposed on individuals by ID documents and other identification procedures. The *kind* of card carried makes a considerable difference to the 'mobility-chances' of the individual concerned, for example. If Chinese people arrive in Canada, their entry visas permit them to study or do business or to engage in tourism. But only certain categories of person can obtain permission to leave China in the first place. It is not even worth attempting to leave China legally if you do not fit the criteria. The would-be visitor is screened both to exit his or her home country and to enter another country. Again, the elasticity of screening processes is evident.

The emerging situation is not a simple one that can be easily captured by binary notions of solidity/liquidity or discipline/ control. While the metaphors of lightness and liquidity do help to indicate ways that social ordering practices have been disembedded[10] from older sedimentary and solid forms, there are also some strong continuities between, for example, the proscribed groups – the 'usual suspects' – in the older, inclusionary spaces and in today's exclusionary regimes. By the same token, the networked, decentralized forms of today's identification regimes should not be understood as somehow loosening the categories or liberating those trapped within certain undesirable identities. The story is much more complex, and the very ways in which identity becomes a mode of governance – especially within post-9/11 states of exception – speak to the persistence of both discipline and control within decentralized and 'light' systems.

New surveillance and identification regimes span these dimensions of today's world, bringing with them both global and local mutations of practice. The quest for common technical standards to facilitate 'interoperability' is an obvious example of the global dimension, with the International Civil Aviation Organization (ICAO) taking the lead in ensuring that passports and other documents can be scanned and read in a 'borderless' world. At the same time, on a local scale, ordinary people are affected in different ways by new surveillance and identification measures. Many discover that their lives are regulated in new ways as a result of the liquefying borders. The border now seems to travel with them in their portable ID documents; the border really does appear to be everywhere.[11]

Governing by Identification

The idea that we are increasingly 'governed by identification' is more than a handy turn of phrase. It points up a crucial shift in modes of governance that is increasingly visible at the start of the twenty-first century, even though its roots lie deep in the twentieth. It can be detected from the abstract and innocuous-sounding notion of 'identity management' that pervades much technical discussion of organizational practice right through to the 'Authorizing, please wait . . .' sign on the LCD screen when one drives up to refuel and is invited to 'pay at the pump' using a credit card. Louise Amoore, who coined the term 'governing by identity' – which I re-use as 'governing by identification' – sees the apparently limitless demands for identification from anyone from a ticket sales clerk to a biometrics software engineer to a security guard to a police officer as indicating a novel mode of governance.[12]

The novelty lies not only in the proliferation of possible agents who might demand ID; the authority by which ID is demanded is also in question. Though the check-in counter agent may be only an airline employee, she can still deny the would-be passenger access to a flight on the basis of inadequate identification. She has become part of the policing process. Indeed, pre-empting the risky passenger is now an aspect of the identification process itself. The idea is not only to check against the records to see who should be included – Amoore gives the example of a mid-twentieth century war-time rationing system – but also to calculate risks to see who should be excluded.

Amoore also shows how identification is now the main means of reconciling mobility with securability. The supposed free flow of people, goods and information within the circuits of global capitalism has to be qualified by the demand for security, by which is meant 'national security'. Thus the so-called 'Security and Prosperity Partnership' in North America (signed in 2005) is intended to promote cooperation on linked matters of security and economic issues between Mexico, the USA and Canada. According to its critics, however, this entails among other things the extension of US no-fly lists – key identification measures – to cover citizens in both Canada and Mexico.[13] Amoore's own illustration of the process of using identity to reconcile mobility with securability is the use of radio frequency identification (RFID) devices in immigration documents that 'convert difference into otherness' in new ways. Now the person on the move as well as the one with the fixed address may be located. Once again, this resonates with the idea that analyses must go beyond the somewhat simplistic binaries mentioned earlier, between solid/liquid and discipline/control.

Lastly, Amoore notes the difficulties in which new identity regimes place conventional privacy discourses. While the ID card, with its photo of the bearer, is one interface between the person and the system, today's modes of identification 'operate primarily via the screen and not via the card'. The projection from the screen, or database, is a person built from fragments, bits and bytes of data, suspicions and prejudices.[14] Other problems than those conventionally addressed by 'privacy' concerns are raised by the projection of the person on the 'stretched screen'. Misidentification by such projections is hard to refute; 'privacy' often misses the point.

The context of Amoore's comments on 'governing by identity' is, of course, the 'war on terror', and this gives a poignant edge to her analysis. For it is in this context particularly that problems with 'misidentification' can have dire consequences for individuals, especially some immigrant groups whose identifying data may in some respects fit the 'terrorist' profile. New ID systems tend to be established precisely because of fears about certain of the most targeted and vulnerable groups in contemporary societies. And in the 'war on terror', as Giorgio Agamben has observed, acts proliferate that 'do not have the value of law but acquire its force'.[15] But one aspect of the identification assemblage is that any ID system may in principle also be co-opted for other purposes. So cell-phone IDs, e-Government records and internet transaction logs may be used not only for more mundane forms of governance, but also in the cause of 'national security'. The means by which one networked database may be linked with another are protocols.

Identification Protocols

The new surveillance and identification regimes must be specified a little more to make clear the connection between 'stretched screens' and actual outcomes for ordinary people. The distributed networks on which contemporary organizations depend are enabled by protocols and standards. As discussed in chapter 3, the protocols are the agreed format for transmitting data between two devices; they enable computers to 'talk' with each other. The standards are formats that have been recognized by a public organization or within an industry. The ICAO standards are a case in point. But standards and protocols are essential for all distributed networks, not just ones that relate to international travel and mobility.

For instance, many computing corporations and other organizations seriously discuss the possibilities of 'ubiquitous computing' (or 'Ambient Intelligence', AmI) in which all manner of devices may collect data from everywhere and communicate those data with each other. This will, they say, produce a seamless digital environment that could 'one day' become the everyday context of social life. Already we see the potential for such ubiquitous computing in machines such as Blackberries that handle and can to an extent interchange text, images, voice, sound and data. Equally, systems such as Skype and other 'Voice-Over Internet Protocols' or VoIPs combine computer, phone, video, document transfer, and so on, in new ways. Protocols are needed for such devices, otherwise the promised 'seamlessness' cannot materialize. The idea of ubiquitous computing is pursued below.

Why is this important for considering identification? Because automated identification, using databases and biometrics, depends on protocols and standards. And for Galloway, as we saw in the previous chapter, protocols are a means of control 'after decentralization'.[16] On the internet, which is a grand distributed network, the TCP/IP protocols enable connections between computers and allow data packets to flow from one device to another. So any machine may be in contact with another. But the internet also depends in part[17] on the Domain Name System (DNS) to map network addresses to network names. This 'map' is a diagram like an inverted tree, each branch of which controls everything below it. Founder of the World Wide Web, Tim Berners-Lee, describes this as the 'one centralized Achilles' heel by which [the Web] can be brought down or controlled'.[18] During the 2007 crackdown on dissidents in Myanmar (formerly Burma), shutting down most of the local internet effectively prevented the outside world knowing what was happening inside the country.[19]

The way protocols work in practice, then, presents the possibility of exclusion. This exclusion could take various forms, precluding certain persons from the benefits of participation in anything from a communication network to a shopping mall. To repeat Galloway's forgivably hyperbolic statement, 'Protocol is to control societies as the panopticon is to disciplinary societies.'[20] This begs many questions, not least the centrality of the panopticon to 'disciplinary societies', but as the principle of contemporary control, the role of protocol does bear analysis and careful critique. It is an area, following Galloway's proposals, that calls for serious and systematic research if we are to understand contemporary modes of technologically mediated surveillance aright. And that possibility of exclusion is a crucial zone for careful critique, because it is also the one promoted by states of exception, the new penology and contemporary cultures of control.[21]

One difficulty with national ID card systems is precisely the range of interoperating organizations and even countries involved. A company-wide ID programme overcomes this relatively easily within a central system. But the protocols for national IDs require standardization and agreement between all the various parties concerned. Also, more than one level of identification or verification is needed, which is why both a PIN, or, more likely, biometric data, is called for to authenticate the card-holder *and* a digital certificate or cryptographic data (the public key infrastructure or PKI) to authenticate the issuing organization (this is the case with the Italian ID mentioned in chapter 1). At the same time, the routing and transmission protocols defined by the government and appointed technology agencies have to be very complex to avoid hijack or interception, which means that card-holders have no knowledge of how their information is accessed or delivered or which routes it takes.[22]

Rather like Lawrence Lessig[23] before him, who focused on the role of 'code' in computer systems, Galloway observes how basic protocol is to distributed networks. It is not as simple as 'rules', but more like 'a mountain trail whose route becomes fixed only after years of constant wear'.[24] It is the apparently practical or sensible way to go, but, as we have seen, it tends to take its users in particular directions. It is a powerful component of contemporary consumer capitalist global relations, and sub-rules flow from it. But at the same time, argues Galloway, protocol is vulnerable to subversion or redirection as codes are developed in open and oppositional ways to those currently dominant. Today's protocols may resemble market economies in their apparently self-driven character, but just like market economies these are subject to ethical critique and political reshaping.

Currently, certain protocols are particularly significant in the world of surveillance, especially when they are institutionalized as standards. In the attempt to ensure that 'national security' priorities and requirements are shared between allies, several proposals have been made about the need for 'interoperability', especially in the field of identification systems. These are visible both in far-reaching plans for national ID card systems and in more modest schemes such as enhanced passports and visas. As we shall see, on other fronts, technological dreams of seamless 'ubiquitous computing' and attempts to curb identity theft provide further impetus to quests for interoperability, and these, too, have identification dimensions.

9/11, Identity Theft and Interoperability

The quest for globally interoperable identification systems comes from two main sources. On the one hand, the post-9/11 'war on terror' has prompted a quest for reliable means of identification that would facilitate the process of preventing terrorists from travelling to targets, or at least from doing so with their weapons in their bags or their vehicles. In response, the ICAO promoted a biometrics-based standard for machine-readable travel documents (MRTDs) in response to which, for example, Canada began field trials of fingerprint and facial recognition technologies for processing temporary resident visa applicants and refugee claimants in October 2006.[25] On the other hand, the rising incidence of 'identity theft' has spurred the search for universally interoperable identification measures to permit the secure use of internet technologies for commercial transactions. To try to ensure that such a standard meets the requirements of Fair Information Practices (FIPs) in Canada, Ontario's Information Privacy Commissioner (IPC), Ann Cavoukian, issued a document based on Kim Cameron's '7 Laws of Identity', also in October 2006.[26]

Although it is by no means clear that these two sources of interest in globally interoperable ID systems would converge in one plastic card (and that Ontario IPC statement, for example, would resist such a move), the twin rationales of opposing terrorism and curbing identity theft also appear in some justifications for developing national ID card systems. In the British case, the Identity Cards Act started life as a primarily anti-terrorism measure, but by the time it became law, curbing identity theft was a key justification. Either way, strong evidence exists of a desire to establish international – or, better, transnational – systems of interoperable identification, some of which point to the potential of national ID cards as a possible vehicle.

The ICAO initiative on MR TDs is a particularly interesting one in this context because it connects with other trends, for example the transfer of passenger name record (PNR) data, especially at the behest of the USA, Advance Passenger Information (API) systems and intergovernmental networks of interoperable data systems to facilitate access to law enforcement and intelligence information across national borders. During 2006, for example, considerable controversy arose over American demands for PNR data – from which passenger profiles may be made and inferences about terrorist connections drawn – from European airline carriers to be passed to border authorities in the USA. The European Court of Justice ruled that this contravened EU data protection law and eventually, after protracted negotiations, a temporary agreement was reached in October that year.[27] The debate continues without resolution, however.

As a coalition of civil liberties and privacy groups observed in an open letter to the ICAO, the organization seems to be 'setting domestic policy, implementing profiling and ID cards where previously none may have existed or enhancing ID documentation through the use of biometrics . . .'.[28] Subsequent events seem to give credence to this view, given that several countries have already complied with the demand to 'upgrade' travel documents to make them not only machine-readable but also biometrics-based and RFID-readable. Other commentators have suggested that the ICAO has been used for 'policy laundering' or that countries may adopt RFID or biometric standards following the 'model' of another country rather than assessing the systems for themselves.

In the 'policy laundering' case, it was suggested by Ian Hosein that when the US Administration failed to obtain approval for a RFID-enabled biometric passport, they circumvented national deliberative practices by turning to the ICAO to find an external 'requirement' for such standards.[29] Jeffrey Stanton proposes an alternative view that, although the operations of the ICAO and government relations with it are somewhat opaque, the situation with RFID-enabled biometric standards for passports is more like 'modelling' than policy laundering. With modelling, one country would follow the legislative or technological lead of another rather than engaging the issues internally. The difference here was that the USA went ahead with the Enhanced Border Security and Enhanced Entry Reform Act, which stipulated the use of RFID-biometric passports before their detailed implementation. They relied on the ICAO – acting as a kind of surrogate national model – to produce a workable standard.[30]

The ICAO's activities may also be seen in terms of a general trend towards the 'securitization of identity'.[31] As the processes of globalization have helped to undermine government activity within territories, so new forms of regulating conduct, often on a transnational basis, have emerged. If people wish to travel, or even see 'freedom of movement' as a right, then to engage that freedom identity must be demonstrated in ways that link individuation and control. To be included as an air traveller, one has to pass through the obligatory access point where identity is required. However, the policing of those access points 'generates novel forms of exclusion'.[32] This means in turn that the activities of such transnational organizations deserve ever more careful scrutiny in the name of an international democratic process.

Another way of putting the above discussion would be to suggest that a global surveillance assemblage[33] is taking shape. Screens are being stretched around the world. The assemblage idea should be read not as a conspiracy to create a system of global surveillance of a top-down kind, but rather as the convergence of a number of items (MRTDs, national ID cards, biometrics, RFIDs, and the like) that simply work together. That the recent origins of this assemblage are the attacks on America on 9/11 and that their consequences could be read by some as a system of domination do not in themselves mean that the emerging assemblage is merely a product of what might be called US imperialism. The sorts of 'desires' that animate the assemblage, say Haggerty and Ericson, include 'control, governance, security, profit and entertainment',[34] to which might be added, in this context, efficient international travel.

Haggerty and Ericson also highlight the role of the body in surveillant assemblages. As they note, the body is first broken down by being abstracted from its territorial settings, and it is then reassembled into different settings by data flows to create a data-double (in our case, in the PNR or the biometric profile). The monitored body is really a kind of cyborg – a fusion of flesh-and-data – and the surveillant assemblage is the means of making visible for specific purposes the body that may or, much more likely, may not be physically present.[35] Much so-called 'border checking' actually occurs upstream of the physical border, where data flow through both airline and customs-and-immigration computer systems.[36] The data-double may be comprised of many kinds of information, from transactions to registration numbers, but in recent years the body itself has become increasingly sought as the source of those data. Although biometric technologies were developed well before 9/11, it was 9/11 that gave them their chance and brought them into public consciousness in unprecedented ways.

The focus here is particularly on the interoperability of the actual and proposed identification and tracking systems represented by MRTDs, such as e-passports and national ID cards, in order to suggest what some of the outcomes – intended or not – may be. As well as the security of the systems concerned (such as the apparent ease of illicit readings of RFID data), and their compliance with data protection regulations and FIPs, there are also broader questions of the paradoxical reinforcement of borders in a supposedly borderless world of travel and trade and, more particularly, how these reinforced borders filter traffic through them. In the next chapter, which discusses biometrics, some of the kinds of exclusion facilitated by 'stretched screens' are made clearer.

Interoperability: Contexts

The idea of internationally compatible identification systems, though not necessarily the term 'interoperability', has been around for some time. The idea of interoperability can be used on a broad level to refer to the means whereby diverse systems and organizations work together, but also to the technical protocols and standards required to enable this. If a system is to be integrated to include a variety of players, then interoperability is vital, whether between organizations or nationally or internationally.

Needless to say, this brings in a political economy issue, as in the case of the complaint from the European Commission in 2005 that Microsoft was restricting the interoperability of non-Microsoft work group servers. For Microsoft, interoperability is a core element of integrated operation, but the issue emerged as one of power and market dominance in an international context. Despite the EU attempt to punish Microsoft with fines,[37] the case is still outstanding at the time of writing. Interoperability clearly has not only technical but contentiously political dimensions.

So where and when are interoperability and its cognates sought? Particularly in the cases of passport systems and policing cooperation, standard means of identifying individuals were sought throughout the twentieth century and even earlier. As Mark Salter observes, the 'modern passport has remained largely unchanged in form and function since its inception in the 1920s'.[38] In the case of international policing, the standardization of identification techniques was also a central goal from the start.

Although the Interpol story began around the same time (the first meeting was held in 1914 and the International Criminal Policing Commission was set up in Vienna in 1923), Interpol itself was not established until after the Second World War.[39] But as Salter also says, after the First World War it was a 'wartime mobility regime' that came into being, placing the security of individual states above the potential for international integration. 'State control of movement trumped individual freedom of movement.'[40] During most of the twentieth century, policing also sought comparable standards for identification to facilitate tracing criminal activity – especially operations targeted at the laundering of the proceeds of drugs and illegal arms trafficking – across borders, and this too has been augmented since 9/11.

Globalization, which by definition has to do with increased mobility of information, goods and persons, raises many issues of secure identification. While globalization produces systems for fast-tracking businesspersons and travellers through airports and immigration checks, it also increases demand for systems that will check identities of migrant workers, immigrants and asylum seekers. Much attention has been paid, since the 1980s, to ways of both improving the ease with which the former group may be

securely and swiftly identified and tightening the systems for checking entry permits, visas and other travel documents held by those
who travel in hope of a better life. The tourist is in part defined by
his or her difference from the vagabond.[41]

The perceived threat of global terrorist activity, however, has
added another dimension to globalization, and stimulated an intensification of security and surveillance measures.[42] This additional
dimension, which actually began in the 1970s with events such as
the abduction and killing of the Israeli team at the 1972 Munich
Olympics and increased IRA activity in the UK, has since 9/11
catalysed not only hard security measures such as upgraded airport
security and moves against terrorist financing organizations, but
soft surveillance measures as well.[43] These soft measures, as Levi
and Wall say, seek to exploit the interactivity of new technologies to identify risk-posing individuals and networks. It is part of a
shift towards planned actuarial strategies relying on the analysis of
secondary data obtained through the assemblage of softwares and
databases to find out more about individuals and groups identified
as risks. The process takes data mining beyond the discovery of
details relating to already suspect persons and towards proactive
surveillance of suspect populations.[44]

For a long time the UK/USA Echelon system for intercepting
communication data (fax, telephone, telex, email) was the most
extensive and ambitious scheme for detecting possible threats to
national interests, but after 9/11 this was joined by even more
large-scale measures such as the ill-named 'Total Information (later,
"Terrorism") Awareness' (TIA) scheme, which joined several
databases using data-search softwares and pattern recognition
technologies to discover infrastructure threats. Although the TIA
scheme was officially closed down in 2003 after vigorous civil liberties opposition, it is unclear that the main thrust of the programme
has been dissipated. In Britain, though no such scheme was set
up, a similar assemblage is in place, using 'Scope', an information-
sharing scheme among the GCHQ (Government Communications
Headquarters), MI5 and MI6 (Military Intelligence, sections 5 and
6). This was to be expanded to up to ten government agencies,
data-sharing programmes between drivers' licence and passport
offices, biometric passports, Eurodac (the EU fingerprint ID

scheme across fourteen member states for tracking asylum seekers and illegal immigrants) and, of course, the largest of all, the national ID scheme. This further development, known as Scope 2, was frozen during 2008.[45]

What these schemes have in common is their attempt to integrate previously separate databases with each other, to harmonize systems within and between different countries and thus to seek forms of interoperability to ensure that standards are equivalent such that what works in one context also works in another. Not only are different components connected or different systems made to work with each other in an effective assemblage, but also, in the effort, the potential targets of surveillance are enlarged hugely. The shift is one that moves from conventionally defined suspect individuals and groups, based on their observed behaviour, to a reconfiguration of whole populations as potentially suspect. In order to prevent or pre-empt attacks, or other forms of violent or illegal behaviour, the activities of large swathes of the population come under scrutiny in the quest to discover hitherto unrecognized links and thus to assure the public that security is sought assiduously.

Interoperability: Cases

Turning from 'contexts' to some further 'cases', this section shows how interoperability has become a goal in both national and transnational policy. It is revealed in the attempts of large-scale, geographically remote organizations to coordinate better their activities, whether within nation-states or between them. Interoperability goals may be seen in three cases here: national ID card systems, digital identity management schemes and biometric passport programmes.

The UK ID card scheme, which became law in 2006, has inter-operability as one of its goals. This is both internal, to provide a universal ID within the UK, eventually for both government and commercial purposes, and external, to offer authentication within the EU as well. The former goal relates to desires for what has been called 'joined-up government' and the latter to a long-term

EU goal[46] of harmonizing ID documents and accepting ID cards as alternatives to passports. The EU Justice and Home Affairs Council established 'minimum security standards' for national ID cards in December 2005, similar to those for the EU biometric passport. These include ICAO interoperability standards for a RFID chip with facial and two fingerprint biometrics.

But a further implication of this expanded power to gather personal data is a subtle shift towards 'actuarial justice' – to which ID schemes arguably contribute[47] – that brings the exceptional powers that are sometimes justified for airports and border posts to interior spaces of the nation-state.[48] Actuarial justice has to do with 'statistically-based standards for identifying the dangerous',[49] but today it is partially superseded by the logic of 'precaution' just because of the growing grey area of uncertainty, especially in relation to anti-terrorism. However, this actually increases the demand for data, just in case, and thus, in a widening feedback loop, the need for greater interoperability. Screens are stretched, again.

The EU i2010 plan stresses that e-Government identity management in the EU should be advanced by addressing interoperability issues as well as future needs, without ignoring differences in legal and cultural practices and the EU framework for data protection. Most governments have acknowledged that an e-Identity programme is essential to future development and several are in the final stages of deployment. However, it appears that a lack of international standards and an absence of legislation have led governments to adopt a piecemeal approach to implementation and interoperability. Many experts in the field (e.g. the European e-Commerce group, eema) believe that there is still much work to be done to achieve a certain level of interoperability between the national e-ID schemes. Interoperability has various clear advantages from both a user side and a government perspective. These include more convenience (fewer cards, fewer PINs), access to more e-services and more secure access, and these real benefits should not be forgotten as the potential downsides are also exposed.

American biometric passports with RFID chips holding a digital photo and personal data began to be issued in August 2006. It was intended that 15 million US citizens would have been issued with them by the autumn of 2007 and that all passports would have

RFID chips by 2016. But at the end of October 2006 all US ports of entry were also supposed to be ready to compare and authenticate data in e-passports from visa waiver programme countries – the UK, France, Germany, Japan, Australia and twenty-two other countries.[50] A metallic mesh is provided to prevent the passports being skimmed, thus protecting against improper access or tracking, and 'Basic Access Control' is supposed to lock the data on the chip. Authentication is required by an optical scan before the data can be read.

Practical questions have been raised, however, both about the security of the mesh protection and the capacity of the system to withstand serious attempts to capture the data.[51] Such questions have yet to be fully addressed, and they stand as a reminder that none of these systems ends up having the capacities in practice that are promised by their promoters and marketers. Policy questions have also been raised, as noted above, about how the RFID-enabled biometric passport standard approved by the ICAO came into being, and – given the likely consequences for 'usual suspects' – about how far the process is a truly democratic one. Chapter 6 picks up issues that relate to ID processes and citizenship.

Towards Ubiquitous Surveillance?

The stretched screens of contemporary surveillance may also be found in the much-heralded world of ubiquitous computing. 'Ubicomp' is worth discussing here because it is a further context for interoperability and ID. Here, computers are built into everyday surfaces of ordinary rooms in buildings. They become, literally, part of the furniture. Ubiquitous computing is thought of as a 'third wave' in computing. The first wave was comprised of mainframes, each shared by many people. The present may be thought of as the second wave, the personal computing era. And the third wave is ubiquitous computing, 'calm technology' in which technological hardware and software recede into the background. Microcomputer chips are embedded in a multitude of everyday devices and environments, each accessible by humans and also communicating with each other. The term was coined by Mark Weiser back in 1988 when he worked at Xerox PARC, but it has really only gained widespread currency in recent years.[52]

Ubiquitous computing magnifies the already existing capacities of networked computer systems to track, record and process personal data, so the same phenomenon could be realistically viewed as ubiquitous surveillance. As well, in order to work at all, means must be found of individual users' identities being authenticated, which calls for modes of self-identification. At the same time, however, ubiquitous computing offers new scope for organizations to identify others, whether consumers or citizens, and this underscores the surveillance potential of such developments.

While ubiquitous computing is the term favoured in North America, the parallel in Europe is known as 'ambient intelligence' (or AmI), whereas in Japan 'ubiquitous networking' translates the same idea.[53] In all cases, however, this emerging phenomenon raises questions about power and control expressed in the protocols and codes that govern the systems. These are accented by post-9/11 developments, by the unforeseeable nature of some consequences of development, and the tendency towards the privatizing of governance as corporations and other private actors take over oversight functions once entrusted to elected governments.[54] While ubiquitous computing or AmI describes well some technological-commercial aspirations, which have their own 'governing by identification' dimensions, it must be recalled that any extension of identification procedures in principle may also be co-opted by national security demands.

With ubiquitous computing, governing by identification becomes even more significant, as users, whether in their private, professional or participatory roles, must often have their identities authenticated in order to continue engaging with the system in question. Already, sensors measuring heart rate and blood pressure can provide real-time remote access to healthcare, and automatic door-opening devices are available domestically with identity verification chips. Shoppers could use location-based discounts and vouchers customized by age, gender, profile and place and available on mobile devices.[55] As noted earlier, if these developments occur, as they appear to be doing at present, then the whole context of human–machine interaction will change, challenging once again the language and tactics used to discuss and assess what is happening.

But how does what was said earlier about 'governing by identification' and about the ways that protocols enable control to continue 'after decentralization' apply to the consumer-client world of AmI and ubiquitous computing? The same questions must be asked: Who authorizes the identification? And how do the tendencies to exclusion by protocol manifest themselves? The modes of identification are generally mandated by a coalition of forces, including corporate bodies, government departments and of course the technically qualified processes within the design and structure of the systems concerned. The tendencies towards exclusion are as evident in the consumer sphere as in the immigration or national security ones. Ever since Oscar Gandy's ground-breaking work on the 'panoptic sort',[56] the potential for negative discrimination and for the exclusion of already-marginalized groups has been clear.[57] The appearance of ubiquitous (consumer) surveillance simply offers opportunities for more of the same.

The familiar language of 'privacy' and 'data protection' along with the principles on which they are based is seriously challenged by ubiquitous computing and AmI. As applications and services are 'personalized' (involving some forms of identity verification protocols) and as data are collected, stored and processed in increasingly invisible and imperceptible ways, with profiles mutating and recombining constantly, not merely the opportunities for but the reality of vastly expanded surveillance capacities will demand radically new approaches to familiar requirements such as consent and accountability. At present, the kinds of proposals made lean towards 'giving individuals more control',[58] but this generally presupposes – optimistically – high levels of knowledgeability among such users. A recent nine-country survey shows that while people in countries such as Canada, France, Spain and the USA have a fairly good grasp of internet and location technologies, others in China, Japan, Mexico and Brazil are not particularly knowledgeable.[59] The field is wide open for genuinely innovative – by which I mean social, political and ethical – proposals for awareness-raising, governance and regulation.

Governing by Identification, the Border Triage and Liquid Controls

The consequences of governing by identification affect mobility and social participation because access and eligibility are determined by the assessments made of profiles obtained in relation to discrete identifications. This is a matter of systems that help to decide fates, and, in particular, the protocols that result in forms of exclusion.

There have always been different strokes for different folks as far as international travel is concerned. As Mark Salter says, there are 'two worlds of travel – a zone in which travel is easy and requires few documents and a zone in which travel is difficult and requires a great number of documents'.[60] The border, whether physical territory or a barrier in virtual space, is the point at which the 'zoning' of travellers occurs. The border checkpoint or immigration control at the airport acts as a filter or, better, a triage to sort out the conditions under which different people may be permitted to travel or not to travel. As noted earlier, Oscar Gandy describes another, consumer, triage in these terms.

The point of what Gandy calls the 'panoptic sort' is to discriminate between different kinds of customers in order to offer them different treatment. The sorting systems characteristic of marketing are also common to the kinds of policing and intelligence gathering that have expanded immensely since 9/11. Thus the identification of individuals is not merely concerned with authentication or verification. It is also to do with acquiring and updating records – hence the need in the case of the national ID for a citizens' registry, and in the case of e-passports for the various databases maintained by customs and immigration. The records, in turn, are used for classification, which has a disciplinary function, and for assessment, which determines everything from levels of service to be offered through to limits on the length of stay or penalties for contravention.

Since Gandy's work was first published in the early 1990s, major changes have occurred that enlarge the capacities of the 'triage' – the screening process has stretched from the consumer context to national and international ones, and consumer surveillance is now but one element in a global triage. That triage, as Salter and others remind us, ensures (by its protocols) that there is a relatively free flow for some and a perilous passage for others. Of course, some of those protocols are of the more conventional type, involving border officials, immigration officers, and the like, but increasingly they rely on databased identification information in order to render their judgements.[61]

Governing by identification achieves what might be called liquid controls. Unlike the solid forms of discipline within territorial spaces about which Michel Foucault wrote, with its separations, mass containment and restrictions on movement, liquid controls are modulating and flexible. This is more like the 'societies of control' idea proposed by Gilles Deleuze. Yet control does not somehow supersede discipline. The two seem to coincide and often mutually support each other. Indeed, there may be disciplinary practices *within* control mechanisms, and vice-versa. ('Enclosure' and 'separation' can hardly be said to have vanished in a world where incarceration rates are at an historical high point, even if control protocols are evident in prison settings.) Galloway's analysis of protocols complements Foucault's idea that biopower – the 'calculated management of life'[62] – is exemplified in the logic of protocols. But following Deleuze, Galloway also insists that this is also a site of resistance.[63]

All these processes are open-ended. The world of protocol is one with built-in possibilities for different modes of governing by identification than those discussed here. How to locate and exploit these possibilities, however, remains moot. Galloway suggests that hacking cultures offer new options for resistance, whereas those involved in the European critique of ubiquitous computing have not lost their optimism for 'giving individuals more control' over their identities. Mark Poster, a leading commentator on the internet and digital technologies, argues that there are 'all kinds of spaces in which copyright law, fixed identities, censorship and so forth are continuously evaded and challenged'.[64] As Poster says, 'the unique communicational architecture of the internet affords potentials for global forms of political organization from below'.[65] Such an outlook is instructive for considering the future of identification protocols and their role in governing by identity.

Conclusion

ID systems today contribute to a new mode of governing by identification and they do so through the use of protocols and standards. Identification generally has broader purposes than just authentication, and this is especially true of national ID systems. They are for classification and assessment – for 'screening' – therefore much hangs on them. In a world where smart ID systems are proliferating, and where they are being used across national borders, global codes are emerging that use similar categories and will – if the EU experience is anything to go by – reinforce already existing inequalities of treatment. But such exclusionary tendencies are also visible in commercial systems and online, as the quest for ubiquitous computing – with its analogous 'ubiquitous surveillance' – makes clear.

Because personal data are sought in order to predict what might happen, it is even more difficult for those attempting to cross borders who in fact have 'nothing to hide' to persuade authorities of that fact. And because the systems rely on biometrics, particularly facial and fingerprint data that inscribe difference in people's bodies, the role of identification cannot be separated from the other processes of classification and assessment. Whether for global mobility or for access and eligibility within AmI regimes, the stretched screens of today's identification systems may be assessed and where necessary challenged through a variety of legal, technological, academic and other means. The days of public debate according to norms of justice and fairness are not over. It is just that the modes and contexts of debate are changing, rapidly and radically.

Increasing global integration and harmonization remove decisions more and more from the local level and human scale as well as introducing other actors (technology experts, entrepreneurs) into the drama. When cultural and national identity has become such a contested dimension of life in the contemporary world, carrying a heavy freight of life-chances and choices, memories and hopes, it is ironic that parallel efforts are made to reduce it to machine-readable formulae and algorithms for ease of bureaucratic, policing and corporate administration. So does this mean 'goodbye, Gerd

Wiesler'? Perhaps not. However human beings are identified by others, and especially by impersonal machine systems, countervailing tendencies appear, challenging and offering alternatives to those identifications. From an historical point of view, where the machine-reduction of human capacities or skills has often been resisted, and the rights of citizens have been restricted by the state, this is not surprising.

Before considering the citizenship implications of new IDs, however, one other dimension deserves discussion: 'body badges'. By body badges I mean that reliance on features of the human body for accurate verification. To examine the minutiae of body data, such as those seen in the fingerprint, the iris scan and facial recognition technology, is as important as examining the global scope of new identification schemes. And as we have already seen, they are already part of the same surveillant assemblage.

5

Body Badges

... through biometrics bodies may become inscribed with identities
shaped by longstanding social and political inequalities.

Irma van der Ploeg[1]

At the end of 2007 and start of 2008 the American Federal Bureau
of Investigation (FBI) announced two major initiatives involving
biometrics. The first is called 'Next Generation Identification', a
$1 billion initiative to build the world's largest database of bodily
characteristics, usable by law enforcement agencies but also by
employers under certain circumstances to collect a variety of
biometric information from many sources for identification and
forensic purposes. The 'long-term goal', says Lawrence Hornak of
CITeR (Center for Identification Technology Research at West
Virginia University), 'is "ubiquitous use" of biometrics.'[2]

The second initiative, called 'Server in the Sky', is an international biometric database that would allow the FBI to cooperate
with other agencies in Australia, Canada, New Zealand and the
UK. The idea is to permit the advanced search and exchange of
biometric information on a global scale. There would be three categories of suspect in the shared system: ' "internationally recognized
terrorists and felons", those who are "major felons and suspected

terrorists", and finally those who are the subjects of terrorist investigations or criminals with international links'.[3]

No one knows at this point (2009) whether these systems will
be fully implemented. However, it is only a very few years since
biometrics moved from the economic doldrums to being seen as a
'solution' to the increasing need for identification. Already, as we
have seen, hopes have been expressed for a 'ubiquitous biometrics',
which suggests great confidence in these products on the part of
both corporations and government-regulated agencies. This dramatic shift indicates at least two things: one, that legitimate status
and access are associated more and more with the production of
some means of identification; and, two, that the means of identification are increasingly associated with biometrics. This is true
not only of law enforcement and intelligence services, but also of
commerce, employment and other areas of life.

Today, as we have seen, we are governed by identification.[4] In
a so-called 'information era', identification has become even more
important than it was in the world of paper-based bureaucracy. The
electronic information infrastructures that permit the processing of
our personal data depend on identification documents and protocols to mediate between individuals and the organizations with
which we relate. The employee authenticates his or her 'identity'
with an access card to enter the workplace, the traveller shows a
passport to board a plane and the patient produces a health card to
prove eligibility for medical services at the hospital. Without the
card, and the databases on which it depends, identity cannot now
be verified. Telling your story no longer suffices. It is displaying
your card that counts.

Now, a further factor has entered the 'governing by identification' equation: biometrics. The fingerprint, once a means of
checking manually for police suspects, is now digitized and found
on databases for instant, remote and automated checking. The
face, once carefully measured and mapped by hand – in Alphonse
Bertillon's nineteenth-century French system, for example[5] – is
now captured by camera to create a template of unique features
that may then be instantly compared with others within the system.
Iris and retinal scans may also be used, but fingers and faces are still
favoured in ID cards, whether in national systems such as in Italy or

in partial systems such as 'enhanced drivers' licences' or photocards.
Taking a sample from your body is increasingly *de rigueur*.

The biometric factor has rapidly moved close to centre-stage in
the development of and debates over ID card systems. The attacks
on America of 9/11 and the 'war on terror' that followed offered a
major opportunity to upgrade identification systems in the relent-
less quest for national security, although the systems proposed were
ones that were generally available already.[6] Moreover, because of
the role played by airports in the original attacks, identification
using biometrics has featured prominently in attempts to strengthen
aviation security but also simply to speed up passenger through-put.
By March 2002 Schiphol Airport at Amsterdam, for example, was
the first to use an iris scan for security checking in its fast-track
Privium system.[7] In 2008 the UK government announced that
the new ID card would be tested for airside workers at two British
airports.[8] Airports already act as data filters[9] for sorting travellers and
their associated luggage within spaces that are closely monitored.
So testing biometrics in airports seems like a natural extension of
existing security practices as well as of airport efficiency measures.

Biometrics are already in use in many existing and proposed
national ID card systems. When the USA endorsed standards issued
by the International Civil Aviation Organization (ICAO) for international passport documents, many other countries seemed to feel
they had no option but to comply as well. After all, the Enhanced
Border Security and Visa Entry Reform Act of 2002 carried an
implied threat to twenty-seven countries, such as Australia, that
they would be dropped from the visa-waiver programme if they
did not themselves adopt a machine-readable biometric passport
by a certain date.[10]

As well, many law enforcement and private industry applications
have encouraged the further use of biometrics. They are used to
regulate movement and access, but also to reinforce transactional
security. Biometrics promoters believe that the potential applications
are manifold, across a range of sectors. The biometrics industries
are still growing steadily, especially since 9/11,[11] and there are signs
that public opinion is generally behind – or at least complacent and
not actively opposed to – the trend towards biometrics in ID documents. For instance, in a Canadian poll in 2007 a high proportion,

72 per cent, agreed with the possibility of introducing a national ID card that would include a photo and fingerprint (compared with 53 per cent somewhat or strongly agreeing in a 2006 poll that also asked about the national register).[12]

The shift to biometric identification is one that both introduces some novelties in the history of identification practices and at the same time confirms some continuities. In what follows, we shall examine three important questions that are raised by this tension: How do we evaluate the claim that biometric identification methods improve on earlier forms of identification? Why the new focus on bodies for identification, and how does this relate to older uses of bodily identification in colonial settings or crime control contexts? What are the deeper cultural meanings of biometrics in relation to contemporary debates over identities and identification?

In answering the first question, some explanations of biometrics – both technical and cultural – are called for, along with an examination and assessment of some of the claims made for biometrics.[13] A further issue concerns who makes those claims, both in the technical literature and in the corporate marketing sphere.[14] The second question, on how far there are continuities as well as new departures in current biometrics, leads back to earlier forms of identification, originating in colonial and crime control contexts, and forward to the potential for ethnic and other disadvantage within the most sophisticated systems available today.[15] The third question draws us back to deeper issues: What does it mean for identification to shift from stories to samples? Can we still sustain a body/data distinction? What are the cultural implications of using the body as a password?[16]

Biometric Solutions

For some, biometric technologies appear as the new silver bullet, the simultaneous 'solution' to a number of problems associated with the organizational desire for positive identification. Biometrics, so the advertisements tell us, is likely to be a vital component in 'tomorrow's' security systems, in government and private enterprise alike. The city-state of Singapore is investing heavily in biometrics, not only for its new biometric passport, but also for systems such as CitiBank's new fingerprint authentication on ordinary accounts. Moreover, given the mobility of those enrolling in biometric schemes, the call for interoperability across borders will foster the quest for international technical standards. The FBI's 'Server in the Sky' proposal to link biometrics databases internationally would clearly require extensive attention to standards to enable the 'Server' to work.

So what is the attraction of biometrics as a 'solution' to identification problems? My, admittedly old, dictionary defines biometrics as the 'quantitative or statistical study of biology', but today's definitions generally assume the enabling presence of information technologies that permit the measurement and analysis of human body characteristics. These include fingerprints, scans of retinas and irises, voice patterns, facial patterns and hand measurements, each of which may be used for authentication purposes. (Other biometrics, such as gait recognition, may be used in military or urban policing contexts, for checking that the correct target or suspect is captured or killed.) In national ID cards, face, finger and iris scans are the main biometrics of choice,[17] with fingerprints still being most popular (used in around 75 per cent of applications) in terms of reliability-for-cost. In order to make use of biometrics, the information technology required comprises a scanning device, software that converts the scanned information into digital form and compares match points, and a database to store the biometric data for comparison. The stored data are usually encrypted for security reasons.[18]

The attraction of biometrics, then, is that identification may be achieved using features that almost all human beings have by virtue of being bodily creatures, in a process that is relatively quick, non-invasive and low-risk (of identity theft, say) for the person identified. It is claimed by biometrics proponents that both security and convenience may be served, which, given again the mobile circumstances within which biometrics tends to be used, is clearly beneficial for all parties. This assumes, of course, that the human body concerned may indeed be enrolled with ease within the system (this is examined later), that the modes of encryption are secure, and that the algorithms for connecting the body data with a particular identity are appropriate and work well. The latter issue is one of authentication or verification. Most uses for biometrics are not, strictly speaking, for identification so much as for verification or authentication. Both identification and verification are ways of recognizing someone, but the latter presents less of a technical challenge than the former. Verification confirms or denies a claimed identity, answering the question of whether this person standing before the immigration official or store clerk is who they say they are. An identification system, on the other hand, is faced with the broader question of 'who is this?', the answer to which must be worked out from a potentially very large list of users in the database of templates. Criminal identification, for example in AFIS – automated fingerprint identification systems – may in some circumstances have to ask the more difficult question. More routine, everyday uses, however, such as access control, computer log-in, welfare disbursement, international border crossing or national ID cards, are, in reality, verification systems.

Even the idea of 'verification' or 'authentication' is questionable, however, if these are taken to refer to the reliability of biometrics for the purposes they are commonly assumed to serve.[19] Many inaccuracies are possible, including those of the test-measures themselves, and of the test-measures being wrongly associated with another identifier or other data. A case in point of the latter concerned Rene Ramon Sanchez, an auto-body worker from the Bronx who apparently had the same fingerprints as Leo Rosario, a drug dealer and candidate for deportation from the USA. Sanchez was arrested several times and spent several months in custody before the error was finally discovered and 'resolved' in 2002. It transpired that after being pulled over on a Driving While Intoxicated charge in 1995, police had wrongly placed his prints on a card that bore the personal details of Rosario and these had entered the criminal justice system.[20] Sanchez still suffers residual negative effects of this misidentification.

Another kind of problem raised by biometrics is associated with the tolerance range within which all matches must be made. Test-measures and reference-measures are bound to vary for a number of reasons, producing both false positives (in which the system wrongly associates an identification with a particular person) and false negatives (in which the right person is rejected). It was presumably a false positive that had an Oregon lawyer jailed as a material witness in the Madrid train bombings until the FBI said they had mistakenly matched his prints with others found near the scene of the attacks.[21]

Any user, such as an airport authority, has a decision threshold at which it makes the choice along a continuum from low to high security. Tighter tolerances make for more false negatives; looser for more false positives. In the former case, still using the airport example, the security would be low and more potential terrorists would escape detection; in the latter, with higher security levels (looser tolerances), innocent persons might be inadvertently caught. These tolerance choices are normally set in the interests of the scheme's primary sponsor and thus may also vary, for instance in the case of airports, where higher traffic will increase demands for easing restrictions on flow, or, in the other direction, when a national alert system has been raised a notch.[22]

Furthermore, matters such as tolerance ranges are not exactly open and obvious, either to members of the public or even to those operating the systems in question. This is significant in the cases mentioned here, not least because civil liberties questions are raised when innocent travellers are needlessly detained as 'suspects'. Like other such technologies, biometrics are, as Lucas Introna says, 'opaque and silent',[23] which makes societal scrutiny difficult. Writing of facial recognition systems (FRSs) of biometrics, Introna observes that, being proprietary software objects, the algorithm codes are hard to access, especially when they are in operation. And yet the implications, especially for marginalized groups, may be significant.

FRSs, often thought to be 'efficient, effective and neutral', may have biases – for instance against African-Americans, Asians, dark-skinned and older people – that become significant in actual social practices. In real-life situations, operators, concerned about the large number of false negatives, are likely to request a higher identification threshold which would in practice render the 'bias groups' more vulnerable to scrutiny. Small differences in identifiability would translate into easier algorithmic identification which, despite a greater likelihood of mistaken identity, would be assumed in fact to be more accurate because the threshold had been set higher. As Introna concludes, 'seemingly trivial differences in recognition rates, within the algorithm, can indeed have important political (ethical) implications for some when it [*sic*] becomes incorporated into a whole set of socio-technical surveillance practices'.[24]

Other issues are addressed later, but before going further, it is worth asking about the claims made for biometrics. The idea that there may be 'biometrics solutions' to security problems is vigorously exploited by corporations and consultants alike, especially as safety and security rise to central importance within the mandates and promises of elected governments. The non-profit International Biometric Industry Association, for example, exists 'to expand opportunities for the industry, advocate government support for the use of biometrics in leading commercial and public-sector applications'.[25] But it is very hard to find independent research that evaluates the claims made for biometrics. A European Union report entitled *Biometrics at the Frontiers: Assessing the Impact on Society*[26] acknowledges some of the limitations, but also assumes the general diffusion of biometrics into commercial sectors. It has as a guiding aim to 'promote a vibrant European biometrics industry'.

By and large, it is left to civil libertarians, human rights groups, privacy advocates, academic networks and others to provide details of where the key lines of biometrics critique lie,[27] although, as we shall see, even some of these may contribute (unwittingly) to the problem. The Liberty and Security report *Trends in Biometrics*, for example, is highly critical of the way that biometrics is being developed in Europe. Not mincing words, they say that:

> Ad hocism, finance and industry drive trends in policies and emerging choices. The EU 25 diverge over the choice of biometrics, ID cards and passports, inter-operability, format, document durability, technical scope of the attendant technology (including document readers, staff training), quality codes of practice, ability and interest in measures to combat malevolent insider action. There are discrepancies between government rhetoric and practice. There are claims that data protection is primary but inadequate attention seems to be

paid to combating opportunities for fraud, including out-sourcing to private sector concerns inside the state or to third states.[28]

The report goes on to substantiate these claims as well as to make constructive proposals regarding the future of biometrics in the EU.

In particular, Juliet Lodge, the author of the Liberty and Security report, argues that there exists a 'triple deficit' in biometrics development in the EU.[29] Technically, the information technology infrastructures are inadequate and incompatible; information processing and exchange is unreliable; questions are raised about interoperability and data-transfer; fears of big system failure, obsolescence and fraud-resilience are not fully addressed. Politically, there is a lack of trust in inter- and intra-agency cooperation; insufficient attention to how ordinary citizens may be included or excluded from full participation because of lack of knowledge for 'informed consent' or the ability of users to pay for mandatory schemes; and public fears about 'Big Brother' in interoperable systems, function creep, malevolent insiders or simple errors. The third area of deficit Lodge calls 'communication', and here the big issue is who drives the agenda, governments or private corporations, plus the concern in Europe (and echoed, of course, in Canada, Mexico and elsewhere) that US demands dominate police and judicial approaches to cooperation.

With serious technical, political and communication problems associated with biometrics,[30] it is worth asking why this technology has achieved such prominence in the early twenty-first century. Clearly, there is more here than meets the eye.[31] Patrick O'Neil suggests several factors are at work here.[32] One is risk perception by the general public. Terrorism is a 'dread risk' where the probability is low but the consequences are perceived as dramatic, possibly horrific, and 'zero-risk' options are favoured that will eliminate rather than merely manage the threat. This then shapes the kinds of choices considered for the prevention of terrorism.

Another key factor exists that helps to explain the rapid post-9/11 recourse to biometric technologies. This is the proclivity in western societies especially to favour high-technology 'solutions' (as opposed to low-tech or non-tech ones), presumably because they appear sufficiently dramatic to address dramatic risks.[33] Yoked comfortably with this, the massive government boost to biometrics industries, especially in post-9/11 USA, indicates the economic incentive to develop such technologies.[34] As O'Neil hints, the high public profile given to information technologies as the tried-and-tested leading edge also supports the notion that IT dependence is appropriate, especially as it also shifts responsibility from fallible human beings.[35] Such factors play into the hands of the marketers of biometrics, but they in turn find supporters, such as politicians and academics, and even critics, who further strengthen their hand.

O'Neil cites the case of David Blunkett, then UK Home Secretary, claiming that biometrics makes identity theft and multiple identities 'impossible' and sociologist Amitai Etzioni assuring fellow Americans that a biometric ID would be 'foolproof'.[36] O'Neil shows that their arguments depend on high rates of success in isolated trials rather than in actual systems and situations, or, with regard to anti-terror tactics, on a conflation of 'information' with 'intelligence' in which the latter would contain some sense of suspects' intentions, rather than the mere cluster of data in 'information'. But civil liberties critics of biometrics may also contribute to an exaggerated sense of the efficacy of biometric technologies through their emphasis on the dangers posed by them (implying that they really do work as advertised).

Thus biometrics has increasingly become the leading choice for identification and especially identity verification systems. It seems to make sense to use the 'body itself' (see below for why this is a problematic idea) both because one does not have to remember something like a password or to carry some item along – although of course PINs *are* still required in many cases and cards containing the data *do* often still have to be carried – and because many assume that both bodies and identities are stable.

However, independent research on biometrics is not easy to find. Companies make large claims for their products, knowing the potential markets are enormous, and governments are seldom qualified to make the necessary technical judgements.[37] Thus the first question, concerning the nature of and claims for biometrics in identification, is one that requires much more research. The issues are complex and the evidence that biometrics 'solutions' are just that is at the very least mixed and often muddled.

Biometrics and Bodies of Information

One of the most striking aspects of identifiers dependent on some bodily trait is their tendency to discriminate inappropriately and unevenly between one group and another.[38] All identification systems are intended to assist in the process of discriminating effectively between population groups, and none will ever be fully satisfactory to all involved. This points up basic issues concerning the ethics of classification. As Lucy Suchman sagely says, all categories have politics.[39] She refers to categories that reveal the intent of their originators, but the consequences of categorizing also require ethical and political scrutiny. In this case, system designers of computer-supported cooperative work categorize in ways that favour discipline and control. Power relationships are also potentially obscured by classification, which is bound to reflect the needs of those classifying, as observed by Bowker and Star in the case of insurance practices.[40] So what asymmetries of power may be revealed in biometric categories?

In his study of 'suspect identities', Simon Cole concludes that while anthropometry (human body measurement for classification) prided itself on being carefully *scientific*, dactyloscopy (examining fingerprints for investigation) was seen as a *technology* with mass application. By this means, he says, '"others" – colonial populations, immigrants, people of colour, women – could be drawn into the web of state-sponsored identification'.[41] In the twenty-first century, things do not appear to have changed significantly. While fingerprinting may have, in some respects, become a universal identification technique regardless of gender, race or social status, biometric identification is still specifically sought in relation to cases of already existing disadvantage (such as welfare recipients) and to immigration (even though the early twentieth-century term 'undesirable aliens' may not so openly be used today).

The Eurodac system (the name originates with 'dactyloscopy'), for example, aims to simplify the comparison of fingerprints of asylum seekers in European Community countries to check that applicants are not simultaneously seeking asylum elsewhere. Established in 2000, Eurodac, an AFIS system, started operation in

2003 and its central unit received its first inspection in March 2006, the details of which were not fully published due to the 'sensitivity' of this information. When the summary document appeared, the European Data Protection Supervisor observed that some searches against fingerprint records had been carried out improperly. It seems that some 'category 3' asylum seekers, those from a third country, staying illegally, had experienced searches beyond those permitted within the Eurodac regulations.[42] It is unclear, moreover, whether the system is really workable in the way that it is promoted.[43]

The second question is how far are there continuities as well as new departures in current biometrics? This question echoes issues about earlier forms of identification, which originate in colonial and crime control contexts, while simultaneously probing the potential for ethnic and other disadvantage within the most sophisticated systems available today. If we take Canada and the USA, for example, contemporary biometric identification has been developed for crime control (law enforcement), social assistance (welfare recipients[44]) and border control (passport issuance) purposes. In each case, already marginalized or disadvantaged persons – criminals, the poor and people of colour – are in view and the aim of these systems is to distinguish between those who should be included and excluded, trusted and mistrusted, and so on. While there are no *prima facie* reasons why using biometric identification in these cases might affect vulnerable groups negatively, the very fact that these are the groups chosen for biometric identification suggests at least that particular care should be taken to ensure that it does not.[45]

Several kinds of questions may be raised about the capacity of biometrics faithfully to capture certain characteristics of different social groups, and to do so in ways superior to earlier modes of identification. The claim is often made that biometrics replaces the subjective eye of the inspector with the objective eye of the scanner, but the problem is that the 'objectivity' is compromised by the ways that key differences – of class, race and gender – are defined. In the nineteenth century, identification practices such as fingerprinting were commended for their ability to distinguish among persons, such as 'orientals', between whom it was allegedly hard to 'tell the difference'. The situation is not dissimilar today, with some groups, such as 'Asian women',[46] being treated within biometrics as relatively inscrutable.

Shoshana Magnet shows how, when biometrics is used in the context of welfare administration in California, stereotypes are reproduced and sometimes reinforced. Whether in relation to immigration or disability, and especially in relation to female welfare claimants, fingerprinting people as part of the checking system for would-be welfare recipients intensifies their criminalization. The stigma of poverty, according to this study, is exacerbated by its increased association with criminality, which is rationalized by the need to reduce fraudulent claims and linked to crime by the use of methods conventionally associated with lawbreakers. Women of colour are particularly hard-hit.[47] Thus the use of biometrics to determine who is eligible for welfare assistance both reduces case-worker discretion and increases the role of governmental rules and regulations in ways that affect social groups rather than just the individuals whose biometrics are sought.[48]

There are further salient aspects of this, however. While negative stereotypes may be biometrically reproduced in the welfare example, it may be shown that the very design of biometrics systems is flawed in complementary ways. The other side of the coin, then, is that as far as 'race' is concerned, some literature on biometrics suggests that the problems with obtaining good results lie with groups other than 'white' ones. This problem arises not at the point of contact where, say, an immigration official checks a record containing biometrics, but long before, at the point of 'enrolment'.

Certain groups are classified as being particularly hard to enrol, and this, when measured, produces 'failure to enrol' rates, or FTEs. This seems to suggest, at the level of biometrics production by the companies involved, that FTEs are highest among non-white groups such as Hispanics, Blacks and Asians, which may at first sight seem to exempt them from the vagaries of biometric identification. However, the corollary of this is, as Joseph Pugliese has argued,[49] that biometrics schemes could be read as privileging whiteness at a very basic level. If biometrics makes whiteness the yardstick for access, then this would clearly be a cause of serious concern.

The Culture of Biometric Identification

The third question draws us back to some basic issues: What does it mean for identification to shift from stories to samples? Can we sustain the common body/data distinction, assumed in modern academic and legal discourses? What are the cultural implications of using the body as a password?

First, a comment on the general issue of reliance on body traces for identification and the verification of identity. Much misunderstanding of biometric identification arises from assumptions about the stability of what we think of as the body and how it is connected with its representation as 'information'. Needless to say, in this area as so many others, hype about the supposed immateriality of information circulating in today's digital media clouds discussion of what is actually going on as people are identified by various biometric means. When measures taken directly from the body are used for identification purposes – the 'body as password' – then this is not merely information about persons.[50] Bodies themselves are being used and experienced in new ways, which properly raises ontological and ethical questions.[51]

In one obvious sense, biometric identification raises cultural and ethical questions beyond those of the pre-electronic uses of body data for identification. In the majority of modern forms of categorization, especially during the twentieth century, most connections between the file and the individual were made on a case-by-case basis, as when, for example, fingerprints found at crime scenes were linked with a suspect. Although Michel Foucault wrote in his *History of Sexuality*[52] about *biopower* as an important modern development in which states control populations and regulate bodies through classification, this concept has become much more salient in recent decades.[53]

Today, categorization is central to identification processes. Searchable databases enable large-scale, real-time categorization, such that suspects (or eligibles, or acceptables) may be generated.[54] Such schemes operate in numerous areas in addition to law enforcement, welfare administration and border controls, including workplace and commercial identification. The idea of biopower as

a means of regulation makes much sense in these contexts, depend
ent as it is on surveillance. Classifying populations, communicating
those classifications and deciding how they are to be acted upon[55] is
exactly what is enabled by surveillance in general and by biometric
identity verification in particular.

Bodies identified using digital codes may be rethought as 'information', as van der Ploeg[56] and, in a slightly different way, Hayles[57]
point out. The familiar modern anatomical-physical descriptions
seem to have less direct resonance in a world where digital media
encompass so many day-to-day relationships. The 'informatized
body' bears some careful consideration. For, I shall argue, while a
distinction is still maintained between the 'body itself' and 'information about the body', the normative, ethical responses will be
inadequate. If the distinction is maintained, potential problems
with biometrics may be limited to matters such as whether the
body to be enrolled has adequate measures from fingers or eyes,
or whether the data that are processed conform to regulations
rooted in some notion of privacy. As van der Ploeg argues, the
idea of 'bodily integrity' may speak to such issues. She draws on
the analogy between X-ray images of the 'inside' of bodies or the
extraction of DNA samples, also from 'inside'.[58]

But the inside/outside distinction is already in trouble here,
because the purpose of using biometrics measures is to generate
information about identity (or at least to connect the 'body' to the
'data').[59] When does the 'body itself' become 'information' is the
query rightly raised by van der Ploeg. Furthermore, this information is even more intimately connected with who 'I' am than my
Social Insurance Number or my bank PIN. The informatized body
requires new ways of thinking about integrity, equal to the shift
from anatomical to data-based definitions of the body. One sug-
gestion would be that ethical treatments of what was once called
'bodily integrity' be expanded to include data purporting to be
about the body, or data extracted from it – such as DNA, discussed
below – thus acknowledging that the 'body' is in part constituted
by what is claimed about it.

It is worth commenting on how information and the body parted
company, or, as Katherine Hayles puts it, how information 'lost its
body'.[60] Hayles observes that information became 'disembodied'

within modern communication systems. What she means is that within electronic media an assumption is made that information and its material context have parted company, and that it is possible to speak of 'disembodied' information. The assumption came to the fore in the mid-twentieth century, during debates over the nature of 'new' communications, but was contested then[61] and Hayles contests it again. While there may be clear advantages for information to float freely through communication networks, apparently unaffected by social, political and cultural contexts, much is erased or ignored in the process.

Writing specifically about the so-called 'surveillance society', I devoted a book chapter to 'disappearing bodies', suggesting, in a parallel way to what Hayles argues, that contemporary communications are increasingly depopulated.[62] That is, we seem to be in the process of constructing a world in which physical bodies are superfluous to communication; the information communicated can be – and often is – seen in isolation from the bodily person who produced it. However, while the distinction may be made for some purposes, as Hayles and others rightly stress, the two can never ultimately be separated. Why? Because those communications involving the body and information about the body in part define the bodily person. My physical being in the world and my social and economic life-chances are actually dependent upon data that are said merely to be 'about me'. Biometrics serves, in van der Ploeg's words, to write these on the body.[63]

One might say that surveillance systems serve to 'bring back' those disappearing bodies, by making them visible to organizations, agencies, authorities, and so on.[64] Surveillance contributes to how the state 'sees' its citizens, for example.[65] The existence of contemporary surveillance systems in a sense reconnects bodily persons with data about them, by constituting them as high-value consumers, terror suspects, loan defaulters, free-flight eligibles, or whatever. So being 'invisible' (or anonymous for that matter) in a surveillance-saturated world becomes increasingly difficult. Surveillance processes thus contribute to what Haggerty and Ericson dub the 'disappearance of disappearance'.[66] Biometrics takes this process even further, implicating 'body data' in the surveillant visibility of 'who we are' at a very basic but highly consequential level.

But this does not complete the picture. For those body data are very restricted in scope, and still refer only to items abstracted from the 'physical' body. They simultaneously ignore the ways in which the body is in part constituted by those criteria that are taken to 'define' it (plus others mentioned in a moment). Surveillance may in some senses make bodies 'reappear', but these are bodies already defined merely in terms of their sameness to other data. Because they are the product of data fragments processed by machines, they are merely rationalized (and reductionistic) 'bodies', as Paul Ricoeur might say.[67] These body identities permit classification and assessment based on 'samples' but exclude the possibility of hearing the voice of the person whose body is under scrutiny, in the form of the 'stories' that he or she might tell. Those stories may well play a critical part in constituting bodies, such that without them the 'body' is incomplete.

Following Ricoeur, then, another avenue of identification opens up, that which he calls the 'self-attesting body'.[68] In contrast with what biometrics offers, which is merely sameness to and difference from other bodies, the self-attesting body is open to Others.[69] The self-attesting body is understood as produced by narratives, by stories and not only by abstract data from the body with which biometrics deals. This takes us back to Bauman's concern (in the introductory epigraph of this book) that speaks of the constant risks of identities constructed for us by others, and the negotiations needed to ensure that channels of communication between these different conceptions of identity are kept open. So even as biometrics plays a role in identification processes, this perspective would emphasize its inadequacy without some corresponding concern with self-attestation.

Why is this so important? Because biometric identification is limited in scope not only insofar as the technologies may not 'work' or that they may be – inadvertently – skewed in favour of particular groups. Biometric identification is limited in scope because it works with a contested definition of 'body', one in which body and information may be conceived as separate entities and where abstracted data act as proxy for other kinds of (inadmissible) definition such as the stories that people (Ricoeur's 'self-attesting bodies') tell. Given that the identities that contemporary biometrics systems are set up to 'verify' are at least in the first instance those of vulnerable and marginalized groups such as terror suspects, welfare recipients and potential offenders, the idea of relying merely on those abstracted data clearly risks injustice.

Beyond Biometrics?

In a chapter concerning the body it is worth mentioning two other emergent issues that relate tangentially to biometrics and about which debate is likely to grow in coming years. One is DNA used for identification and the other is the use of RFID implants into the body to keep track of identifiable persons in real time. The UK has the largest DNA databank in the world (established in 1995), used primarily for forensic criminal investigation. The techniques of using DNA found in blood, body fluids, hair or human tissues to establish reliable links between suspects, crimes and victims are widespread. And since a 2005 US FDA (Food and Drug Administration) ruling permitted the limited use of RFID implants in humans, new questions have been raised about this technology too. While DNA depends on what might be called body data, it is not normally considered a biometric (even though some dub it the 'ultimate biometric'). And while biometrics may be used in conjunction with a RFID chip inserted in the body, implants raise other issues beyond those generated by biometrics.

The National DNA Database in the UK contains data on 5.2 per cent of the British population, as contrasted with the equivalent database in the USA, which covers only 0.5 per cent of the American population. Although it was set up in 1995 to help investigate the most serious of crimes, such as rape and murder, it was expanded between 2000 and 2005 to include eventually almost all the active criminal population.[70] Not only this. It also includes anyone arrested for a recordable offence, whether charged or convicted or not, and even some volunteers such as crime-scene eye-witnesses. In England, details are retained on the database even if the person concerned is innocent. In addition, as with other surveillance technologies, it soon becomes apparent that specific kinds of sorting are prevalent. Given the features mentioned above, plus discriminatory policing, some sectors of the population are more likely to be profiled than others. Nearly 40 per cent of black males are profiled, compared with 9 per cent of white and 13 per cent of Asian males.[71]

Analogous inequalities reappear in other contexts where DNA is used, as well. Healthcare services and especially medical insurance companies rely increasingly on identifiable genetic data for predicting future healthcare needs, and these are also of great interest to some employers. If such bodies know in advance of health complications, this could clearly affect the individual negatively. This is the kind of scenario that appears fictionally in the 1997 movie *Gattaca*, where a 'genetic underclass' experiences systematic disadvantage at the hands of the genetically privileged or 'valid'. If DNA is ever seriously proposed as part of a potential national ID scheme – molecular biologist Leroy Hood once suggested that 'your entire genome and medical history will be on a credit card'[72] – these are the kinds of questions about which citizens will no doubt seek reassurance.

Apparently also in the realm of science fiction until a few years ago, RFID chip implants for humans could also be generally used as a means of personal identification. The durable chip, the size of a grain of rice, could 'hold or link to information about the identity, physiological characteristics, health, nationality and security clearances' of the person in whom it is embedded.[73] The fact that the FDA now permits its medical use in the USA, and that it is used from Mexico (as a security device for vulnerable officials) to Spain (the Baja Beach Club in Barcelona was first to have customers voluntarily chipped for ID and credit card transactions), suggests that the RFID implant may become more widely used.

Many of the same questions raised about national IDs also appear in preliminary ethical, social and political critiques of RFID implants. Would all medical uses involve informed consent? How voluntary would they be if they were applied to, say, guest workers? What would prevent tracking and tracing of a very intrusive kind? As well, without encryption, the security of the data may be at risk, and as with other identification systems, risks of function creep are enormous. Additionally, the fact of embedding the device inside human flesh raises issues not encountered with ID simply carried on a person, those of bodily integrity. True, bodily integrity is already compromised, say some, by some aspects of biometrics, but an implant would seem to ratchet this up to another level.[74]

Conclusion

Issues of biometric identification raise questions at several levels, from the basic 'does it work?' to 'how just and fair are the consequences?' and 'what are the cultural meanings of data-defined bodies?' Some of the most pressing ones will not properly be resolved while only one or another level of questions is addressed. Obtaining independent research on the first question is difficult, given the involvement of technology companies that produce and distribute biometrics 'solutions' in the processes of government procurement. Equally, with the second question, we have seen that fundamental questions – such as whether biometrics systems as currently calibrated might privilege whiteness – do not seem to be asked, at least not in places where it counts. Clearly, such processes have different origins and effects in different countries. But if there is a significant issue here, then it has even broader implications if the third area of data-defined bodies has traction. For if it is shown that today's biometrics technologies are 'racially' skewed – and more research is required here – then this has profound ontological as well as ethical consequences for the industry, for users and for ordinary citizens and consumers touched by them.

Biometrics today is embedded not merely in processes of establishing verified identities at borders, and thus affecting physical movement. It is also implicated in identification in general, in the shift towards governing by identity. In this way it affects trade as much as travel, for example. Familiar, and crucial, questions about function creep, privacy violations and data misuse do indeed deserve debate, and this is one area where valuable research and policy work is ongoing.[75] Relevant activity should not stop there, however. Those questions open up others, for example of social stigma resulting from the data mining and profiling in which biometrics is increasingly featured. In van der Ploeg's words in the epigraph opening this chapter, 'bodies may become inscribed by identities shaped by longstanding social and political inequalities'. This shifts the debate more decisively into realms of civil liberties, human rights and social justice.

Such issues, in turn, may be construed in the conventional – and valuable   language of trust between citizens and the state, but it is also by definition an international and a global issue, as the quest for interoperability of standards – for instance in the 'Server in the Sky' – demonstrates. But all these questions also hinge on the even larger one of how humanness is defined in a digital era. If informatized bodies define humanness in ways that transcend older anatomical-physical definitions of the body, and yet ignore the stories of the self-attesting body, then this calls not only for caution in making assumptions about body data being mere 'immaterial' information, but also for serious and informed debate about how, when and under what circumstances biometric identification is permissible. Regrettably, entrepreneurs, politicians and pundits currently dominate what debate there is.

Which brings us back to the question of what national IDs mean today for 'ordinary citizens'. They, not merely the entrepreneurs and politicians, are the ones affected most immediately by national IDs. Biometric identification is just one dimension of the quest for new IDs, which, as we have seen, has a mixed historical background, always entails social sorting, is driven not only by 'the state' but also by technology corporations and the 'technologic' of protocols, and which is expanding on a global scale. But if national IDs are meant to identify citizens, then what are the ongoing implications for those citizens? Are those political economies and technologies that inform new IDs an add-on, or are they contributing to a new kind of citizenship, the cyber-citizen? And do citizens have a voice in decisions about modes of citizen identification?

6

Cyber-Citizens

The alien living with you must be treated as one of your native-born.
Love him as yourself, for you were aliens in Egypt.

Leviticus 19:34

For most people, citizenship is a precious thing even though it
may not fully be appreciated until it is threatened. After Slovenia
gained its independence in 1991, ethnic Slovenians were offered
automatic citizenship while other residents had six months to
apply. Soon, 171,000 people born in other ex-Yugoslav republics
became citizens but, inexplicably, 18,305 did not; their names
were quietly purged from the national registry. Some even had to
watch their ID papers torn up in front of them. Barred from social
services, jobs and housing, they only realized one by one that they
had lost their citizenship and only slowly started to organize to
publicize their plight. They call themselves the 'Erased'. Slovenian
courts ruled in 1999 and 2003 that the name purging was illegal,
but the struggle for recognition continues and some of the Erased
are still in limbo.[1]

Thus far this book has explored the development and meaning
of ID card systems, and in this chapter the issue of citizenship
is addressed directly, along with its close cousin, democracy.

Although in Western Europe and North America popular concepts of citizenship were relatively settled in the mid-twentieth century, they are now in flux, especially in situations of global mobility that have increased since then. Who may be included and who, for whatever reason, excluded is a question raised especially by people who travel for survival rather than for business or tourism and by those already resident within a given society who may suffer some form of disadvantage and deprivation.

The case of national ID documents is striking because the cards may be read very differently by those who are offered them. On the one hand, they represent the tissue linking citizens to their rights and entitlements, as in the Slovenian case. Groups that wish for one reason or another to strengthen their sense of national identity – in Hungary, Palestine, Quebec, for instance – will welcome markers such as ID cards. In Palestine, where holding a computerized ID is the prerequisite for a work permit in Israel, people in situations of unemployment and poverty long for a card.[2] And although there may or may not be an actual ID card involved, Simon Szreter argues that in many poor countries in Latin America, Asia and Africa, 'identity registration' should be regarded as a human right. Such public acknowledgement of the individual's existence, he insists, is vital both to civil and political rights and to economic development.[3]

On the other hand, ID card systems may be experienced as a means to exclude, and to restrict or prohibit the participation of, certain groups. In earlier chapters, egregious cases have been highlighted where ID systems have been implicated in unfairness, negative discrimination, unnecessary suffering and, at the extreme, genocide. Even in some more 'liberal democratic' contexts the use of new ID cards seems to reduce citizenship to mere 'identity management' which, at least as far as the 'war on terror' is concerned, is preoccupied with discriminating between 'friend and enemy'.[4] As Benjamin Muller asserts in this context, 'Less concerned with your identity or origin, identity management is preoccupied with discriminating between qualified and disqualified bodies.'[5] Either positively or negatively, then, ID card systems point up the importance of citizenship, whether as a perceived lack or as a precious link.

Specific systems, such as the American Real ID system, may also be seen from more than one perspective. On the one hand, it is clear that the attacks of 9/11 prompted the Real ID system for enhancing drivers' licences, which may also be seen as a *de facto* national identification system. The Department of Homeland Security defines the official uses made of the cards, including for boarding commercial flights, or entering federal buildings or nuclear plants. The same authority defines 'terrorist activity' and believes that the improved personal information retrieval facilitated by linking state drivers' licence records will aid its discovery. This ID system is clearly about knowing who are enemies and who are friends.

The 2005 law that mandated the Real ID system is supported among others by the right-wing Heritage Foundation and a number of anti-immigrant groups because it further restricts immigration by introducing stricter standards, especially for asylum seekers. Citizenship is harder to attain. But there is also widespread and multi-pronged opposition to the law. Variously, the restrictions to free movement, the increase in government power, likely security failures (making things like identity theft more not less likely), the loss of habeas corpus for refugees and asylum seekers and the potential for closing borders to legitimate entrants are all cited by its opponents as problems.

At the same time, the Real ID system may be seen as a logical outgrowth of the so-called 'information revolution', particularly, suggests Kelly Gates, in respect of three dimensions:[6] one, the increasing call for 'tokens of trust'[7] within bureaucratic systems that are increasingly distant from the citizens and consumers they serve; two, the need for access controls in both public and private information networks and for which personal data are a vital component; and, three, the ways that identification is progressively becoming central for access to the rights and responsibilities of citizenship. This approach stresses the long-term trends giving rise to Real ID, which connect it with the more general growth of online government services.

Questions of identification, surveillance, democracy and, thus, citizenship are central to national ID systems. Given the importance of electronic records in national registries, which enhance surveillance capacities significantly, it is no stretch to see these as test cases of 'cyber-citizenship'. The same goes for all new ID systems, dependent as they are on networked computer databases and – especially since 9/11 – harnessed to goals such as national security, understood primarily as anti-terrorism. Critics argue that numerous values taken for granted in western liberal democracies are imperilled by post-9/11 measures. The monitoring of movement, encouraging spying on neighbours, detention without trial and even the use of torture are now countenanced, plus, in this context, the massive processing of personal data in quest of national identification. Even those systems that downplay the relation of identification to national security still raise questions about democracy and citizenship just because they touch directly on governance, and the terms of membership in the nation-state.

Of course, the idea of 'cyber-citizens' in the chapter title could conjure up a range of possible meanings, from the enthusiastic worlds of e-Democracy and fresh opportunities for citizen participation through to the multi-player online simulation game based on Google maps. In the context of identification systems and surveillance, however, cyber-citizens may be thought of as the product of new information-technology-based modes by which governments register and interact with populations of nation-states. On the one hand, this offers new vistas for accuracy and efficiency, and for citizen access to government departments and information. This is the e-Government aspiration. On the other, cyber-citizenship may be thought of in relation to a political extension of the original meaning of 'cybernetics', a means of control through feedback loops. In this case it glosses the ways in which stereotypes and cumulative disadvantage may be reinforced, as the feedback loops created serve purposes inimical to democratic recognition and participation.[8]

New national ID systems and their surrogates – such as 'enhanced drivers' licences' – relate directly to citizenship and indirectly to democracy. But how should these systems be evaluated with respect to citizenship and democracy? Polarized positions clearly will not do, not least because it is unlikely to be a zero-sum game between greater efficiency or greater disadvantage. Social advantage or disadvantage may be reproduced more or less efficiently. Access to government information may be opened up, strategically sanctioned or shut down very effectively in either case. Nor can researchers point to already-existing systems to indicate what sorts of experience other countries have had with large-scale national ID systems. Japan has an advanced registration system but few corresponding cards as such, and Malaysia, for all the technological sophistication of its multi-purpose card system, has had very limited roll-out as yet. The most advanced systems are scarcely off the ground.

The only way to obtain some kind of evaluative stance is to place such emerging systems in context, both historical and comparative. This chapter addresses four questions, starting with the historical. One, how has citizenship been understood in modern times? Understanding this helps us see how contemporary modes of identification may affect it, for better or for worse. Two, what sorts of governance are represented by new identification systems, and what do these say about citizenship? Or, put another way, what kinds of citizens are produced by new IDs? Three, what kinds of identification and social sorting are enabled by new ID systems? And, in particular, how are Others defined and treated in new ID systems? Four, how can ordinary citizens make a difference to how we are classified and administered through new ID systems?

Modern Citizenship in Tension

In democratic societies, being committed to citizenship has generally meant something like this. Rather than suffering from the vagaries of arbitrary rule, in which citizens may have demands made of them at any time, citizens hold, in the right to assemble, in elections and in the opportunity to run for office, the means to hold government accountable. This also presupposes that citizens exercise political judgement, a notion that is less prominent in liberal versions. Citizenship, then, confers certain rights and privileges on citizens as well as demanding some duties and obligations. But how is fairness ensured, such that citizens are assured of equality before the law or that citizens may vote only once in an election?

The answer is that the very advent of modern forms of citizenship assumes identification. There has to be some listing of names for taxation, conscription, voting or entitlements. This was, more patchily, the case with some antique civilizations, too. Citizenship was often linked with city-states from the culture of ancient Athens onwards. Western notions of citizenship are associated with status and city-membership – the French *citoyen* or Spanish *ciudadano* expresses this neatly and sums up the ways that protection and entitlements are available in the autonomous city. As Engin Isin expresses it, 'the city was the battleground *through which* groups have defined their identities, staked their claims, waged their battles, and articulated citizenship rights, obligations and principles . . .'.[9]

The growth of citizenship in the West depended on the cultures of Abrahamic faiths with their characteristic values relating to the person, universal social membership and history understood as social change.[10] The epigraph above taken from the Old Testament book of Leviticus reminds the Hebrew people that they should care for the alien, just because they too were once *gerim* – vulnerable sojourners and, in this case, slaves – in Egypt, and is a classic expression of this.[11] Roman law in European city-states added a secular dimension, so that citizenship became secular solidarity where nationalism replaced religious symbolism and solidarity.

Citizenship expanded to nation-states as they developed over the past two hundred years, and these are the primary contexts within which citizenship is conceived in modern times. This is where notions of 'national citizenship' took off. The now somewhat derelict welfare state model, often associated with T.H. Marshall's sociology of citizenship, had everything to do with citizen entitlement within the nation-state. The idea was that citizenship would assure the worker of at least a minimum of protection against the vicissitudes of life in the forms of sickness, accident or unemployment. This commitment had grown out of earlier securing of civil rights – common law, habeas corpus and the jury system – and political rights in parliament and an extended franchise.

Issues of gender and of race and ethnicity have challenged some of Marshall's tenets by raising the question of rapidly changing identities.[12] But not only race and gender. The development of state health and welfare systems along with general government administration involved the gargantuan growth of bureaucracy during the twentieth century. Indeed by the 1970s some were starting to ask whether this was in fact stifling the very tasks that welfare states were set up to serve. Complete collapse was averted – at least temporarily – in the 1980s by the application of computer technologies, although these, too, were a mixed blessing. They helped rationalize some services, bringing some genuine benefits, but in the process often increased the already-growing gap between officials and the general public while simultaneously systematizing surveillance over some populations in particular.[13]

If we view new ID systems in the context of administrative development and the technological upgrading of bureaucratic processes, then the best that can be said is that their likely outcomes are ambiguous with respect to citizenship and democracy. State welfare systems certainly began to creak under the weight of their own administration. Solutions to that situation involved the spread of surveillance, which today is accelerating under the newer banner of national security and includes national ID card systems. In this light, IDs may be seen more consequentially as a crucial moment in the drift towards a generalized surveillance that is rapidly becoming the dominant organizing principle of contemporary institutions. Could they be part of a sea change in modes of governance?

From some points of view, newer citizenship models may be less benign than the bureaucratic-technical one. Their origins and consequences may actually be disturbing to democratically minded citizens. After all, as we have seen, some dimensions of new ID systems originate in colonial, crime control and war-time conditions, each of which suggests that something deeply abnormal necessitates extraordinary measures. It is about these kinds of issues that political thinking and judgement are urgently required on matters surrounding ID card systems.

Add to that the fact that identification is a basic component of surveillance systems that today are characterized overwhelmingly by their classificatory methods, intended to place people in different categories so that each group may be treated differently. This is illustrated by the case (from chapter 2) of British people applying online for drivers' licences and being assigned 'trust scores' or being

assessed for housing benefits and being categorized according to
'risk scores'. How much of this is understood by 'ordinary citizens'
going about their everyday lives? Not only this, classification is
sometimes carried out in part by means of biometrics, which tends
in practice to prefer body data over personal narrative, especially in
those cases for which biometrics is often said to be superior: vulnerable groups such as those on welfare, parole or seeking refugee
or asylum status.

Looking at the contemporary comparative scene, it is clear
that globalization processes have helped to highlight a number
of new questions about citizenship, identity and identification.
Indeed, struggle over these matters is partly what constitutes globalization. Writing of the fast-changing world of contemporary
claims to membership of nation-states, Gerard Delanty concludes
that citizenship is no longer defined only by nationality and the
nation-state, but is increasingly de-territorialized and fragmented
into separate discourses of rights, participation, responsibility and
identity.[14] Equally, citizenship is no longer exclusively about struggles for social equality – the dominant post-war mode of struggle
– but has become a major site of battles over cultural identity and
demands for the recognition of group difference. This cannot but
be evident in current debates over ID systems.

The relationships between identification, citizenship and democracy are worth examining more closely. The call for universal IDs
may mask fears about particular groups in the population, groups
that have been historically marginalized and disadvantaged. After
all, as historian Valentin Groebner rightly says, 'The position of the
excluded, of the non-identified, is forever evident in the history
of identification. The presence of the excluded actually frames
identification . . . .'[15] The technical trends – inseparable from the
corporate trends that support and promote them – have already
been shown to lend themselves to a new actuarialism and, even
more, a new precautionary principle that fosters social sorting, a
process which in its current form leaves much to be desired from
a democratic viewpoint. The current context of the security state,
already growing but significantly reinforced after 9/11, also serves
to indicate at least some of the political and policy priorities guiding
the emergence of ID systems.

Globalization, Consumerism and Citizenship

It is no accident that new IDs generally come in generic credit card format, that they often have multiple purposes that include commercial transactions, and that they offer 'identity management' opportunities. They reflect, or are *produced* by, the world that has made them. That world is increasingly accustomed to carrying cards that have the same format. Credit cards, drivers' licences and membership cards all have barcodes and serial numbers, and they all carry names, dates and sometimes photos and other verification devices. New IDs are for security, entitlement, travel and transactions. Some, like the Malaysian *MyKad*, have commercial features built in, while others are platforms that may permit these to be added later. And they all fall within the identity management rubric, which places them on a continuum with internet access and denial protocols.

Equally, however, new ID systems may be thought of as *producing* new kinds of citizens or at least of perpetuating and reproducing certain kinds of citizenship. New national ID card systems are appearing at a time when notions of national citizenship have attracted considerable criticism. Citizenship has always been a contested concept, of course, but there are significant ways in which new IDs reflect some important dimensions of today's world that challenge older views of citizenship. In particular, many have observed how the figure of the consumer has become in many ways more salient to social life than citizenship and at the same time globalization has thrown doubt on the category of national citizenship as international migration raises issues of political membership *beyond* the nation-state. New ID card systems reflect these emphases on consumption and on globalization and should provoke fresh thinking on citizenship.

There are some further ways in which new IDs reflect consumer and global conditions. The intention of many governments, not to mention some powerful lobbies in Europe and North America, is to ensure some degree of interoperability between ID card systems. In Europe, new ID cards are already machine-readable in countries geographically remote from the one in which they were issued.

They relate to nationality but also beyond. However, it could also be argued that new IDs speak to issues of the displacement of active citizenship by consumer behaviour and to the fragmentation of national identity by the forces of globalization. If so, and if this prompts doubts about how positive this may be for the life-chances of citizens and the prospects for democratic participation, one might also ask whether IDs may be used in the service of responsible, participatory citizenship and of cosmopolitanism.

These two dimensions of debates over citizenship may be seen, for example, in the work of Zygmunt Bauman, who paints a bleak picture of an emerging world where what he sees as the one-dimensional freedom of the consumer marketplace eclipses any notion of active citizenship. Having redefined freedom in relation to consumer choice, governments support this shift by restricting the poor, and non-consumers generally, to places and to conditions that separate them from the consuming majority. At the same time, global capitalism is still in rapid ascendancy, largely unfettered by the rules and regulations that nation-states were once able to impose. The unpredictable fortunes of such global capitalism affect everyone for better or worse, although consumers enjoy mobility while poorer sections of the populace are trapped by their locality.[16]

Noting the shift away from citizenship to consumer concerns, Bauman also points out that political power 'sails away from the street and the marketplace, from assembly halls and parliaments . . . beyond the reach of citizens' control, into the extraterritoriality of electronic networks',[17] which could well be a comment on ID card systems, too. This shift undoubtedly permits the discourse around ID cards to be phrased in terms of 'identity' rather than 'identification' and helps to render fuzzy who is included and who is excluded. In the UK, former Prime Minister Tony Blair once claimed that a 'sense of citizenship and belonging' is fostered by IDs. Perhaps he had in mind the sense of gratitude experienced by those once denied human rights elsewhere, who are granted citizenship in the UK. But this ignores the other side of the coin, in which 'citizenship' seems to connote inclusion while 'terrorists' and other 'troublemakers' are lumped together with the 'strangers' and 'Others' of whom Bauman writes as potentially excluded categories.

The sociologist T.H. Marshall, whose ideas were forged in the welfare state era, worked with an inclusive model of citizenship.[18] Bauman's work resonates with this and with a sense of the possibilities for democratic politics, where a concept like 'responsibilities' is equally important. Bauman also has much to say about the weakening of social bonds under the pressure of individualism, and he takes the view that recovering some meaningful modes of citizenship is the only way to recover a sense of common, public and private good.[19] Whether such citizenship could be expressed by or symbolized in new ID card systems, which seem primarily to be about permitting access, or authorizing certain kinds of transactions, or checking that their bearers have legitimate business in the place where they are found, remains to be seen.

In fact, it is difficult to see what large-scale contribution new IDs could make to the 'solidarity' aspect of citizenship, or, for that matter, to democratic participation. Indeed, if the British case is anything to go by, the new ID was itself introduced despite efforts to involve ordinary citizens in informed debate (the academic London School of Economics [LSE] report on the UK ID card was treated to *ad hominem* attacks and official opprobrium, for example), which augurs badly for future democratic participation in relation to the system. New IDs seem to have more in common with what David Garland calls the 'culture of control', which falls back on technical means of organizing societies in a context of broadly neoliberal anti-welfare policies. Such outlooks are 'more exclusionary than solidaristic, more committed to social control than to social provision and more attuned to the private freedoms of the market than the public freedoms of universal citizenship'.[20]

We return to the question of inclusion and exclusion in a moment. First, it is worth pausing to consider not only the broader context within which new ID cards are being introduced, which affects the meanings attached to them, but also the possible effects of the new IDs themselves. There are at least two more specific ways in which new electronic IDs are likely to affect the experiences and processes of citizenship.

First, multi-purpose IDs may be used for commercial exchanges as well as for entitlement and access to government services (whether this is deliberately intended or an 'unanticipated' consequence of their use). This fits with the fact that such IDs are also the product of more than one sector. This is the 'card cartel' in which not only government departments but also technology corporations and even, by shaping infrastructural possibilities, the standards and protocols themselves are involved in the production of new ID systems. Thus governing by identification is a process that may be stretched across different institutional areas – not just government administration and crime control – and is symbolized and made operational by those new IDs. Practical government is thus given a technological frame that facilitates what has been evident to political theorists for some time, that we are 'governed' by corporate and technical decisions as well as laws and administrative rules.

Second, if new IDs grant a new kind of universality of governance across once discrete institutional areas, they also encourage a new spatial reach. Those ID cards and documents as markers of citizenship are not only available at borders. Their use encourages the notion that the border is everywhere, including – echoing but not embracing older versions of citizenship – in the city. For many who will be negatively affected by ID cards, it will be in urban areas, not necessarily at physical borders. But this is also true of those advantaged by ID cards. In China, for instance, ID cards really act as badges of urban citizenship, the privileges of which far outstrip the expectations of rural dwellers. And in other countries, especially in the global north, where residents with ambiguous loyalties and origins – immigrants and migrant workers especially – make up significant proportions of urban dwellers, this sense of the border being 'everywhere' is likely to be accentuated by the use of new IDs, particularly when they have multiple purposes. This brings us to the question of how new IDs relate to social sorting and to Otherness.

Citizenship, Social Sorting and the Other

The third question to be addressed is: What kinds of identification and social sorting are enabled by new ID systems? And in particular, how are Others defined and treated in new ID systems? This question has in a sense haunted the different dimensions of what has been discussed in this book. How to deal with colonial and criminal Others prompted some of the oldest forms of modern identification, which in turn helped to produce the very Others they denoted. Identification systems are by definition sorting systems and – again by definition – national ID schemes distinguish between citizens and Others. The use of biometrics in ID systems tends to create sets of Others that may be unanticipated, but that often have an uncanny resemblance to the 'usual suspects' – in the actual as well as metaphorical sense of that word – who are so often marginalized in today's world.

New ID systems exhibit several characteristics that relate to their social sorting capacities and thus to their treatment of Others. These in turn have a strong bearing on citizenship. The features of ID systems, referred to earlier but noted here briefly in turn, are as follows. They are remote, interoperable, categorical, they tend to conflate risks, bodily and behavioural, and, lastly, they are exclusionary.

First, identification is remote. The frequency of face-to-face identifications is further reduced with digitization. When the face fades, it is easy for identification to become a mere matter of types and categories as it is, by definition, in bureaucratic systems. Only now, identification practices occur not merely in offices but within computer systems. When migrant workers, immigrants or asylum seekers are involved, this happens at a physical distance from borders, crossings or checkpoints. New ID card systems affect citizenship both within the territory of a given nation-state and beyond it. Didier Bigo and Elspeth Guild, for instance, highlight the process of 'policing at a distance' or remote control.[21] They describe this phenomenon in the European context, but it can also be seen in the efforts to harmonize border controls across the North American countries.

In Europe the Schengen visa policies that began in the 1980s meant that countries both issued and verified at borders passports and travel documents but also established intergovernmental agreements, common databases, good practices, common manuals and eventually a common visa. Thus the so-called 'technologies of control' are far from the border itself. Who belongs or does not belong is determined not at the border but remotely. Foreign officials at the EU frontier are involved, along with private security firms sometimes charged with checking documents. Insofar as the checking is done in embassies and consulates, it also deals in remote time – would-be travellers across borders may be deemed undesirable on the basis of what they may do, or what medical conditions they may experience, in the future. The actuarial principle has never been stronger.

Second, identification systems are (at least intended to be[22]) interoperable. It is important to remember – ironically – that national ID card systems do not necessarily stand alone within the boundaries of a given nation-state. Increasingly, they relate both to the corresponding systems in other countries and to the identification systems of other organizations. Put the other way round, ID systems expand governance beyond the nation-state both internationally and organizationally. Interoperability means that common standards and protocols develop that affect all countries that adopt national ID systems, globally. And governing by identification means that all organizations contribute to governance using identification methods, not just organizations associated directly with the nation-state.

The fact that new IDs may be internationally interoperable does not indicate that some cosmopolitan globalism is informing the concept of citizenship involved. To the contrary, the idea of interoperability is generally taken to be a device for strengthening security – policing, border controls and military intelligence – on an international level. The idea is to be able to respond more efficiently to so-called 'security threats'. This may have some beneficial effects, at least in principle. In practice, however, such interoperable systems tend to reproduce the distinctions and divisions between what Bauman calls 'globals' and 'locals', which are now overlaid with 'trusted traveller' and 'suspected terrorist' categories generated by the backlash of 9/11 responses.[23]

Third, it need hardly be said that new ID systems are categorical. In the case of the UK ID card, while the attacks of 9/11 were a significant factor in promoting the idea of a national system, it was 'asylum abuses' that gave the initial impetus to the political promotional campaign. Then Home Secretary David Blunkett said that he wanted the ID cards because 'I do want to know who is here. . . . I want to know whether they're working legally. I want to know whether they are drawing on services legally.'[24] Indeed, at the time the proposed cards were referred to as 'Entitlement Cards', with the express purpose of permitting checks on employment, health and education to ascertain who was and who was not benefiting legally. The promotional emphasis was on reducing numbers of asylum cases rather than on checking the stories of those applying for that status from situations of persecution or torture.

However, fourthly, those categories may easily become conflated. In the later twentieth century, governments with ageing populations and low birth rates began to rely more heavily on foreign migrant labour to keep their economies going while at the same time attempting to placate those in their populations who argued that migration should be minimized. Add to this the more recent post-9/11 concerns about state security and the shoring up of borders, and it is not difficult to see how the categories of migrants, refugees and asylum seekers might be confused.[25] While migrant workers contribute to growth, they are often seen as parasitic on the host society health and welfare system. This is very clear in a country like Japan, where only 'ethnic' Japanese may hold full citizenship, although similar situations exist elsewhere, too.

A related development involves interim forms of citizenship, such as the Canadian 'Maple Leaf' card, which defines migrants in a way that ensures certain rights and freedoms, but not yet as full citizens. As Isin and Turner argue, this kind of 'interim form' has further implications when one considers the possibilities for broader conceptions of citizenship, perhaps including a more global dimension.[26] One still requires a more local basis for citizenship because rights and obligations are in reciprocal relation, and this implies territory. But could there be a 'cosmopolitan citizen'? Citizenship is both a legal status that confers an identity – often expressed in an identity card or passport – and a social status that determines the redistribution and recognition of economic and cultural capital. Now that social relations spill over national borders in unprecedented ways in a globalizing world, some rights and responsibilities are respected – or not – in much more international settings.

Fifth, new ID systems depend on bodily and behavioural traits.

Although there are ongoing debates over the modes of verification in new ID systems, it does seem that contemporary emphases placed on biometrics could deepen the difficulties of groups that are already marginalized. There are a number of reasons for this, one of which is the downplaying of verbal evidence from those whose cases are deemed questionable. Again, this is not a new issue, but rather one that has been exacerbated by the dependence on electronic databases, just because their use tends to diminish the opportunities for discussion and discretion.[27] Apart from the questions about how well biometrics systems perform, it is important to note that the codes that determine in which category individuals are placed are related to bodily and behavioural characteristics. This means that the decisions made about the prospects for individuals in questionable categories are likely to be even further abstracted from the struggles and stories of everyday life of which vulnerable people are likely to be most acutely aware.

At the same time, the biometric and information technology systems that support them enable borders to be re-defined in some dramatic ways. As Irma van der Ploeg suggests, especially when using biometrics, the border becomes 'part of the embodied identity of certain groups of people, verifiable at any of the many points of access to increasingly interconnected databases'.[28] Some identities thus produced, she goes on, are more habitable than others, which is why research on IDs must ever be mindful of ethical and political issues. Beyond this, as biometric standards are adopted, such that the body becomes a password, systems may be linked with other identifying technologies such as RFID, location technologies and ubiquitous computing (or AmI, Ambient Intelligence, discussed earlier).[29]

Sixth, and lastly, new ID systems are exclusionary. Although the language of 'identity management' would seem to offer a neutral approach to identification, especially at national borders, there is nothing neutral about these processes in practice. Identity management is now the mantra of border-controlling authorities, but it is important to note that these strategies emerged not from the task at hand – determining who should be a legitimate traveller within or outside the nation-state – but from the realm of internet security in an era of electronic commerce. The language of identity management is used for the protection of online systems from hackers and fraudsters in both public and private contexts. It represents the search for means of preventing access for some and permitting it for others, generally for commercial reasons. Fear of loss to the public purse is the driving force behind identity management, and it is worth exploring what such practices really have in common with the far from merely technical and commercial matter of who is a *bona fide* citizen or traveller.[30]

In light of this it is difficult to disagree with the conclusion of Didier Bigo that new IDs often connect not with a surveillance *pan*opticon but with a *ban*opticon.[31] Unlike rights-based notions of citizenship, in which all find a place and at the very least a social safety net, or its related panopticon, which includes everyone in the gaze, new IDs seem to be geared to singling out exceptions – those to be excluded or sequestered as undesirable – as quickly and efficiently as possible. Once again, this is not a novel situation, but is accentuated by the electronic databases and global dimensions of new ID systems. Moreover, if many post-9/11 events are anything to go by, this occurs with relatively little concern about which innocent individuals might be negatively affected. The concern with national security (often translated into simpler terms of personal safety) in particular trumps civil liberties and privacy concerns, especially in the USA.

The new modes of citizenship that appear to be emerging at the same time as and to some extent to be aligned with national and other ID systems exhibit characteristics quite at odds with the inclusionary models of citizenship that welfare states aspired to in the post-war period. However one examines them, their exclusionary features stand out. Of course, there are also continuities with previous systems, which, despite their apparent inclusionary spirit, were in fact in practice negatively disposed towards particular groups. But the new modes, often stripped of their previously discretionary possibilities for compassionate or affirmative action, tend to single out particular groups for less than favourable attention.

Such groups may be thought of as the Other, whose existence stands as a warning and as a limit to those currently enjoying full citizenship entitlements, privileges and rights. They include Bauman's 'flawed consumers',[32] would-be immigrants who now seek asylum or refugee status, and of course the stereotypical 'bad guys' of contemporary anti-terrorist and crime control rhetoric. One difficulty of such Others, in current identification regimes is that their ranks may expand at will or whim – through slight statistical adjustments expressed in the algorithms controlling entry or eligibility. Hence the frequently expressed fears, to take one example, that the 'war on terror' is really a 'war on immigrants'.

For anyone taking seriously the ethical critique of new identification modes, the treatment of the Other raises basic questions of justice and humanity, not merely of citizenship. Following Emmanuel Levinas, Bauman places moral responsibility for the Other at the existential core of the human condition.[33] On this reading, citizenship schemes should take special care with those whose lives are already marginalized by colour, gender, religion or ethnic or national background. It is hard to resist the conclusion that from one point of view national ID card schemes will effectively entrench existing disadvantage and vulnerability by automating difference and conducting the relevant assessments remotely.

IDs and Prospects for Citizenship

The fourth and final question is: How can ordinary citizens make a difference to how new ID systems are developed? Without wishing to minimize the ways that citizen registration and ID documents are vital for healthy democracy, much of our discussion thus far has necessarily centred on the negative consequences for citizenship of developing new ID systems. While acknowledging that new IDs do not bear the blame alone for this situation – they are being developed in contexts where 'national identity' and identification are already problematic and controversial – it is worth turning the question around to ask whether some less circumscribed modes of citizenship could affect positively the development of new ID systems.

Questions to be asked include: Is there scope for developing ID schemes that avoid some of the negative consequences mentioned here? Can anything be done to change the direction of current developments? What effect do forms of organized opposition have on the progress of new ID card systems? Is it possible to engage with forms of 'participatory design' in planning ID systems? The last question is particularly important. The idea of participatory design has a fairly long pedigree going back to trades union involvement in production processes in the 1970s and 1980s. It now looks to practitioners, especially actual or potential users, to be actively involved in the assessment, design and development of technological systems and could in principle be ideally suited to the appropriate shaping of new IDs.[34]

In some major cases, the implementation of new ID schemes has been thwarted or at least slowed down by means of organized opinion and informed opposition.[35] The proposed Access Card in Australia became the focus of bitter political wrangling during 2007 and was eventually shelved after Kevin Rudd replaced John Howard as Prime Minister following the general election at the end of the year. The appearance of the INES (*identité nationale eléctronique sécurisée*) in France has been put back indefinitely (at the time of writing, early 2009) by the efforts of a coalition of groups opposed to the scheme, who produced a report and petition that both questioned its details and suggested that the social pact between citizen and state in France would be shattered by the new card.[36]

In Japan, the *Juki-Net* system of national registration was vigorously opposed by many municipalities before it was launched in 1999, and this opposition is ongoing. When the corresponding *Juki-Card* was issued in 2003, further opposition surfaced, which ensured up to 2007 that less than 1 per cent of the Japanese population actually uses the ID card.[37] Similarly, in the USA, a number of states have refused to comply with the requirements of the Real ID for data sharing. Various ultimatums have been issued – the latest for 11 May 2008 – to try to pull the recalcitrant states into line. But as several state governors (in Idaho, Maine, Montana, New Hampshire, Oklahoma, South Carolina and Washington) have signed bills refusing to comply with the act and yet others have stated their opposition, it appears that the impasse will continue for some time to come. Exactly how this will work out under the new Administration is unclear. President Obama made very little direct comment on the scheme in the run-up to his election.[38]

Less dramatically, but very much in keeping with the 'democratic participation' dimensions of citizenship, a number of proposals have been made by those working on the design of ID card systems. In 2006 the LSE report on the proposed UK ID card system, though roundly attacked as flawed, actually made a number of constructive proposals as to how an ID card system might be set up in more secure and less contentious ways than the one legislated. Equally, in Canada, concrete suggestions have been made about developing ID systems in ways that preserve anonymity and avoid the risks associated with a single unique identifier.[39] In both cases, arguments have been promoted that show how, for example, 'participatory design' processes could – and in some cases do – contribute to a more democratically accountable mode of creating ID card systems.

Equally, the work of information commissioners and privacy commissioners, along with non-government organizations such as the Electronic Privacy Information Centre (USA), should not be underestimated.[40] While in European countries debates often centre on national ID card systems (or on components of them such as biometrics or RFID), in Canada and the United States issues hinge rather on enhanced drivers' licences. In this case, on the Canadian side, privacy commissioners issued a joint communiqué in 2008 calling on governments to ensure that personal data remain in Canada, that RFID systems are secure, and that there be 'meaningful and independent oversight of how the U.S. Customs and Border Protection (a unit of the U.S. Department of Homeland Security) receives and uses the personal information of Canadians'.[41] Such steady work at a policy level is vital.

Even more broadly, there is every reason for citizens and consumers themselves to ask organizations that demand ID to explain themselves. With the rise of new ID systems, and the general securitizing of ID, the everyday material practices of politics have – at least in the plastic cards – become very visible. However, it is that less-easily-visible world of the database network, the 'iceberg below the surface', that requires exposure and explanation. These networks are now deeply involved in the politics of democracy and deserve to be explored as such. ID systems both express the ways that citizens are governed – through self-discipline, control, and the like – and, by categorizing people, variously, as immigrants, resident aliens, migrant workers or aboriginals, actually constitute people as citizens.

Avenues exist for citizen information and involvement in ID card system debates. Sometimes these are specific and local, such as the NO2ID campaign in the UK, sometimes transnational, such as Privacy International. Civil liberties groups also take up ID issues, again either as national groups, such as the Korean People's Solidarity for Participant Democracy, which is especially critical of the South Korean national registration system, or, as with the Canadian International Civil Liberties Monitoring Group, as coalitions of concerned citizens' groups and non-government organizations of various stripes. Many of these are documented in Colin Bennett's *Privacy Advocates* book,[42] which also includes examples of artistic and web-based groups that both question current ID developments and offer alternative perspectives on their potential direction.

Such questioning, whether at the level of workplace, bank or border-crossing IDs, is an appropriate but at present under-used mode of political involvement. One of the major obstacles lies in the consumerist cultures that spawn new IDs, in which convenience and comfort – undeniably desirable at one level – masquerade as priorities. Until the means are found of making the iceberg of social sorting databases visible above the surface, it will be hard to persuade some ordinary citizens and consumers that they should care about anything beyond the supposed security and ease of access that is promised to those who can get their hands on new IDs of whatever sort.

Conclusion

Electronic and biometric identification systems are increasingly part of everyday life in many countries around the world. The idea that we are governed by identification actually means that many other agencies than only the nation-state are involved in governance, and this has implications for the kinds of citizenship that are now possible and, for that matter, desirable. The debates over

ID card systems cannot be understood without considering the broader context of controversies over citizenship and democracy, but equally those questions themselves raise identification issues. In a globalizing world with its high mobility rates, more and more people are associated with states but not necessarily with nations, and it is just this ambiguity that national ID cards address. Does this migrant worker qualify for state health benefits? Might this international student have ties to proscribed organizations and thus be a threat to state security? Could this tourist intend to stay beyond the date specified in her visa? These sorts of questions speak to the matter of today's ambiguous identities that ID cards can attempt to encompass.

New IDs may be considered as a stand-in[43] for the kinds of political identities that are important in the twenty-first century. As far as citizenship is concerned, the sorts of characteristics exhibited by new IDs make it clear that citizenship is generally circumscribed, related to nationality but also to country-of-origin, ethnicity, gender and even religion. The politics of identity is obscured by or at best subsumed under new regimes of identity management. Thoughtful, organized and mobilized citizens, willing to state their misgivings about new IDs *and* to propose some more democratic alternatives to whatever valid problems they are intended to address, have the opportunity to speak to just such a circumstance.

New IDs also point up some of the ways in which basic concepts of government, democracy and politics stand in need of overhaul. I alluded above to the way that ID cards express at least two new senses of citizenship. They speak of the actual forms of governance emerging today, from multiple sources – corporations as well as government departments – in what used to be thought of as separate 'public' and 'private' spheres, which guide everyday actions and attitudes of belonging, responsibility, and so on. And they also help to create the subject as a 'citizen', especially through the social and demographic categories by which citizens are sorted. This in turn suggests a move away from the idea of democracy as the political 'view from below' (complementing the shift from government as the merely political 'view from above') towards more nuanced concepts such as 'civil society'.[44] Of course, civil society is as contested a concept as any in political sociology, but it does serve to draw attention to the role of ordinary people in local contexts, thus bringing loftier notions of citizenship down to earth, to the importance of having social ideals, and to the need to deliberate openly on these.

What would a focus on the latter two dimensions contribute to ID system development? If care for the Other is indeed basic to human sociality, and if the key test of government legitimacy is that the most vulnerable are cared for, this does yield some strong social ideals to frame alternative modes of identification practice to many discussed here. All too often, suspicion and the concomitant breakdown of trust characterize the development of new IDs. Those, for example, who work at a grassroots level with immigrant groups are well placed to comment on appropriate ways of developing ID systems, to try to foster trust and inclusion in that context. If new IDs with their remote functioning and biometric tests make systems deaf to people's stories, is there no way to overcome this?[45] This book has indicated some dismal dimensions of the emerging world to which new IDs sometimes contribute. Although words like love, care and trust seem alien from technology, policy and analysis alike, does it have to be this way?

As for the deliberative contexts for developing ID systems, we have seen that in many cases they are woefully inadequate. When introducing systems that touch raw nerves of inclusion and exclusion in the territories of nation-states, or that serve to determine who may board a flight or even, more mundanely, that assess eligibility for help with housing, the language encountered is that of 'identity management'. And the behind-the-scenes reality is one of social sorting, on criteria that are often opaque to the citizen, claimant or consumer, and reflect the interests of the organization rather than those whom it claims to serve. Here above all there is a paramount need for public discussion and responsiveness – seen, for instance, in the idea of 'identity assurance' rather than identity management (mentioned in the introduction).

At present, by contrast, the very production of new IDs tends to restrict political dissent and to curtail the efforts of those who propose modifications in the kinds of functions such cards have. This is certainly true in major cases such as that of the UK, USA and Japan. ID card systems are the product of a growing coalition between various groups: high-technology hardware and software providers; corporations such as banks for whom the card may also have benefits; and government departments.[46] And their effects tend to be felt most strongly and most negatively among the most vulnerable sectors of the population: immigrants, suspected terrorists and welfare claimants. If the measure of good government is the extent to which the weakest are protected from the worst eventualities, then ID cards can hardly be said to enhance such government.

New IDs all too often do what computer networks (on which they depend) generally do best: they contribute to a culture of control. As we have seen, the nature of this control is telling. It is by definition digital[47] and relates to governance in general, across a range of social realms. It is the product of a long-term historical shift that is visible in the rise of management approaches and neo-liberal political economies.[48] And in utilizing computer networks it supports a move away from conventional disciplines associated with modernity (and as analysed by Foucault). They move towards mere control or audio-visual protocols, as Gilles Deleuze calls them.[49] These in turn deflect attention from the demands of morality and democracy to the calculable, to relations determined by computer codes that express social categories. New IDs 'sort things out'[50] in new ways, the consequences of which have yet fully to be seen. Moreover, they do this remotely and using biometric measures, thus removing these markers of identity even further from the struggles of daily life and the sphere of political debate.

That the securitizing of identity is also occurring at a juncture when the conventional rule of (inter)national law is being set aside in favour of states of emergency within the so-called 'war on terror' increases the likelihood that in some contexts new IDs may be used to categorize and disadvantage certain vulnerable groups even further.[51] Add to this the evident power of high-technology corporations and the apparent willingness of governments to embrace the 'solutions' they proffer and the situation seems still gloomier, at least from the perspective of the politics of recognition and of human rights.

But none of this is inevitable, and the development of electronics-based ID card systems is still in its relative infancy. Yet if the current trends are to be questioned or even re-directed, not only will clear, critical scholarship be required, but also the political will to put first the interests of citizens and would-be citizens who are registered in ID systems. The abstraction of personal data and the emphasis on precautionary measures within security-obsessed regimes create considerable obstacles to such hopes. But that does not mean that holding such hopes or acting upon them is futile. Indeed, only such hopes and action, yoked with sensitive investigation, will contribute to a future in which identities are not overshadowed by identifications.

Notes

Introduction

1 Zygmunt Bauman 2004, *Identity*, Cambridge: Polity, 13.
2 See David Lyon and Colin J. Bennett 2008, 'Introduction' to Bennett and Lyon, eds, *Playing the Identity Card: Surveillance, Security and Identification in Global Perspective*, London and New York: Routledge.
3 See Elia Zureik, Lynda Harling-Stalker, Emily Smith, David Lyon and Yolande E. Chan, eds, forthcoming, *Privacy and Surveillance: International Survey*, Montreal and Kingston: McGill-Queen's University Press.
4 James B. Rule 1973, *Private Lives, Public Surveillance*, London: Allen Lane Press.
5 See Mark Salter 2003, *Rights of Passage: The Passport in International Relations*, Boulder, CO: Lynne Rienner Publishers; and John Torpey 2000, *The Invention of the Passport: Surveillance, Citizenship and the State*, Cambridge and New York: Cambridge University Press.
6 Nikolas Rose 1999, *Powers of Freedom*, Cambridge and New York: Cambridge University Press, 240.
7 Nicholas Abercrombie, Stephen Hill and Bryan Turner 1986, *Sovereign Individuals of Capitalism*, London: Allen and Unwin; Jane Caplan and John Torpey, eds, 2001, *Documenting Individual Identity*, Princeton:

Princeton University Press; and Richard Jenkins 2004, *Social Identity*, London and New York: Routledge.

8 Ayse Ceyhan, ed., 2007, *Identifier et surveiller: Les technologies de sécurité*, Paris: L'Harmattan (*Cultur et Conflits* 64), 8.

9 See Roger Clarke 1997, 'Chip-based ID: Promise and peril', available at *www.anu.edu.au/people/Roger.Clarke/DV/IDCards97.html*, accessed 17 December 2008.

10 Caterina Frois 2008, 'Personal databases and surveillance in Portugal: Analysis of a transitional process', Sheffield conference of the Surveillance Network, April.

11 Miriam Lips, John A. Taylor and Joe Organ 2007, 'Identity management as public innovation: Looking beyond ID cards and authentication systems', in Victor J.J.M. Bekkers, Hein P.M. van Duivenboden and Marcel Thaens, eds, *ICT and Public Innovation: Assessing the Modernisation of Public Administration*, Amsterdam: IOS Press.

12 Erving Goffman 1959, *The Presentation of Self in Everyday Life*, New York: Anchor.

13 James Crosby 2008, *Challenges and Opportunities in Identity Assurance*, London: HMSO.

14 E.g. LSE 2005, *The Identity Project*, London: LSE Department of Information Systems.

15 Gary T. Marx 2006, 'Varieties of personal information as influences on attitudes towards surveillance', in Kevin D. Haggerty and Richard V. Ericson, eds, *The New Politics of Surveillance and Visibility*, Toronto: University of Toronto Press, 107.

16 Charles Raab 2005, 'Perspectives on "personal identity"', *BT Technology Journal*, 23:4, 15–24.

17 Raab 2005, 16.

18 See the brief discussion in David Lyon 2007, *Surveillance Studies: An Overview*, Cambridge: Polity, 89–92 and Jenkins 2004.

19 Michael Dillon 2002, 'Network-centric warfare and the state of emergency', *Theory, Culture and Society*, 19:4, 71–9.

20 For a Christian theological account of some of the issues of identity, in a colonial African context, see Kwame Bediako 1992, *Theology and Identity*, Oxford: Regnum Books.

21 Miroslav Volf 1996, *Exclusion and Embrace: A Theological Exploration of Identity, Otherness and Reconciliation*, Nashville, TN: Abingdon, especially chapter 3.

22 David Lyon 1994, *The Electronic Eye: The Rise of Surveillance Society*, Cambridge: Polity.

23 Zygmunt Bauman 2000, *Liquid Modernity*, Cambridge: Polity.

24 If ID systems started from the assumption made by the Crosby Report (see n. 13 above) that the interests of the card-holder, not the system operator, should be paramount, very different consequences would follow.

25 Ceyhan 2007, 13.

26 Ceyhan 2007, 13.

27 Emmanuel Levinas 1961, *Totality and Infinity: An Essay in Exteriority*, Pittsburgh: Duquesne University Press, 24.

28 Cited in Zygmunt Bauman 1993, *Postmodern Ethics*, Oxford and Cambridge, MA: Blackwell, 149.

29 Charles Taylor 1994, 'The politics of recognition', in Amy Guttman, ed., *Multiculturalism: Examining the Politics of Recognition*, Princeton: Princeton University Press, 25.

30 Bauman 2004, 21.

31 This is a near-quote from Bauman (2004, 21) and rests on ideas from Giorgio Agamben 2000, *Means without Ends*, Minneapolis: University of Minnesota Press.

32 I gratefully take my cue here from the challenging reflections of Volf (1996).

33 David Lyon, ed., 2003c, *Surveillance as Social Sorting: Privacy, Risk and Digital Discrimination*, London and New York: Routledge.

34 Simone Browne 2007, Trusted Travelers: The Identity-Industrial Complex, Race and Canada's Permanent Resident Card, PhD dissertation, Toronto: UT-OISE.

35 Elia Zureik with Karen Hindle 2004, 'Governance, security and technology: The case of biometrics', *Studies in Political Economy*, 73, 113–37.

36 Statewatch 2005, 'EU: Biometrics – from visas to passports to ID cards', available at *www.statewatch.org/news/2005/jul/09eu-passports-id-cards.htm*, accessed 17 December 2008.

37 Ellen Nakashima 2008, 'US seeks data exchange', *Washington Post*, 8 July, D01, available at *www.washingtonpost.com/wp-dyn/content/article/2008/07/07/AR2008070702459.html?referrer=emailarticle*, accessed 17 December 2008.

38 Selya Benhabib 2004, *The Rights of Others: Aliens, Residents and*

Citizens, Cambridge and New York: Cambridge University Press, 1.

Chapter 1 Demanding Documents

1 Valentin Groebner 2007, *Who Are You? Identification, Deception, and Surveillance in Early Modern Europe*, New York: Zone Books, 237.

2 Summing up in the case of *Willock* v. *Muckle* (1951). (Mr Willock was a British motorist who refused to continue showing his ID card in peacetime, arguing that this was a war measure.)

3 See Dennis Gaffney 2000, 'Tricks of the trade: African Americana', Antiques Roadshow, PBS, 17 July, available at *www.pbs.org/wgbh/roadshow/tips/africanamericana.html*, accessed 18 December 2008.

4 Herbert L. Dreyfus and Paul Rabinow 1982, *Michel Foucault: Beyond Structuralism and Hermeneutics*, Chicago: University of Chicago Press, 119.

5 Valentin Groebner 2001, 'Describing the person, reading the signs in late medieval and Renaissance Europe: Identity papers, vested figures and the limits of identification', in Jane Caplan and John Torpey, eds, *Documenting Individual Identity*, Princeton: Princeton University Press.

6 Tracy Wilkinson 2008, 'Italy criticized for fingerprinting Gypsies', *Los Angeles Times*, 11 July, available at *www.latimes.com/news/nationworld/world/europe/la-fg-gypsies11-2008jul11,0,3931207.story*, accessed 18 December 2008.

7 Jane Caplan and John Torpey, eds, 2001, *Documenting Individual Identity*, Princeton: Princeton University Press.

8 Kristin Ruggiero 2001, 'Fingerprinting and the Argentine plan for universal identification in the late nineteenth and early twentieth centuries', in Jane Caplan and John Torpey, eds, *Documenting Individual Identity*, Princeton: Princeton University Press.

9 Jon Agar 2005, 'Identity cards in Britain: Past experience and policy implications', *History and Policy*, Policy Paper 33, available at *www.historyandpolicy.org/archive/policy-paper-33.html*, accessed 18 December 2008.

10 A key source for this is Chandak Sengoopta 2003, *Imprint of the Raj*, London: Macmillan.

11 See, further, Stephen Kern 2003, *The Culture of Time and Space* (second edition), Cambridge, MA: Harvard University Press.

12 James Scott 1998, *Seeing Like a State: How Certain Schemes to Improve the Human Condition Have Failed*, New Haven: Yale University Press.

13 John Torpey 2000, *The Invention of the Passport: Surveillance Citizenship and the State*, Cambridge and New York: Cambridge University Press.

14 See also Veena Das and Deborah Poole, eds, 2004, *Anthropology in the Margins of the State*, New Delhi: Oxford University Press.

15 Torpey 2000, 12.

16 Scott 1998.

17 Richard Ericson and Kevin Haggerty 1997, *Policing the Risk Society*, Toronto: University of Toronto Press, 111.

18 Torpey 2000.

19 This is a reference to the principles on which the Canadian confederation was built in 1867; 'Peace, Order and Good Government'.

20 Victoria Hui 2005, *War and State Formation in Ancient China and Early Modern Europe*, Cambridge and New York: Cambridge University Press.

21 R.F. Willetts, *The Civilization of Ancient Crete*, Troy, MI: Phoenix Press, 88.

22 Edward Higgs 2004, *The Information State in England: The Central Collection of Information on Citizens, 1500–2000*, London: Palgrave.

23 Scott 1998, 71.

24 Higgs 2004, 42.

25 T.H. Marshall 1950, *Citizenship and Social Class*, Cambridge: Cambridge University Press.

26 Engin Isin and Bryan Turner 2007, 'Investigating citizenship: An agenda for citizenship studies', *Citizenship Studies*, 11:1, 5–17.

27 C.B. MacPherson 1962, *The Political Theory of Possessive Individualism: Hobbes to Locke*, Oxford: Oxford University Press.

28 Gérard Noiriel 1996, *The French Melting Pot: Immigration, Citizenship and National Identity*, Minneapolis: University of Minnesota Press.

29 Noiriel 1996, 60.

30 Zygmunt Bauman 1991, *Modernity and the Holocaust*, Cambridge: Polity.

31 Edwin Black 2001, *IBM and the Holocaust*, New York: Crown.

32 See Keith Breckenridge 2008, 'The elusive panopticon: The HANIS project and the politics of standards in South Africa', in Colin J. Bennett and David Lyon, eds, *Playing the Identity Card: Surveillance,*

Security and Identification in Global Perspective, London and New York: Routledge.

33 Timothy Garton Ash 1998, *The File: A Personal History*, New York: Vintage Books.

34 David Shearer 2004, 'Elements near and alien: Passportization, policy and identity in the Stalinist state 1932–1952', *Journal of Modern History*, 76, 837–8.

35 Shearer 2004, 838.

36 Shearer 2004, 839.

37 John Torpey 1998, 'Coming and going: On the state monopolization of the "legitimate means of movement"', *Sociological Theory*, 16:3, 254.

38 Marc Garcelon 2001, 'Colonizing the subject: The genealogy and legacy of the Soviet internal passport', in Jane Caplan and John Torpey, eds, 2001, *Documenting Individual Identity*, Princeton: Princeton University Press, 84.

39 Garcelon 2001, 98.

40 Christian Parenti 2003, *The Soft Cage: Surveillance in America from Slavery to the War on Terror*, New York: Basic Books, 14.

41 Parenti 2003, 15.

42 A photo of the tin badge is available at Michael Riley 2006, 'The slave hire badges of Charleston, South Carolina', *Heritage-Slater Americana News*, 28 April, 2:3, available at *historical.ha.com/common/newsletter. php?id=1651/*, accessed 19 December 2008.

43 Parenti 2003, 25.

44 A photo of the pass is available at *cofc.cdmhost.com/cdm4/item_viewer. php?CISOROOT=/p246801coll5&CISOPTR=4&CISOBOX=1&R EC=1/*, accessed 19 December 2008.

45 Shuddhabrata Sengupta 2003, 'Signatures of the Apocalypse', *Mute*, 3 July, available at *www.metamute.org/en/Signatures-of-the-Apocalypse/*, accessed 19 December 2008; see also Taha Mehmood 2008, 'India's new ID card: Fuzzy logics, double meanings and ethnic ambiguities', in Colin J. Bennett and David Lyon, eds, *Playing the Identity Card: Surveillance, Security and Identification in Global Perspective*, London and New York: Routledge.

46 Sengupta 2003.

47 Peter Uvin 1997, 'Prejudice, crisis and genocide in Rwanda', *African Studies Review*, 40:2, 95.

48 Timothy Longman 2001, 'Identity cards, ethnic self-perception and genocide in Rwanda', in Jane Caplan and John Torpey, eds, *Documenting Individual Identity*, Princeton: Princeton University Press, 346,

49 Longman 2001, 350.

50 Longman 2001, 352.

51 Longman 2001, 356.

52 Simon Cole 2001, *Suspect Identities: A History of Fingerprinting and Criminal Identification*, Cambridge, MA and London: Harvard University Press, 7.

53 Georg Simmel 1950, 'The Stranger', in *The Sociology of Georg Simmel*, ed. K.H. Wolff, Glencoe, IL: Free Press.

54 Cole 2001.

55 Cole 2001, 13.

56 Cole 2001, 21.

57 See, e.g., Max Houck 2007, *Forensic Science: Modern Methods of Solving Crime*, Westport, CT: Greenwood, 64.

58 Cole 2001, 121.

59 Cole 2001, 132.

60 Cole 2001, 249.

61 See Scott 1998, 371 n. 38.

62 Christopher Dandeker 1990, *Surveillance, Power and Modernity*, Cambridge: Polity, 93.

63 Dandeker 1990, 101.

64 Dandeker 1990, 107; and David Lyon 2003b, *Surveillance after September 11*, Cambridge: Polity.

65 Higgs 2004, 133.

66 Agar 2005.

67 Much of the material in this paragraph is derived from Jon Agar's work; the quote is from Jon Agar 2001, '"Modern horrors": British identity and identity cards', in Jane Caplan and John Torpey, eds, *Documenting Individual Identity*, Princeton: Princeton University Press, 104.

68 Agar 2005, 2.

69 Agar 2005, 3.

70 Linda Colley 1996, *Britons: Forging the Nation 1707–1837*, London: Vintage 37.

71 Nikolas Rose 1999, *Powers of Freedom*, Cambridge and New York: Cambridge University Press, 47.

72 Rule 1973.

73 Ian Hacking 1990, *The Taming of Chance*, Cambridge: Cambridge University Press.

74 Scott 1998, 83.

75 Scott 1998, 83.

76 The classic sources for understanding the development of the passport are Torpey 2000 and Mark Salter 2003, *Rights of Passage: The Passport in International Relations*, Boulder, CO: Lynne Rienner Publishers.

77 See, e.g., Nadia Abu-Zahra 2007, 'IDs and territory: Population control for resource expropriation', in Deborah Cowen and Emily Gilbert, eds, *War, Citizenship, Territory*, London: Taylor and Francis.

Chapter 2 Sorting Systems

1 Geoffrey Bowker and Susan Leigh Star 1999, *Sorting Things Out: Classification and Its Consequences*, Cambridge, MA: MIT Press, 225.

2 Scott Thompson 2008, 'Who's absent, is it you? Identification technology and categorical tightness in Canada's national registration program 1940–1945', presented at *(In)Visibilities: The Politics, Practice and Experience of Surveillance in Everyday Life*, the 3rd Surveillance & Society Conference, University of Sheffield, 2–3 April, Sheffield, UK.

3 Samantha Hanig 2006, 'Pentagon surveillance of student groups as security threats extended to monitoring email', *Chronicle of Higher Education*, 6 July.

4 Richard Jenkins 2004, *Social Identity*, London and New York: Routledge, 165.

5 See Kirstie Ball, Elizabeth Daniel, Sally Dibb and Maureen Meadows 2009, 'Democracy, surveillance and "knowing what's good for you": The private sector origins of profiling and the birth of "citizen relationship management"', in Kevin Haggerty and Minas Samatas, eds, *Surveillance and Democracy*, London and New York: Routledge.

6 David Lyon 2002, 'Everyday surveillance: Personal data and social classifications', *Information, Communication and Society*, 5:2, 242–57; and Lyon, ed., 2003c, *Surveillance as Social Sorting: Privacy, Risk and Digital Discrimination*, London and New York: Routledge.

7 Oscar Gandy 2006, 'Data mining, surveillance and discrimination in the post-9/11 environment', in Kevin Haggerty and Richard Ericson,

eds, *The New Politics of Surveillance and Visibility*, Toronto: University of Toronto Press.

8 David Lyon 2004a, *ID Cards: Social Sorting by Database*, Issues Brief of the Oxford Internet Institute, available at *www.oii.ox.ac.uk/resources/publications/IB3all.pdf*, accessed 19 December 2008.

9 For further details on the Italian Identity Card in Figure 2.1, see 'LaserCard and Ritel team on production of Italian citizen ID card encoders', Reuters, 2 June 2008, available at *www.reuters.com/article/pressRelease/idUS104009+02-Jun-2008+BW20080602*, accessed 19 December 2008; and 'Baltimore Technologies provides secure new infrastructure for Italian government's new electronic identity card project', Business Wire, 15 May 2001, available at *findarticles.com/p/articles/mi_m0EIN/is_2001_May_15/ai_74502263*, accessed 19 December 2008. In addition: OECD 2004, *The Security Economy* Paris: OECD.

10 Summaries of the survey findings are in Elia Zureik with Emily Smith, Lynda Harling-Stalker and Shannon Yurke 2006, 'International surveillance and privacy opinion research', The Surveillance Project, Queen's University, Kingston, Ontario, 13 November, *www.surveillanceproject.org/research/intl_survey/*, accessed 31 December 2008; and a fuller discussion is available in David Lyon 2009, 'National ID card systems and social sorting: International public opinion', in Elia Zureik, Lynda Harling-Stalker, Emily Smith, David Lyon and Yolande E. Chan, eds, *Privacy and Surveillance: International Survey*, Montreal and Kingston: McGill-Queen's University Press.

11 See David Lyon and Felix Stalder 2003, 'ID cards and social classification', in David Lyon, ed., *Surveillance as Social Sorting: Privacy, Risk, and Digital Discrimination*, London and New York: Routledge.

12 See Irma van der Ploeg 2005, *The Machine-Readable Body*, Maastricht: Shaker.

13 Alexander Galloway 2004, *Protocol: How Control Exists after Decentralization*, Cambridge, MA: MIT Press.

14 See William G. Staples 2000, *Everyday Surveillance: Vigilance and Visibility in Postmodern Life*, Lanham, MD: Rowman and Littlefield; and David Lyon 2007, *Surveillance Studies: An Overview*, Cambridge: Polity.

15 James Scott 1998, *Seeing Like a State: How Certain Schemes to Improve the Human Condition Have Failed*, New Haven: Yale University Press.

16 See John Torpey 2000, *The Invention of the Passport: Surveillance, Citizenship and the State*, Cambridge and New York: Cambridge University Press; and Mark Salter 2003, *Rights of Passage: The Passport in International Relations*, Boulder, CO: Lynne Rienner Publishers.

17 Nicholas Abercrombie, Stephen Hill and Bryan Turner 1986, *Sovereign Individuals of Capitalism*, London: Allen and Unwin; Anthony Giddens 1987, *The Nation-State and Violence*, Cambridge: Polity.

18 Edwin Black 2001, *IBM and the Holocaust*, New York: Crown; and Timothy Longman 2001, 'Identity cards, ethnic self-perception and genocide in Rwanda', in Jane Caplan and John Torpey, eds, *Documenting Individual Identity*, Princeton: Princeton University Press.

19 But see, for example, cautionary comments by Keith Breckenridge 2008, 'The elusive panopticon: The HANIS project and the politics of standards in South Africa', in Colin J. Bennett and David Lyon, eds, *Playing the Identity Card: Surveillance, Security and Identification in Global Perspective*, London and New York: Routledge; and 2005, 'The biometric state: The promise and peril of digital government in the New South Africa', *Journal of South African Studies*, 31:2, 267–82.

20 John Taylor, Miriam Lips and Joe Organ 2007, 'Information-intensive government and the layering and sorting of citizenship', *Public Money and Management*, 27:2, 161–4.

21 Taylor et al. 2007, 164.

22 See Andrew Clement, Krista Boa, Simon Davies and Gus Hosein 2008, 'Towards national ID policies for Canada: Federal initiatives and alternative principles', in Colin J. Bennett and David Lyon, eds, *Playing the Identity Card: Surveillance, Security and Identification in Global Perspective*, London and New York: Routledge.

23 See Simon Cole 2001, *Suspect Identities: A History of Fingerprinting and Criminal Identification*, Cambridge, MA and London: Harvard University Press.

24 See, e.g., Roger Clarke 2006b, 'National identity schemes: The elements', 8 February, available at *www.anu.edu.au/people/Roger.Clarke/DV/NatIDSchemeElms.html*, accessed 19 December 2008.

25 Roger Clarke 1988, 'Information technology and dataveillance', *Communications of the ACM*, 31:5, 499.

26 Gary T. Marx and Nancy Reichman 1984, 'Routinizing the discovery of secrets', *The American Behavioral Scientist*, 27:4, 423–52.

27 See, e.g., Bruce Rocheleau 2006, *Public Management Information Systems*, Hershey, PA and London: Idea Group Publishing, 262.

28 Lawrence Lessig 1999, *Code and Other Laws of Cyberspace*, New York: Basic Books 151

29 Oscar Gandy 1993, *The Panoptic Sort: A Political Economy of Personal Information*, Boulder, CO: Westview.

30 See Ian Hacking 1990, *The Taming of Chance*, Cambridge: Cambridge University Press; and 2002, *Historical Ontology*, Cambridge, MA: Harvard University Press.

31 Lessig 1999.

32 Such as the UK Data Protection Act 1998.

33 For a critical view from a computer scientist, see Roger Clarke's work on national ID systems: Roger Clarke 2006a, 'National identity cards? Bust the myth of "security über alles"!', 28 January, available at *www.anu.edu.au/people/Roger.Clarke/DV/NatID-BC-0602.html*, accessed 22 December 2008.

34 Felix Stalder and David Lyon 2003, 'ID cards and social classification', in David Lyon, ed., *Surveillance as Social Sorting: Privacy, Risk and Digital Discrimination*, London and New York: Routledge.

35 Didier Bigo 2002, 'Security and immigration: Toward a critique of the governmentality of unease', *Alternatives*, 27, 81.

36 Didier Bigo 2004, 'Globalized in-security: The field of the professionals of unease management and the ban-opticon', *Traces: A Multilingual Journal of Cultural Theory*, 4, 1–33.

37 See, *inter alia*, David Lyon 2003b, *Surveillance after September 11*, Cambridge: Polity; and Kirstie Ball and Frank Webster, eds, 2003, *The Intensification of Surveillance*, London: Pluto.

38 See *www.icao.int/mrtd/Home/Index.cfm/*.

39 See Armand Mattelart 2007, *La globalisation de la surveillance*, Paris: La Découverte.

40 Oscar Gandy 2006b, 'Quixotics unite! Engaging the pragmatists on rational discrimination', in David Lyon, ed., *Theorizing Surveillance: The Panopticon and Beyond*, Cullompton, UK: Willan.

41 Kevin Haggerty and Richard Ericson 2000, 'The surveillant assemblage', *British Journal of Sociology*, 51:4, 605–22.

42 Nancy Lewis 2005, "Expanding surveillance: Connecting biometric information systems to international police cooperation', in Elia

Zureik and Mark Salter, eds, *Global Surveillance and Policing: Borders, Security and Identity*, Cullompton, UK: Willan.

43 James B. Rule 1973, *Private Lives, Public Surveillance*, London: Allen Lane Press.

44 See House of Commons Science and Technology Committee 2006, 'Scientific advice, risk and evidence: How government handles them', available at *www.parliament.uk/parliamentary_committees/science_and_technology_committee/sag.cfm*, accessed 22 December 2008.

45 Lucia Zedner 2007, 'Fixing the future: The precautionary principle as security technology', paper presented at Technologies of In/Security, Oslo University, April.

46 See, *inter alia*, Elia Zureik with Karen Hindle 2004, 'Governance, security and technology: The case of biometrics', *Studies in Political Economy*, 73, 113–37.

47 Kevin Dougherty 2008, 'Some border stories fuel the notion of a "war on tourism"', *Montreal Gazette*, 24 May, available at *www.canada.com/montrealgazette/news/saturdayextra/story.html?id=c1141f79-2b8e-430f-a701-6d713fd5647e*, accessed 22 December 2008.

48 See Jamie Doward 2006, 'The Karachi connection: From Pakistan to Britain, the remarkable story of an international web of terror', *The Observer*, 13 August, available at *www.guardian.co.uk/world/2006/aug/13/terrorism.jamiedoward*, accessed 29 January 2009.

49 See Eric Lipton and Scott Shane 2006, 'Plot shows need for more passenger data, officials say', *New York Times*, 15 August, available at *www.nytimes.com/2006/08/15/world/europe/15visa.html?_r=1&oref=slogin*, accessed 22 December 2008.

50 See the Australia Privacy Foundation website: *www.privacy.org.au/Campaigns/ID_cards/index.html*.

51 There is disagreement, however, as to who is responsible for ID card developments within the EU. See 'EU: Biometrics and national ID cards back on the table', Statewatch News Online, 2006, available at *www.statewatch.org/news/2006/jul/09eu-id-cards.htm*, accessed 22 December 2008.

52 Available at *www.publications.parliament.uk/pa/cm200708/cmselect/cmhaff/58/5802.htm*, accessed 22 December 2008.

53 Available at *www.lse.ac.uk/collections/PressAndInformationOffice/NewsAndEvents/archives/2005/IDCard_FinalReport.htm*, accessed 22 December 2008.

54 Mary Kaldor 2005, 'What is human security?', in David Held, Anthony Barnett and Caspar Henderson, eds, *Debating Globalization*, Cambridge: Polity.

55 Owen Bowcott 2008, 'CCTV boom has failed to slash crime, say police', *The Guardian*, 6 May, available at *www.guardian.co.uk/uk/2008/may/06ukcrime1*, accessed 29 January 2009.

Chapter 3 Card Cartel

1 This website is no longer functioning.

2 Quoted in Naomi Klein 2007, *The Shock Doctrine: The Rise of Disaster Capitalism*, Toronto: Knopf Canada, 369.

3 See 'LaserCard Corporation on winning team for Angola national ID card project', Business Wire, 17 January 2008, available at *findarticles.com/p/articles/mi_m0EIN/is_2008_Jan_17/ai_n24232620*, accessed 22 December 2008; Kunle Adirinokun 2008, 'New ID card scheme to gulp N30 billion', *This Day*, 2 July, available at *allafrica.com/stories/printable/200807020735.html*, accessed 22 December 2008.

4 Seth Grimes 2003, 'Shared risk, shared rewards', *Intelligent Enterprise*, 1 September, 28, cited in Kelly Gates 2006, 'Identifying the 9/11 "faces of terror"', *Cultural Studies*, 20:4–5, 423.

5 See Robert O'Harrow 2005, *No Place to Hide*, New York: Free Press.

6 OECD 2004, *The Security Economy*, Paris: OECD.

7 Elia Zureik with Karen Hindle 2004, 'Governance, security and technology: The case of biometrics', *Studies in Political Economy*, 73, 113–37.

8 See Lucas Introna 2007, 'Making sense of ICT, new media and ethics', in Robin Mansell, Christanthi Avgerou, Danny Quab and Roger Silverstone, eds, *The Oxford Handbook of Information and Communication Technologies*, Oxford and New York: Oxford University Press, 325.

9 Richard Jenkins 2004, *Social Identity*, London and New York: Routledge, 3–6; Georg Simmel 1950, 'The Stranger', in *The Sociology of Georg Simmel*, ed. K.H. Wolff, Glencoe, IL: Free Press, 30.

10 See Simone Browne 2007, Trusted Travelers: The Identity-Industrial Complex, Race and Canada's Permanent Resident Card, PhD dissertation, Toronto: UT-OISE.

11 Richard Jones 2000, 'Digital rule', *Punishment and Society*, 2:1, 5–22.

12 Lucia Zedner 2008, 'Epilogue: The inescapable insecurity of security technologies?', in Katja Frank Aas, Helene Oppen Gundhus and Heidi Mork Lomell, eds, *Technologies of InSecurity: The Surveillance of Everyday Life*, New York and London: Routledge.

13 Nikolas Rose 1999, *Powers of Freedom*, Cambridge and New York: Cambridge University Press, 240–6.

14 John Torpey 2000, *The Invention of the Passport: Surveillance, Citizenship and the State*, Cambridge and New York: Cambridge University Press.

15 Rose 1999, 243.

16 Torpey 2000, 4.

17 Cf. Andreas Mehler 2004, 'Oligopolies of violence in Africa south of the Sahara', *Nord–Sud Aktuell*, 18:3, 539–48.

18 Torpey 2000, 167.

19 Torpey 2000, 165.

20 Torpey 2000, 166.

21 James Scott 1998, *Seeing Like a State: How Certain Schemes to Improve the Human Condition Have Failed*, New Haven: Yale University Press.

22 Torpey 2000, 166.

23 Rose 1999, 166.

24 Rose 1999, 246.

25 John Schwartz 2003, 'Venture to offer ID card for use at security checks', *New York Times*, 23 October, available at *http://query.nytimes.com/gst/fullpage.html?res=980DEED71731F930A15753C1A965 9C8B63&n=Top/Reference/Times%20Topics/Subjects/P/Prices%20 (Fares,%20Fees%20and%20Rates)*, accessed 29 January 2009.

26 Louise Amoore 2008, 'Governing by identity', in Colin J. Bennett and David Lyon, eds, *Playing the Identity Card: Surveillance, Security and Identity in Global Perspective*, London and New York: Routledge.

27 David Lyon 2003b, *Surveillance after September 11*, Cambridge: Polity, 91–4.

28 House of Commons Science and Technology Committee 2006, 'Scientific advice, risk and evidence: How government handles them', 31, available at *www.parliament.uk/parliamentary_committees/ science_and_technology_committee/sag.cfm*, accessed 22 December 2008.

29 See Andrew Barry 2001, *Political Machines: Governing a Technological Society*, New York: Athlone Press.

30 Budi Putra 2006, 'HP proposes a national identity system in Indonesia',

Asia Cnet.com, 3 November, available at *asia.cnet.com/blogs/toekangit/ post.htm?id=61964396*, accessed 23 December 2008.

31 O'Harrow 2005, 6.

32 O'Harrow 2005, 300.

33 Thomas H. Kean, chair, 2005, *Final Report on 9/11 Commission Recommendations*, 4, available at *www.9-11pdp.org/press/2005-12-05_ report.pdf*, 4, accessed 29 January 2009.

34 'ITAA White Paper: REAL ID means real privacy protection', Tax Press Release, 8 May 2007, available at *www.itaa.org/taxfinance/release. cfm?ID=2445*, accessed 23 December 2008.

35 O'Harrow 2005, 119f.

36 Further work is required to discover how far this concept is translated (and translatable) for other language groups whose users embrace these practices.

37 See, e.g., Langdon Winner 2002, 'Complexity, trust and terror', *Tech Knowledge Revue*, 3:1, available at *http://www.netfuture.org/2002/ Oct2202_137.html*, accessed 23 December 2008.

38 See, e.g., Bruno Latour 2005, *Reassembling the Social: An Introduction to Actor-Network-Theory*, Oxford and New York: Oxford University Press.

39 Lawrence Lessig 1999, *Code and Other Laws of Cyberspace*, New York: Basic Books, 6; see also Martin Dodge and Rob Kitchen 2005, 'Codes of life: Identification codes and the machine-readable world', *Environment and Planning D: Society and Space*, 23, 851–81.

40 See, e.g., Ganaele Langlois 2005, 'Networks and layers: Technocultural encodings of the World Wide Web', *Canadian Journal of Communication*, 30:4, available at *http://www.cjc-online.ca/viewarticle.php?id=1586*, accessed 23 December 2008.

41 Alexander Galloway 2004, *Protocol: How Control Exists after Decentralization*, Cambridge, MA: MIT Press, 13.

42 See, e.g., David Lyon, ed., 2006b, *Theorizing Surveillance: The Panopticon and Beyond*, Cullompton, UK: Willan.

43 Galloway 2004, 242.

44 NECCC 2002, *Identity Management: A White Paper*, New York: The National Electronic Commerce Coordinating Council, 10.

45 See also Jason Pridmore and David Lyon 2007, 'Customer relationship management as surveillance', unpublished paper, The Surveillance Project, Queen's University, Kingston, Ontario.

46 Kelly Gates 2006, 'Identifying the 9/11 "faces of terror"', *Cultural Studies*, 20:4–5, 417–40; and Benjamin Muller 2004, '(Dis)Qualified bodies: securitization, citizenship and "identity management"', *Citizenship Studies*, 8:3, 279–94.

47 Muller 2004, 291.

48 Dean Wilson 2006, 'Biometrics, borders and the ideal suspect', in Sharon Pickering and Leanne Weber, eds, *Borders, Mobility and Technologies of Control*, Berlin: Springer-Verlag.

49 Martin Heidegger 1977, *The Question Concerning Technology and Other Essays*, New York: Harper Torchbooks.

50 E.g. David Garland 2001, *The Culture of Control*, Chicago: University of Chicago Press.

51 Heidegger 1977; and Introna 2007.

52 Mark Salter 2003, *Rights of Passage: The Passport in International Relations*, Boulder, CO: Lynne Rienner Publishers, 55–6.

53 Vincent Mosco 2004, *The Digital Sublime: Myth, Power and Cyberspace*, Cambridge MA: MIT Press.

54 Jones 2000.

55 See Louise Amoore and Marieke de Goede 2005, 'Governance, risk and dataveillance in the war on terror', *Crime, Law and Social Change*, 43, 149–73.

56 See Oscar Gandy 2006, 'Data mining, surveillance and discrimination in the post-9/11 environment', in Kevin Haggerty and Richard Ericson, eds, *The New Politics of Surveillance and Visibility*, Toronto: University of Toronto Press.

Chapter 4 Stretched Screens

1 Interview with Gordon Brown, UK Prime Minister, reported in Vikram Dodd and Richard Norton-Taylor 2007, 'Britain failing to check migrants on terror database, says Interpol chief', *The Guardian*, 9 July, available at *www.guardian.co.uk/society/2007/jul/09/asylum. terrorism*, accessed 31 December 2008.

2 In FIDIS (*Future of Identity in the Information Society*), Executive Summary, D4.1, 8, available at *www.fidis.net/fileadmin/fidis/deliverables/ fidis-wp4-del4.1.account_interoperability.pdf*, accessed 31 December 2008.

3 Dodd and Norton-Taylor 2007.

4 See Anne Frieberg 2006, *Virtual Window*, Cambridge, MA: MIT Press.

5 See William Connolly 1991, *Identity/Difference: Negotiations of Political Paradox*, Minneapolis: University of Minnesota Press, 64,

6 Keith Breckenridge 2008, 'The elusive panopticon: The HANIS project and the politics of standards in South Africa', in Colin J. Bennett and David Lyon, eds, *Playing the Identity Card: Surveillance, Security and Identification in Global Perspective*, London and New York: Routledge, 53.

7 A helpful discussion of the ICAO and the passport is found in Jeffrey M. Stanton 2008, 'ICAO and the biometric RFID passport: History and analysis', in Colin J. Bennett and David Lyon, eds, *Playing the Identity Card: Surveillance, Security and Identification in Global Perspective*, London and New York: Routledge.

8 The term 'liquid' is used in several contexts by Zygmunt Bauman, e.g. Bauman 2000, *Liquid Modernity*, Cambridge: Polity.

9 See the discussions in Mark Salter, ed., 2008, *Politics at the Airport*, Minneapolis: University of Minnesota Press.

10 See Anthony Giddens 1990, *The Consequences of Modernity*, Cambridge: Polity.

11 See David Lyon 2005a, 'The border is everywhere: ID cards, surveillance and the other', in Elia Zureik and Mark Salter, eds, *Global Surveillance and Policing: Borders, Security and Identity*, Cullompton, UK: Willan.

12 Louise Amoore 2008, 'Governing by identity', in Colin J. Bennett and David Lyon, eds, *Playing the Identity Card: Surveillance, Security and Identification in Global Perspective*, London and New York: Routledge.

13 See website Integrate This! Challenging the Security Prosperity Partnership of North America at *canadians.org/integratethis/backgrounders/guide/ABCs.html*, accessed 31 December 2008.

14 Louise Amoore 2007, 'Vigilant visualities: The watchful politics of the war on terror', *Security Dialogue*, 38:2, 139–56.

15 Cited in Amoore 2008.

16 Alexander Galloway 2004, *Protocol: How Control Exists after Decentralization*, Cambridge, MA: MIT Press.

17 It is worth stressing, however, that the internet is always volatile, in flux. In some ways addressability is becoming less central as keywords and search phrases – as on Google – become the mode of access, rather

than addresses. Some network technologies, such as gaming or messaging, do not require the DNS at all.

18 Quoted in Galloway 2004, 10.

19 David Pallister 2007, 'Junta tries to shut down internet and phone links', *The Guardian*, 27 September, available at *www.guardian.co.uk/international/story/0,,2177641,00.html*, accessed 31 December 2008.

20 Galloway 2004, 13.

21 See Giorgio Agamben 2004, *State of Exception*, Chicago: University of Chicago Press; and David Garland 2001, *The Culture of Control*, Chicago: University of Chicago Press.

22 Teddy Hsu 2003, 'Security requirements and application scenarios for national identification card schemes', available at *72.14.205.104/search?q=cache:PHcZZafeCGkJ:icsa.cs.up.ac.za/issa/2003/Publications/012.pdf+id+protocols+national+id+card+systems&hl=en&ct=clnk&cd=3&gl=ca&client=firefox-a*, accessed 31 December 2008.

23 Lawrence Lessig 1999, *Code and Other Laws of Cyberspace*, New York: Basic Books.

24 Galloway 2004, 244.

25 Citizenship and Immigration Canada (CIC), in partnership with the Canada Border Services Agency (CBSA), began a six-month operational Biometrics Field Trial on 19 October 2006. The Field Trial involves the introduction of fingerprint and facial recognition technologies to the processing of temporary resident visa applicants (students, workers and visitors) and refugee claimants. It tested the impact of these technologies on CIC and CBSA operations, and it also evaluated their usefulness in detecting fraud and facilitating legitimate travel. The Field Trial also helped CIC assess the merits of making significant technology investments to gather and verify biometric data at visa offices and ports of entry. Results of the Field Trial are available at *www.cic.gc.ca/english/department/atip/pia-biometrics.asp*.

26 Ann Cavoukian 2006, *7 Laws of Identity*, Toronto: IPC. The original '7 Laws of Identity' came from Kim Cameron. See Joshua Trupin 2006, 'The 7 Laws of Identity', *Technet Magazine*, July, available at *technet.microsoft.com/en-us/magazine/cc160959.aspx*, accessed 31 December 2008.

27 See Stephen Mulvey 2006, 'What the US knows about visitors', BBC News, 1 October, available at *news.bbc.co.uk/2/hi/europe/5390074.stm*, accessed 31 December 2008.

28 See *www.privacyinternational.org/issues/terrorism/rpt/icaoletter.pdf*, accessed 31 December 2008.

29 Ian Hosein 2004, 'The sources of laws: Policy dynamics in a digital and terrorized world' *The Information Society*, 20:3, 107–99.

30 Stanton 2008, 265.

31 Nikolas Rose 1999, *Powers of Freedom*, Cambridge and New York: Cambridge University Press, 240.

32 Rose 1999, 246.

33 Kevin Haggerty and Richard Ericson 2000, 'The surveillant assemblage', *British Journal of Sociology*, 51:4, 605–22.

34 Haggerty and Ericson 2000, 609.

35 David Lyon 2001, *Surveillance Society: Monitoring Everyday Life*, Buckingham: Open University Press, 47.

36 Colin J. Bennett 2006, 'What happens when you buy an airline ticket?', in Kevin Haggerty and Richard Ericson, eds, *The New Politics of Surveillance and Visibility*, Toronto: University of Toronto Press; and David Lyon 2006a, 'Airport screening, surveillance and social sorting: Canadian responses to 9/11 in context', *Canadian Journal of Criminology and Criminal Justice*, 48:3, 397–411.

37 See 'Brussels poised to fine Microsoft', BBC News, 27 June 2006, available at *news.bbc.co.uk/2/hi/business/5120536.stm*, accessed 31 December 2008.

38 Mark Salter 2003, *Rights of Passage: The Passport in International Relations*, Boulder, CO: Lynne Rienner Publishers, 4; see also John Torpey 2001, 'The Great War and the birth of the modern passport system', in Jane Caplan and John Torpey, eds, *Documenting Individual Identity*, Princeton: Princeton University Press.

39 The Nazi government in Germany took over the ICPC in 1938, leading to the withdrawal of other nations and the organization's collapse. It was revived on a Belgian initiative in 1946 and Interpol was set up with headquarters in Paris.

40 Salter 2003, 81.

41 See Zygmunt Bauman 1998a, *Globalization: The Human Consequences*, Cambridge: Polity.

42 Kirstie S. Ball and Frank Webster, eds, 2003, *The Intensification of Surveillance*, London: Pluto; and David Lyon 2003b, *Surveillance after September 11*, Cambridge: Polity.

43 Michael Levi and David Wall 2004, 'Technologies, security and

privacy in the post-9/11 European information society', *Journal of Law and Society*, 31:2, 194–220.

44 Levi and Wall 2004, 199–200.

45 See 'Government halts work on Scope intelligence network', *The Register*, 16 July 2008, available at *www.theregister.co.uk/2008/07/16/ scope_network_frozen/*, accessed 31 December 2008.

46 Dating from 1983. See Adrian Beck and Kate Broadhurst 1998, 'Compulsion by stealth: Lesson from the European Union on the use of national identity cards', *Public Administration*, 76, 779–92.

47 Dean Wilson 2006, 'Biometrics, borders and the ideal suspect', in Sharon Pickering and Leanne Weber, eds, *Borders, Mobility and Technologies of Control*, Berlin: Springer-Verlag; and Eyal Weizman 2007, *The Hollow Land: Israel's Architecture of Occupation*, London: Verso.

48 Malcom M. Feely and Jonathan Simon 2006, 'The new penology: Notes on the emerging strategy of corrections and its implications', *Criminology*, 30:4, 449–74.

49 Richard Ericson 2007, *Crime in an Insecure World*, Cambridge: Polity.

50 Roy Mark 2006, 'US e-Passports hitting market', Internet News, 23 October, available at *www.internetnews.com/security/article.php/ 3639411*, accessed 2 February 2009.

51 See, e.g., Will Sturgeon 2006, 'Biometric passport cracked and cloned', CNet News, 4 August, available at *news.cnet.com/8301-10784_3-6102333-7.html*, accessed 31 December 2008.

52 See Mark Weiser 1993, 'Hot topics: Ubiquitous computing', *IEEE Computer*, October. Version available at *www.ubiq.com/hypertext/ weiser/UbiCompHotTopics.html*, accessed 31 December 2008.

53 David Wright, Serge Gutwirth, Michael Friedewald, Elena Vildjiounaite and Yves Punie, eds, 2007, *Safeguards in a World of Ambient Intelligence*, New York: Springer.

54 Wright et al. 2007, 4.

55 Maya Gadzheva 2008, 'Privacy in the age of transparency: The new vulnerability of the individual', *Social Science Computer Review*, 26:1, 62.

56 Oscar Gandy 1993, *The Panoptic Sort: A Political Economy of Personal Information*, Boulder, CO: Westview.

57 See also Jason Pridmore 2008, Loyal Subjects? Consumer Surveillance in the Personal Information Economy. PhD dissertation, Queen's University, Kingston, Ontario.

58 E.g. Gadzheva 2008; and Wright et al. 2007.

59 Further information on the international survey, conducted at Queen's University, Kingston, Ontario, in 2006–7, is available at Elia Zureik with Emily Smith, Lynda Harling-Stalker and Shannon Yurke 2006, 'International surveillance and privacy opinion research', The Surveillance Project, Queen's University, Kingston, Ontario, 13 November, *www.surveillanceproject.org/research/intl_survey*, accessed 31 December 2008.

60 Salter 2003, 20.

61 See, e.g., the discussion of the Allenby crossing between the occupied Palestinian Territories and Israel in Elia Zureik 2001, 'Constructing Palestine through surveillance practices', *British Journal of Middle Eastern Studies*, 8:2, 205–8: and in Weizman 2007.

62 Michel Foucault 1978, *The History of Sexuality*, vol. 1, New York: Vintage, 138–40.

63 Galloway 2004, 16.

64 Mark Poster 2005, 'Hardt and Negri's information empire: A critical response', *Cultural Politics*, 1:1, 110.

65 Poster 2005, 112.

Chapter 5 Body Badges

1 Irma van der Ploeg 2005, *The Machine-Readable Body*, Maastricht: Shaker, 78.

2 Ellen Nakashima 2007, 'FBI prepares vast database of biometrics', *Washington Post*, 22 December, A01, available at *www.washingtonpost.com/wp-dyn/content/article/2007/12/21/AR2007122102544_pf.html*, accessed 2 January 2009.

3 Owen Bowcott 2008, 'FBI wants instant access to British identity data', *The Guardian*, 16 January, available at *www.guardian.co.uk/print/0,,332065468-105744,00.html*, accessed 2 January 2009.

4 Louise Amoore 2008, 'Governing by identity', in Colin J. Bennett and David Lyon, eds, *Playing the Identity Card: Surveillance, Security and Identification in Global Perspective*, London and New York: Routledge.

5 See contributions to Jane Caplan and John Torpey, eds, 2001, *Documenting Individual Identity*, Princeton: Princeton University Press.

6 For a legal view of this see M.G. Milone 2001, 'Biometric surveillance: Searching for identity', *Business Lawyer*, 57:1, 497–513.

7 CNN 2002, 'Schiphol back eye scan security', available at *http://*

archives.cnn.com/2002/WORLD/europe/03/27/schiphol.security/index. html, accessed 2 January 2009.

8 'People "can't wait for ID cards"', BBC News, 7 November 2008, available at *http://news.bbc.co.uk/2/hi/uk_news/politics/7712275.stm*, accessed 2 January 2009.

9 David Lyon 2003a, 'Airports as data filters: Converging surveillance systems after September 11', *Information, Communication and Ethics in Society*, 1:1, 13–20. See also Peter Adey 2007, '"May I have your attention": Airport geographies of spectatorship, position and (im)mobility', *Environment and Planning D: Society and Space*, 25, 516–36; and Mark Salter, ed., 2008, *Politics at the Airport*, Minneapolis: University of Minnesota Press.

10 See Jeffrey M. Stanton 2008, 'ICAO and the biometric RFID passport: History and analysis', in Colin J. Bennett and David Lyon, eds, *Playing the Identity Card: Surveillance, Security and Identification in Global Perspective*, London and New York: Routledge.

11 Elia Zureik with Karen Hindle 2005, 'Governance, security and technology: The case of biometrics', *Studies in Political Economy*, 73, 113–37; and Kelly Gates 2008, 'Biometrics and post-9/11 technostalgia', *Social Text*, 83, 35–54.

12 Angus Reid Global Monitor 2007, 'Canadians open to national ID card', available at *www.angus-reid.com/polls/view/16691*, accessed 2 January 2009. The figure was considerably lower in the GPD survey in 2006, but the question was connected with one about the accompanying database (see chapter 2).

13 Lucas Introna and David Wood 2004, 'Picturing algorithmic surveillance: The politics of facial recognition systems', *Surveillance and Society*, 2:2–3, 177–98.

14 Dean Wilson 2008, 'Australian biometrics and global surveillance', *International Criminal Justice Review*, 17:3, 207–19.

15 Jeremy Wickins 2007, 'The ethics of biometrics: The risk of social exclusion from the widespread use of electronic identification', *Science and Engineering Ethics*, 13, 45–54; Lucas Introna 2005, 'Disclosive ethics and information technology: Disclosing facial recognition systems', *Ethics and Information Technology*, 7, 75–86; Philip E. Agre 2003, 'Your face is not a bar code: Arguments against automatic face-recognition in public places', available at *http://polaris.gseis.ucla.edu/pagre/bar-code.html*, accessed 2 January 2009.

16 Heather Murray 2007, 'Monstrous play in negative spaces: Illegible bodies and the cultural construction of biometric technology', *The Communication Review*, 10:4, 347–65.

17 National ID 2005, 'Survey Part One; National ID – Europe', *Biometric Technology Today*, 2007, October, available at *www.sciencedirect.com/ science?_ob=ArticleURL&_udi=B6W70-4PMSV7V-M&_user=10&_rdoc = 1&_fmt = &_orig = search&_sort = d&view = c&_acct = C000050221&_ version = 1&_urlVersion = 0&_userid = 10&md5 = haefaab9073f8032fd3fa 6bc18332706, accessed 2 January 2009.*

18 See, e.g., Ann Cavoukian and Alex Stoianov 2007, *Biometric Encryption*, Toronto: IPC, available at *www.ipc.on.ca/images/Resources/up-1bio_ encryp.pdf*, accessed 2 January 2009.

19 See, e.g., Roger Clarke 2002, 'Biometrics' inadequacies and threats, and the need for regulation', available at *www.anu.edu.au/people/Roger. Clarke/DV/BiomThreats.html*, accessed 2 January 2009.

20 Benjamin Weiser 2004, 'Can prints lie? Yes, man finds to his dismay', *New York Times*, 31 May, available at *query.nytimes.com/gst/fullpage. html?res = 9D07EED91F3EF932A05756C0A9629C8B63&n = Top/ Reference/Times%20Topics/People/W/Weiser,%20Benjamin*, accessed 2 January 2009.

21 Weiser 2004.

22 Adey 2007; see also Salter 2008.

23 Introna 2005, 77.

24 Introna 2005, 85.

25 See *www.ibia.org/aboutibia*.

26 European Communities 2005, *Biometrics at the Frontiers: Assessing the Impact on Society*, available at *http://ec.europa.eu/justice_home/doc_centre/ freetravel/doc/biometrics_eur21585_en.pdf*, accessed 2 January 2009.

27 E.g. Privacy International 2004, 'Files and biometric identifiers on more than a billion passengers to be computerised and shared globally by 2015', media release, available at *www.privacyinternational.org/ article.shtml?cmd%5B347%5D=x-347-62397*, accessed 2 January 2009; EPIC 2006, 'Biometric identifiers', available at *www.epic.org/privacy/ biometrics*, accessed 2 January 2009; Shoshana Magnet 2007, 'Are biometrics race-neutral?', 5 June, available at *www.anonequity.org/weblog/ archives/2007/06/are_biometrics_raceneutral.php*, accessed 2 January 2009; and Liberty and Security 2006, *Trends in Biometrics*, available at *www.libertysecurity.org/article1191.html*, accessed 2 January 2009.

28 Liberty and Security 2006, 1.

29 See also Juliet Lodge, ed., 2007, *Are You Who You Say You Are? The EU and Biometric Borders*, Nijmegen: Wolf Legal Publishers.

30 Murray 2007; Wilson 2008; and Zureik with Hindle 2005.

31 Of course one could cite parallel problems in related areas such as CCTV. See, e.g., Benjamin Goold 2004, *CCTV and Policing: Public Area Surveillance and Police Practices in Britain*, Oxford: Oxford University Press, 20–39.

32 Patrick O'Neil 2005, 'Complexity and counter-terrorism: Thinking about biometrics', *Studies in Conflict and Terrorism*, 28, 547–66.

33 See Vincent Mosco 2004, *The Digital Sublime: Myth, Power and Cyberspace*, Cambridge, MA: MIT Press.

34 Naomi Klein 2007, *The Shock Doctrine: The Rise of Disaster Capitalism*, Toronto: Knopf Canada, 339–69.

35 O'Neil 2005, 559.

36 Amitai Etzioni 2002, 'You'll love those national ID cards', *Christian Science Monitor*, 14 January, available at *www.csmonitor.com/2002/0114/p11s1-coop.html*, accessed 2 January 2009.

37 One criticism of the UK ID Card proposal made by the London School of Economics team was that biometrics systems had been adopted *before* full trials had occurred: LSE 2005, *The Identity Project*, London: LSE Department of Information Systems.

38 See, e.g., Benjamin Muller 2004, '(Dis)Qualified bodies: Securitization, citizenship and identity management', *Citizenship Studies*, 8:3, 279–94.

39 Lucy Suchman 1993, 'Do categories have politics?', *Computer-Supported Cooperative Work*, 2:3, 177–90.

40 Geoffrey Bowker and Susan Leigh Star 1999, *Sorting Things Out: Classification and Its Consequences*, Cambridge, MA: MIT Press, 70.

41 Simon Cole 2001, *Suspect Identities: A History of Fingerprinting and Criminal Identification*, Cambridge, MA and London: Harvard University Press, 166.

42 EDPS 2007, *Summary Report of the European Data Protection Supervisor on the Eurodac Audit, 2006*, available at *www.libertysecurity.org/IMG/pdf_07-11-09_Eurodac_audit_summary_EN.pdf*, accessed 2 January 2009.

43 See, e.g., Irma van der Ploeg 1999, 'The illegal body: "Eurodac" and the politics of biometric identification', *Ethics and Information Technology*, 1:4, 295–302.

44 See, e.g., Magnet 2007.

45 See also the Australian case: Wilson 2008.

46 Magnet 2007, n. 45.

47 Shoshana Magnet 2008, 'Bio benefital Technologies of criminaliza-tion, biometrics and the welfare system', in Sean Hier and Joshua Greenberg, eds, *Surveillance and Social Problems*, Halifax: Fernwood.

48 Robin Rogers-Dillon 2004, *The Welfare Experiments: Politics and Policy Evaluation*, Stanford: Stanford Law and Politics.

49 Joseph Pugliese 2005, '*In silico* race and the heteronomy of biometric proxies: Biometrics in the context of civilian life, border security and counter-terrorism laws', *The Australian Feminist Law Journal*, 23, 1–32.

50 Agre 2003.

51 Van der Ploeg 2005, 79f.

52 Michel Foucault 1976, *The History of Sexuality*, vol. 1, New York: Vintage.

53 See also Ian Hacking 1982, 'Biopower and the avalanche of printed numbers', *Humanities in Society*, 5, 279–95.

54 Van der Ploeg 2005, 83.

55 See Richard Ericson and Kevin Haggerty 1997, *Policing the Risk Society*, Toronto: University of Toronto Press, 90.

56 Van der Ploeg 2005.

57 Katherine Hayles 1992, *How We Became Posthuman: Virtual Bodies in Cyberspace, Literature and Informatics*, Chicago: University of Chicago Press.

58 Van der Ploeg 2005, 94.

59 In passing, it should also be noted that similar problems arise in relation to the use of implants containing RFID chips and in some cases – such as offenders on probation or with a curfew – GPS devices, both for verifying identities and for connecting those identified bodies with a specific location.

60 Hayles 1992.

61 For instance by Donald MacKay 1969, *Information, Mechanism and Meaning*, Cambridge, MA: MIT Press.

62 David Lyon 2001, *Surveillance Society: Monitoring Everyday Life*, Buckingham: Open University Press, chap. 1.

63 Van der Ploeg 2005, chap. 3.

64 Lyon 2001, chap. 1.

65 James Scott 1998, *Seeing Like a State: How Certain Schemes to Improve the Human Condition Have Failed*, New Haven: Yale University Press.

66 Kevin Haggerty and Richard Ericson 2000, 'The surveillant assemblage', *British Journal of Sociology*, 51:4, 605–22.

67 Paul Ricoeur 1992, *Oneself as Another*, Chicago: University of Chicago Press, 23; see also Lyon 2001, 162.

68 Ricoeur 1992, 23.

69 See also Ayse Ceyhan 2008, 'Technologization of security: Management of uncertainty and risk in an age of biometrics', *Surveillance and Society*, 5:2, 102–23.

70 Clive Norris 2006, Expert Report: Criminal Justice, in *A Report on the Surveillance Society*, London: Office of the Information Commissioner.

71 James Randerson, 'DNA of 37% of black men held by police', *The Guardian*, 5 January, available at *www.guardian.co.uk/world/2006/jan/05/race.ukcrime*, accessed 2 January 2009.

72 Cited in Dorothy Nelkin and Lori Andrews 2003, 'Surveillance creep in the genetic age', in David Lyon, ed., *Surveillance as Social Sorting*, London and New York: Routledge, 108.

73 Kenneth R. Foster and Jan Jaeger 2007, 'RFID inside', *IEEE Spectrum*, March, available at *www.spectrum.ieee.org/mar07/4939*, accessed 2 January 2009.

74 See van der Ploeg 2005.

75 See, e.g., the work of the European Court of Human Rights 2005, *Progress Report on the Application of the Principles of Convention 108 to the Collection and Processing of Biometric Data*, available at *www.coe. int/t/e/legal_affairs/legal_co-operation/data_protection/documents/reports_and_studies_of_data_protection_committees/2O-Biometrics(2005)_en.asp*, accessed 2 January 2009.

Chapter 6 Cyber-Citizens

1 See the Open Society summary at *www.justiceinitiative.org/db/resource2?res_id=103920*, accessed 2 January 2009.

2 See Amira Hass 2007, 'The yearnings for a magnetic card', *Haaretz*, 9 May, available at *www.haaretz.com/hasen/spages/857291.html*, accessed 2 January 2009.

3 Simon Szreter 2007, 'The right of registration: Development, identity ⌐

registration, and social security – a historical perspective', *World Development*, 35:1, 67–86.

4 Benjamin Muller 2006, '(Dis)Qualified bodies: Securitization, citizenship and identity management', *Citizenship Studies*, 8i3, 279 94.

5 Muller 2006, 290.

6 Kelly Gates 2008, 'The United States Real ID Act and the securitization of identity', in Colin J. Bennett and David Lyon, eds, *Playing the Identity Card: Surveillance, Security and Identification in Global Perspective*, London and New York: Routledge.

7 The phrase is from Anthony Giddens 1990, *The Consequences of Modernity*, Cambridge: Polity, 26 which is cited by Gates 2008, 219, and discussed in surveillance contexts in David Lyon 2001, *Surveillance Society: Monitoring Everyday Life*, Buckingham: Open University Press.

8 See, e.g., the discussion in Barry Hague and Brian Loader 1999, *Digital Democracy: Discourse and Decision Making in the Digital Age*, London and New York: Routledge.

9 Engin Isin 2002, *Being Political*, Minneapolis: University of Minnesota Press, 51.

10 See Bryan Turner, ed., 1993, *Citizenship and Social Theory*, London: Sage, 12.

11 See, e.g., Christiana Van Houten 1991, *The Alien in Biblical Law*, Sheffield: Sheffield Academic Press; and Nick Spencer 2004, *Asylum and Immigration: A Christian Perspective on a Polarised Debate*, Milton Keynes: Paternoster Press, 88–9.

12 Engin Isin and Bryan Turner 2007, 'Investigating citizenship: An agenda for citizenship studies', *Citizenship Studies*, 11:1, 5–17.

13 See, e.g., John Gilliom 2001, *Overseers of the Poor*, Chicago: University of Chicago Press.

14 Gerard Delanty 2000, *Citizenship in a Global Age: Society, Culture, Politics*, Buckingham: Open University Press.

15 Valentin Groebner 2007, *Who Are You? Identification, Deception and Surveillance in Early Modern Europe*, New York: Zone Books, 255.

16 Zygmunt Bauman 1998a, *Globalization: The Human Consequences*, Cambridge: Polity.

17 Zygmunt Bauman 2000, *Liquid Modernity*, Cambridge: Polity, 40.

18 See Turner 1993.

19 Bauman 2000, 40.

20 David Garland 2001, *The Culture of Control*, Chicago: University of Chicago Press, 193.

21 Didier Bigo and Elspeth Guild 2005, 'Policing at a distance: Schengen to visa policies', in Didier Bigo and Elspeth Guild, eds, *Controlling Frontiers: Free Movement into and within Europe*, London: Ashgate.

22 Keith Breckenridge cautions that interoperability may not be a workable goal: Breckenridge 2008, 'The elusive panopticon: The HANIS project and the politics of standards in South Africa', in Colin J. Bennett and David Lyon, eds, *Playing the Identity Card: Surveillance, Security and Identification in Global Perspective*, London and New York: Routledge.

23 Bauman 1998a.

24 Quoted in Alan Travis 2003, 'ID cards to cut asylum abuses', *The Guardian*, 23 May, available at *www.guardian.co.uk/politics/2003/may/23/immigration.immigrationandpublicservices*, accessed 5 January 2009.

25 Isin and Turner 2007, 10.

26 Isin and Turner 2007.

27 Groebner 2007, 258.

28 Irma van der Ploeg 2005, *The Machine-Readable Body*, Maastricht: Shaker, 133.

29 See David Wright, Serge Gutwirth, Michael Friedewald, Elena Vildjiounaite and Yves Punie, eds, 2007, *Safeguards in a World of Ambient Intelligence*, New York: Springer.

30 See also Muller 2004.

31 Didier Bigo 2004, 'Globalized in-security: The field of the professionals of unease management and the ban-opticon', *Traces: A Multilingual Journal of Cultural Theory*, 4, 1–33.

32 Zygmunt Bauman 1998b, *Work, Consumerism and the New Poor*, Buckingham: Open University Press.

33 While Bauman (1993, *Postmodern Ethics*, Oxford and Cambridge, MA: Blackwell) uses Levinas, however, he seems to neglect the transcendent dimension of Otherness that Levinas affirms. Levinas also insists that we recognize the 'infinite in the Other' as a proper starting point for ethics. Without that, one might argue, it is hard to resist either the self-indulgent consumerism or the fear-culture dependence on 'national security' that characterizes today's 'liquid modernity'.

34 See *http://cpsr.org/issues/pd/*, accessed 5 January 2009.

35 See Colin J. Bennett 2008, *The Privacy Advocates: Resisting the Spread of Surveillance*, Cambridge, MA: MIT Press.

36 See Pierre Piazza and Laurent Laniel 2008, 'The INES biometric card and the politics of national identity assignment in France', in Colin J. Bennett and David Lyon, eds, *Playing the Identity Card: Surveillance, Security and Identification in Global Perspective*, London and New York: Routledge.

37 See Midori Ogasawara 2008, 'A tale of the colonial age or the banner of a new tyranny: National identification card systems in Japan', in Colin J. Bennett and David Lyon, eds, *Playing the Identity Card: Surveillance, Security and Identification in Global Perspective*, London and New York: Routledge; and David Murakami Wood, David Lyon and Kiyoshi Abe 2007, 'Surveillance in urban Japan: An introduction', *Urban Studies*, 43:3, 551–68.

38 Ryan Singel 2008, 'New Real ID rules to shut down nation's airports in May?', *Wired*, 11 January, available at *blog.wired.com/27bstroke6/2008/01/new-real-id-rul.html*, accessed 5 January 2009.

39 Andrew Clement, Krista Boa, Simon Davies and Gus Hosein 2008, 'Towards national ID policies for Canada: Federal initiatives and alternative principles', in Colin J. Bennett and David Lyon, eds, *Playing the Identity Card: Surveillance, Security and Identification in Global Perspective*, London and New York: Routledge.

40 See, e.g., *epic.org/privacy/id-cards/* or *www.ico.gov.uk/about_us/news_and_views/current_topics/identity_cards.aspx* for some useful updated information on ID card systems (accessed 5 January 2009).

41 See *www.privcom.gc.ca/media/nr-c/2008/nr-c_080205_e.asp*, accessed 5 January 2009.

42 Bennett 2008.

43 See Darin Barney 2000, *Prometheus Wired: The Hope for Democracy in the Age of Network Technology*, Vancouver: UBC Press, chapter 7.

44 Michael Edwards 2004, *Civil Society*, Cambridge: Polity.

45 This comment does not exclude the possibility that fraudulent claims may well be made by those seeking entry into a new country. My argument is that stories should be heard, from compassion in the first instance. Discretion is two-edged, and this is not to deny appropriate refusal to certain would-be border entrants.

46 This is discussed in chapter 3 as the 'oligopolization of the means of identification'.

47 See Richard Jones 2000, 'Digital rule', *Punishment and Security*, 2:1, 5–22.
48 Garland 2001.
49 Gilles Deleuze 1992, 'Postscript on the societies of control', *October*, 59, 3–7.
50 See comments on 'sorting things out' in South Africa under apartheid, in Geoffrey Bowker and Susan Leigh Star 1999, *Sorting Things Out: Classification and Its Consequences*, Cambridge, MA: MIT Press.
51 Dean Wilson 2006, 'Biometrics, borders and the ideal suspect', in Sharon Pickering and Leanne Weber, eds, *Borders, Mobility and Technologies of Control*, Berlin: Springer-Verlag.

Bibliography

Abercrombie, Nicholas, Stephen Hill and Bryan Turner (1986) *Sovereign Individuals of Capitalism*, London: Allen and Unwin.

Abu-Zahra, Nadia (2007) 'IDs and territory: Population control for resource expropriation', in Deborah Cowen and Emily Gilbert, eds, *War, Citizenship, Territory*, London: Taylor and Francis.

Adey, Peter (2007) '"May I have your attention": Airport geographies of spectatorship, position and (im)mobility', *Environment and Planning D: Society and Space*, 25, 516–36.

Agamben, Giorgio (1997) *State of Exception*, Chicago: University of Chicago Press.

Agar, Jon (2001) '"Modern horrors": British identity and identity cards', in Jane Caplan and John Torpey, eds, *Documenting Individual Identity*, Princeton: Princeton University Press.

Agar, Jon (2005) 'Identity cards in Britain: Past experience and policy implication', *History and Policy*, Policy Paper 33, November, available at *www.historyandpolicy.org/archive/policy-paper-33.html*, accessed 18 December 2008.

Agre, Philip E. (2003) 'Your face is not a bar code: Arguments against automatic face-recognition in public places', available at *http://polaris.gseis.ucla.edu/pagre/bar-code.html*, accessed 2 January 2009.

Amoore, Louise (2007) 'Vigilant visualities: The watchful politics of the war on terror', *Security Dialogue*, 38:2, 139–56.

Amoore, Louise (2008) 'Governing by identity', in Colin J. Bennett and David Lyon, eds, *Playing the Identity Card: Surveillance, Security and Identification in Global Perspective*, London and New York: Routledge.

Amoore, Louise and Marieke de Goede (2005) 'Governance, risk and dataveillance in the war on terror', *Crime, Law and Social Change*, 43, 149–73.

Ball, Kirstie, Elizabeth Daniel, Sally Dibb and Maureen Meadows (2009) 'Democracy, surveillance and "knowing what's good for you": The private sector origins of profiling and the birth of "citizen relationship management"', in Kevin Haggerty and Minas Samatas, eds, *Surveillance and Democracy*, London and New York: Routledge.

Ball, Kirstie and Frank Webster, eds (2003) *The Intensification of Surveillance*, London: Pluto.

Barney, Darin (2000) *Prometheus Wired: The Hope for Democracy in the Age of Network Technology*, Vancouver: UBC Press.

Barry, Andrew (2001) *Political Machines: Governing a Technological Society*, New York: Athlone Press.

Bauman, Zygmunt (1991) *Modernity and the Holocaust*, Cambridge: Polity.

Bauman, Zygmunt (1993) *Postmodern Ethics*, Oxford and Cambridge, MA: Blackwell.

Bauman, Zygmunt (1998a) *Globalization: The Human Consequences*, Cambridge: Polity.

Bauman, Zygmunt (1998b) *Work, Consumerism and the New Poor*, Buckingham: Open University Press.

Bauman, Zygmunt (2000) *Liquid Modernity*, Cambridge: Polity.

Bauman, Zygmunt (2004) *Identity*, Cambridge: Polity.

Beck, Adrian and Kate Broadhurst (1998) 'Compulsion by stealth: Lesson from the European Union on the use of national identity cards', *Public Administration*, 76, 779–92.

Bediako, Kwame (1992) *Theology and Identity*, Oxford: Regnum Books.

Benhabib, Selya (2004) *The Rights of Others: Aliens, Residents and Citizens*, Cambridge and New York: Cambridge University Press.

Bennett, Colin J. (2006) 'What happens when you buy an airline ticket?', in Kevin Haggerty and Richard Ericson, eds, *The New*

Politics of Surveillance and Visibility, Toronto: University of Toronto Press.

Bennett, Colin J. (2008) *The Privacy Advocates: Resisting the Spread of Surveillance*, Cambridge, MA: MIT Press.

Bigo, Didier (2004) 'Globalized in-security: The field of the professionals of unease management and the ban-opticon', *Traces: A Multilingual Journal of Cultural Theory*, 4, 1–33.

Bigo, Didier and Elspeth Guild (2005) 'Policing at a distance. Schengen to visa policies', in Didier Bigo and Elspeth Guild, eds, *Controlling Frontiers: Free Movement into and within Europe*, London: Ashgate.

Black, Edwin (2001) *IBM and the Holocaust*, New York: Crown.

Bowker, Geoffrey and Susan Leigh Star (1999) *Sorting Things Out: Classification and Its Consequences*, Cambridge, MA: MIT Press.

Breckenridge, Keith (2005) 'The biometric state: The promise and peril of digital government in the New South Africa', *Journal of South African Studies*, 31:2, 267–82.

Breckenridge, Keith (2008) 'The elusive panopticon: The HANIS project and the politics of standards in South Africa', in Colin J. Bennett and David Lyon, eds, *Playing the Identity Card: Surveillance, Security and Identification in Global Perspective*, London and New York: Routledge.

Broeders, Dennis (2007) 'The new digital borders of Europe: EU databases and the surveillance of irregular migrants', *International Sociology*, 22:1, 71–92.

Browne, Simone (2007) Trusted Travelers: The Identity-Industrial Complex, Race and Canada's Permanent Resident Card, PhD dissertation, Toronto: UT-OISE.

Caplan, Jane and John Torpey, eds (2001) *Documenting Individual Identity*, Princeton: Princeton University Press.

Cavoukian, Ann (2006) *7 Laws of Identity*, Toronto: IPC.

Cavoukian, Ann and Alex Stoianov (2007) *Biometric Encryption*, Toronto: IPC, at *www.ipc.on.ca/images/Resources/up-1bio_encryp.pdf*, accessed 2 January 2009.

Ceyhan, Ayse, ed. (2007) *Identifier et surveiller: Les technologies de sécurité*, Paris: L'Harmattan (*Cultur et Conflits* 64).

Ceyhan, Ayse (2008) 'Technologization of security: Management of uncertainty and risk in an age of biometrics', *Surveillance and Society*, 5:2, 102–23.

Clarke, Roger (1988) 'Information technology and dataveillance', *Communications of the ACM*, 31:5, 498–512.

Clarke, Roger (1997) 'Chip-based ID: Promise and peril?', available at *www.anu.edu.au/people/Roger.Clarke/DV/IDCards97.html*, accessed 8 November 2008.

Clarke, Roger (2002) 'Biometrics' inadequacies and threats, and the need for regulation', available at *www.anu.edu.au/people/Roger.Clarke/DV/BiomThreats.html*, accessed 2 January 2009.

Clarke, Roger (2006a) 'National identity cards? Bust the myth of security über alles!', 28 January, available at *www.anu.edu.au/people/Roger.Clarke/DV/NatID-BC-0602.html*, accessed 22 December 2008.

Clarke, Roger (2006b) 'National identity schemes: The elements', 8 February, available at *www.anu.edu.au/people/Roger.Clarke/DV/NatIDSchemeElms.html*, accessed 19 December 2008.

Clement, Andrew, Krista Boa, Simon Davies and Gus Hosein (2008) 'Towards national ID policies for Canada: Federal initiatives and alternative principles', in Colin J. Bennett and David Lyon, eds., *Playing the Identity Card: Surveillance, Security and Identification in Global Perspective*, London and New York: Routledge.

Cole, Simon (2001) *Suspect Identities: A History of Fingerprinting and Criminal Identification*, Cambridge, MA and London: Harvard University Press.

Colley, Linda (1996) *Britons: Forging the Nation 1707–1837*, London: Vintage.

Connolly, William (1991) *Identity/Difference: Democratic Negotiations of Political Paradox*, Minneapolis: University of Minnesota Press.

Crosby, James (2008) *Challenges and Opportunities in Identity Assurance*, London: HMSO.

Damani, Ernesto, Sabrina De Capitani di Vimercati and Pierangela Samarati (2003) 'Managing multiple and dependable identities', *IEEE Internet Computing*, 7:6, 29–37, available at *spdp.dti.unimi.it/papers/RI-5.pdf*, accessed 2 February 2009.

Dandeker, Christopher (1990) *Surveillance, Power and Modernity*, Cambridge: Polity.

Das, Veena and Deborah Poole, eds (2004) *Anthropology in the Margins of the State*, New Delhi: Oxford University Press.

Delanty, Gerard (2000) *Citizenship in a Global Age: Society, Culture, Politics*, Buckingham: Open University Press.

Deleuze, Gilles (1992) 'Postscript on the societies of control', *October*, 59, 3–7.

Dillon, Michael (2002) 'Network-centric warfare and the state of emergency', *Theory, Culture and Society*, 19:4, 71–9.

Dodge, Martin and Rob Kitchen (2005) 'Codes of life: Identification codes and the machine-readable world', *Environment and Planning D: Society and Space*, 23, 851–81.

Dreyfus, Herbert L. and Paul Rabinow (1982) *Michel Foucault: Beyond Structuralism and Hermeneutics*, Chicago: University of Chicago Press.

EDPS (2007) *Summary Report of the European Data Protection Supervisor on the Eurodac Audit, 2006*, available at *www.libertysecurity.org/IMG/pdf_07-11-09_Eurodac_audit_summary_EN.pdf*, accessed 2 January 2009.

EPIC (2006) 'Biometric identifiers', available at *www.epic.org/privacy/biometrics*, accessed 2 January 2009.

Ericson, Richard (2007) *Crime in an Insecure World*, Cambridge: Polity.

Ericson, Richard and Kevin Haggerty (1997) *Policing the Risk Society*, Toronto: University of Toronto Press.

Etzioni, Amitai (2002) 'You'll love those national ID cards', *Christian Science Monitor*, 14 January, available at *www.csmonitor.com/2002/0114/p11s1-coop.html*, accessed 2 January 2009.

European Communities (2005) *Biometrics at the Frontiers: Assessing the Impact on Society*, available at *ec.europa.eu/justice_home/doc_centre/freetravel/doc/biometrics_eur21585_en.pdf*, accessed 2 January 2009.

European Court of Human Rights (2005) *Progress Report on the Application of the Principles of Convention 108 to the Collection and Processing of Biometric Data*, available at *www.coe.int/t/e/legal_affairs/legal_co-operation/data_protection/documents/reports_and_studies_of_data_protection_committees/2O-Biometrics(2005)_en.asp*, accessed 2 January 2009.

Feely, Malcom M. and Jonathan Simon (2006) 'The new penology: Notes on the emerging strategy of corrections and its implications', *Criminology*, 30:4, 449–74.

Finn, Jonathan (2005) 'Photographing fingerprints: Data collection and the state', *Surveillance and Society*, 3:1, 21–44.

Foucault, Michel (1978) *The History of Sexuality*, vol. 1, New York: Vintage.

French, Martin (2007) 'In the shadow of Canada's camps', *Social and Legal Studies*, 16:1, 49–69.

Frieberg, Anne (2006) *Virtual Window*, Cambridge, MA: MIT Press.

Frois, Caterina (2008) 'Personal databases and surveillance in Portugal: Analysis of a transitional process', Sheffield conference of the Surveillance Studies Network, April.

Gadzheva, Maya (2008) 'Privacy in the age of transparency: The new vulnerability of the individual', *Social Science Computer Review*, 26:1, 60–74.

Galloway, Alexander (2004) *Protocol: How Control Exists after Decentralization*, Cambridge, MA: MIT Press.

Gandy, Oscar (1993) *The Panoptic Sort: A Political Economy of Personal Information*, Boulder, CO: Westview.

Gandy, Oscar (2006a) 'Data mining, surveillance and discrimination in the post-9/11 environment', in Kevin Haggerty and Richard Ericson, eds, *The New Politics of Surveillance and Visibility*, Toronto: University of Toronto Press.

Gandy, Oscar (2006b) 'Quixotics unite! Engaging the pragmatists on rational discrimination', in David Lyon, ed., *Theorizing Surveillance: The Panopticon and Beyond*, Cullompton, UK: Willan.

Garcelon, Marc (2001) 'Colonizing the subject: The genealogy and legacy of the Soviet internal passport', in Jane Caplan and John Torpey, eds, *Documenting Individual Identity*, Princeton: Princeton University Press.

Garland, David (2001) *The Culture of Control*, Chicago: University of Chicago Press.

Garton Ash, Timothy (1998) *The File: A Personal History*, New York: Vintage Books.

Gates, Kelly (2005) 'Biometrics and post-9/11 technostalgia', *Social Text*, 83, 35–54.

Gates, Kelly (2006) 'Identifying the 9/11 "faces of terror"', *Cultural Studies*, 20:4–5, 417–40.

Gates, Kelly (2008) 'The United States Real ID Act and the securitization of identity', in Colin J. Bennett and David Lyon, eds, *Playing the Identity Card: Surveillance, Security and Identification in Global Perspective*, London and New York: Routledge.

Giddens, Anthony (1987) *The Nation-State and Violence*, Cambridge: Polity.

Giddens, Anthony (1990) *The Consequences of Modernity*, Cambridge: Polity.

Gilliom, John (2001) *Overseers of the Poor*, Chicago: University of Chicago Press.

Goffman, Erving (1959) *The Presentation of Self in Everyday Life*, New York: Anchor.

Goold, Benjamin (2004) *CCTV and Policing: Public Area Surveillance and Police Practices in Britain*, Oxford: Oxford University Press.

Groebner, Valentin (2001) 'Describing the person, reading the signs in late medieval and Renaissance Europe: Identity papers, vested figures and the limits of identification', in Jane Caplan and John Torpey, eds, *Documenting Individual Identity*, Princeton: Princeton University Press.

Groebner, Valentin (2007) *Who Are You? Identification, Deception, and Surveillance in Early Modern Europe*, New York: Zone Books.

Hacking, Ian (1982) 'Biopower and the avalanche of printed numbers', *Humanities in Society*, 5, 279–95.

Hacking, Ian (1990) *The Taming of Chance*, Cambridge: Cambridge University Press.

Hacking, Ian (2002) *Historical Ontology*, Cambridge, MA: Harvard University Press.

Haggerty, Kevin and Richard Ericson (2000) 'The surveillant assemblage', *British Journal of Sociology*, 51:4, 605–22.

Haggerty, Kevin and Richard Ericson, eds (2006) *The New Politics of Surveillance and Visibility*, Toronto: University of Toronto Press.

Hague, Barry and Brian Loader, eds (1999) *Digital Democracy: Discourse and Decision Making in the Information Age*, London and New York: Routledge.

Hayles, Katherine (1999) *How We Became Posthuman: Virtual Bodies in Cyberspace, Literature and Informatics*, Chicago: University of Chicago Press.

Heidegger, Martin (1977) *The Question Concerning Technology and Other Essays*, New York: Harper Torchbooks.

Higgs, Edward (2004) *The Information State in England: The Central Collection of Information on Citizens, 1500–2000*, London: Palgrave.

Hosein, Ian (2004) 'The sources of laws: Policy dynamics in a digital and terrorized world', *The Information Society*, 20:3, 187–99.

Houck, Max (2007) *Forensic Science: Modern Methods of Solving Crime*, Westport, CT: Greenwood.

House of Commons Science and Technology Committee (2006)

'Scientific advice, risk and evidence: How government handles them', available at *www.parliament.uk/parliamentary_committees/science_and_technology_committee/sag.cfm*, accessed 22 December 2008.

Hui, Victoria (2005) *War and State Formation in Ancient China and Early Modern Europe*, Cambridge and New York: Cambridge University Press.

Introna, Lucas (2005) 'Disclosive ethics and information technology: Disclosing facial recognition systems', *Ethics and Information Technology*, 7, 75–86.

Introna, Lucas (2007) 'Making sense of ICT, new media and ethics', in Robin Mansell, Christanthi Avgerou, Danny Quab and Roger Silverstone, eds, *The Oxford Handbook of Information and Communication Technologies*, Oxford and New York: Oxford University Press.

Introna, Lucas and David Wood (2004) 'Picturing algorithmic surveillance: The politics of facial recognition systems', *Surveillance and Society*, 2:2–3, 177–98.

Isin, Engin (2002) *Being Political*, Minneapolis: University of Minnesota Press.

Isin, Engin and Bryan Turner (2007) 'Investigating citizenship: An agenda for citizenship studies', *Citizenship Studies*, 11:1, 5–17.

Jenkins, Richard (2004) *Social Identity*, London and New York: Routledge.

Jones, Richard (2000) 'Digital rule', *Punishment and Society*, 2:1, 5–22.

Kaldor, Mary (2005) 'What is human security?', in David Held, Anthony Barnett and Caspar Henderson, eds, *Debating Globalization*, Cambridge: Polity.

Kaluzynski, Martine (2001) 'Republican identity: Bertillonage and government technique', in Jane Caplan and John Torpey, eds, *Documenting Individual Identity*, Princeton: Princeton University Press, 123–38.

Kean, Thomas H., chair (2005) *Final Report on 9/11 Commission Recommendations*, available at *www.9-11pdp.org/press/2005-12-05_report.pdf*, accessed 29 January 2009.

Kern, Stephen (2003) *The Culture of Time and Space* (second edition), Cambridge, MA: Harvard University Press.

Klein, Naomi (2007) *The Shock Doctrine: The Rise of Disaster Capitalism*, Toronto: Knopf Canada.

Langlois, Ganaele (2005) 'Networks and layers: Technocultural encodings of the World Wide Web', *Canadian Journal of Communication*, 30:4, available at *www.cjc-online.ca/viewarticle.php?id=1586*, accessed 23 December 2008.

Latour, Bruno (2005) *Reassembling the Social: An Introduction to Actor-Network-Theory*, Oxford and New York: Oxford University Press.

Lessig, Lawrence (1999) *Code and Other Laws of Cyberspace*, New York: Basic Books.

Levi, Michael and David Wall (2004) 'Technologies, security and privacy in the post-9/11 European information society', *Journal of Law and Society*, 31:2, 194–220.

Lewis, Nancy (2005) 'Expanding surveillance: Connecting biometric information systems to international police cooperation', in Elia Zureik and Mark Salter, eds, *Global Surveillance and Policing*, Cullompton, UK: Willan.

Liberty and Security (2006) *Trends in Biometrics*, available at *www.libertysecurity.org/article1191.html*, accessed 2 January 2009.

Lips, Miriam, John A. Taylor and Joe Organ (2007) 'Identity management as public innovation: Looking beyond ID cards and authentication systems', in Victor J.J.M. Bekkers, Hein P.M. van Duivenboden and Marcel Thaens, eds, *ICT and Public Innovation: Assessing the Modernisation of Public Administration*, Amsterdam: IOS Press.

Lodge, Juliet, ed. (2007) *Are You Who You Say You Are? The EU and Biometric Borders*, Nijmegen: Wolf Legal Publishers.

Longman, Timothy (2001) 'Identity cards, ethnic self-perception and genocide in Rwanda', in Jane Caplan and John Torpey, eds, *Documenting Individual Identity*, Princeton: Princeton University Press.

LSE (2005) *The Identity Project*, London: LSE Department of Information Systems.

Lyon, David (1994) *The Electronic Eye: The Rise of Surveillance Society*, Cambridge: Polity.

Lyon, David (2001) *Surveillance Society: Monitoring Everyday Life*, Buckingham: Open University Press.

Lyon, David (2002) 'Everyday surveillance: Computer codes and mobile bodies', *Information, Communication and Society*, 5:2, 242–57.

Lyon, David (2003a) 'Airports as data filters: Converging surveillance systems after September 11', *Information, Communication, Ethics in Society*, 1:1, 13–20.

Lyon, David (2003b) *Surveillance after September 11*, Cambridge: Polity.

Lyon, David, ed. (2003c) *Surveillance as Social Sorting: Privacy, Risk, and Digital Discrimination*, London and New York: Routledge.

Lyon, David (2004a) *ID Cards: Social Sorting by Database*, Issues Brief of the Oxford Internet Institute, available at *www.oii.ox.ac.uk/resources/publications/IB3all.pdf*, accessed 19 December 2008.

Lyon, David (2004b) 'Globalizing surveillance: Sociological and comparative perspectives', *International Sociology*, 19:2, 135–49.

Lyon, David (2005a) 'The border is everywhere: ID cards, surveillance and the Other', in Elia Zureik and Mark Salter, eds, *Globalizing Surveillance: Borders, Security and Identity*, Cullompton, UK: Willan.

Lyon, David (2005b) 'A sociology of information', in Craig Calhoun, Chris Rojek and Bryan Turner, eds, *A Handbook of Sociology*, London and New York: Sage.

Lyon, David (2006a) 'Airport screening, surveillance and social sorting: Canadian responses to 9/11 in context', *Canadian Journal of Criminology and Criminal Justice*, 48:3, 397–411.

Lyon, David (ed.) (2006b) *Theorizing Surveillance: The Panopticon and Beyond*, Cullompton, UK: Willan.

Lyon, David (2007) *Surveillance Studies: An Overview*, Cambridge: Polity.

Lyon, David (2009) 'National ID card systems and social sorting: International public opinion', in Elia Zureik, Lynda Harling-Stalker, Emily Smith, David Lyon and Yolande E. Chan, eds, *Privacy and Surveillance: International Survey*, Montreal and Kingston: McGill-Queen's University Press.

Lyon, David and Colin J. Bennett (2008) 'Introduction' to Colin J. Bennett and David Lyon, eds, *Playing the Identity Card: Surveillance, Security and Identification in Global Perspective*, London and New York: Routledge.

Lyon, David and Felix Stalder (2003) 'ID cards and social classification', in David Lyon, ed., *Surveillance as Social Sorting: Privacy, Risk, and Digital Discrimination*, London and New York: Routledge.

MacKay, Donald (1969) *Information, Mechanism and Meaning*, Cambridge, MA: MIT Press.

MacPherson, C.B. (1962) *The Political Theory of Possessive Individualism: Hobbes to Locke*, Oxford: Oxford University Press.

Magnet, Shoshana (2007) 'Are biometrics race-neutral?', 5 June, available at *www.anonequity.org / weblog / archives / 2007 / 06 / are _ biometrics_race neutral.php*, accessed 2 January 2009.

Magnet, Shoshana (2008) 'Bio-benefits: Technologies of criminalization, biometrics and the welfare system', in Sean Hier and Josh Greenberg, eds, *Surveillance and Social Problems*, Halifax: Fernwood.

Marshall, T.H. (1950) *Citizenship and Social Class*, Cambridge: Cambridge University Press.

Marx, Gary T. (2006) 'Varieties of personal information as influences on attitudes towards surveillance', in Kevin Haggerty and Richard Ericson, eds, *The New Politics of Surveillance and Visibility*, Toronto: University of Toronto Press.

Marx, Gary T. and Nancy Reichman (1984) 'Routinizing the discovery of secrets', *The American Behavioral Scientist*, 27:4, 423–52.

Mattelart, Armand (2007) *La globalisation de la surveillance*, Paris: La Découverte.

Mehler, Andreas (2004) 'Oligopolies of violence in Africa south of the Sahara', *Nord–Süd Aktuell*, 18:3, 539–48.

Mehmood, Taha (2008) 'India's new ID card: Fuzzy logics, double meanings and ethnic ambiguities', in Colin J. Bennett and David Lyon, eds, *Playing the Identity Card: Surveillance, Security and Identification in Global Perspective*, London and New York: Routledge.

Milone, M.G. (2001) 'Biometric surveillance: Searching for identity', *The Business Lawyer*, 57:1, 497–513.

Mosco, Vincent (2004) *The Digital Sublime: Myth, Power and Cyberspace*, Cambridge, MA: MIT Press.

Muller, Benjamin (2004) '(Dis)Qualified bodies: Securitization, citizenship and identity management', *Citizenship Studies*, 8:3, 279–94.

Murakami Wood, David, David Lyon and Kiyoshi Abe (2007) 'Surveillance in urban Japan: A critical introduction', *Urban Studies*, 44:3, 551–68.

Murray, Heather (2007) 'Monstrous play in negative spaces: Illegible bodies and the cultural construction of biometric technology', *The Communication Review*, 10:4, 347–65.

National ID (2005) 'Survey Part One: National ID – Europe', *Biometric Technology Today*, October, available at *www.sciencedirect.com/science?_ob=ArticleURL&_udi = B6W70-4PMSV7V-M&_user = 10&_rdoc = 1&_fmt = &_orig = search&_sort = d&view = c&_acct = C000050221&_version = 1&_urlVersion = 0&_userid = 10&md5 = baefaab9073f8032fd3fa6be18332706*, accessed 2 January 2009.

NECCC (2002) *Identity Management: A White Paper*, New York: The National Electronic Commerce Coordinating Council.

Nelkin, Dorothy and Lori Andrews (2003) 'Surveillance creep in the genetic age', in David Lyon, ed., *Surveillance as Social Sorting*, London and New York: Routledge.

Noiriel, Gérard (1996) *The French Melting Pot: Immigration, Citizenship and National Identity*, Minneapolis: University of Minnesota Press.

Norris, Clive (2006) Expert Report: Criminal Justice, in *A Report on the Surveillance Society*, London: Office of the Information Commissioner.

O'Harrow, Robert (2005) *No Place to Hide*, New York: Free Press.

O'Neil, Patrick (2005) 'Complexity and counter-terrorism: Thinking about biometrics', *Studies in Conflict and Terrorism*, 28, 547–66.

OECD (2004) *The Security Economy*, Paris: OECD.

Ogasawara, Midori (2008) 'A tale of the colonial age or the banner of a new tyranny: National identification card systems in Japan', in Colin J. Bennett and David Lyon, eds, *Playing the Identity Card: Surveillance, Security and Identification in Global Perspective*, London and New York: Routledge.

Parenti, Christian (2003) *The Soft Cage: Surveillance in America from Slavery to the War on Terror*, New York: Basic Books.

Piazza, Pierre and Laurent Laniel (2008) 'The INES biometric card and the politics of national identity assignment in France', in Colin J. Bennett and David Lyon, eds, *Playing the Identity Card: Surveillance, Security and Identification in Global Perspective*, London and New York: Routledge.

Poster, Mark (2005) 'Hardt and Negri's information empire: A critical response', *Cultural Politics*, 1:1, 101–17.

Pridmore, Jason (2008) Loyal Subjects? Consumer Surveillance in the Personal Information Economy. PhD dissertation, Queen's University, Kingston, Ontario.

Pridmore, Jason and David Lyon (2007) 'Customer relationship management as surveillance', unpublished paper, The Surveillance Project, Queen's University, Kingston, Ontario.

Privacy International (2004) Report on Biometrics, available at *www. privacyinternational.org/article.shtml?cmd % 5B347 % 5D = x-347-62397*, accessed 2 January 2009.

Pugliese, Joseph (2005) '*In silico* race and the heteronomy of biometric proxies: Biometrics in the context of civilian life, border security and counter-terrorism laws', *The Australian Feminist Law Journal*, 23, 1–32.

Putra, Budi (2006) 'HP proposes a national identity system in Indonesia', Asia Cnet.com, 3 November, available at *asia.cnet.com/blogs/toekangit/post.htm?id=61964396*, accessed 23 December 2008.

Raab, Charles (2005) 'Perspectives on "personal identity"', *BT Technology Journal*, 23:4, 15–24.

Ricoeur, Paul (1992) *Oneself as Another*, Chicago: University of Chicago Press.

Rose, Nikolas (1999) *Powers of Freedom*, Cambridge and New York: Cambridge University Press.

Rotenberg, Marc (2006) 'Real ID, real trouble?', *Communication of the ACM*, 49:3, 128.

Ruggiero, Kristin (2001) 'Fingerprinting and the Argentine plan for universal identification in the late nineteenth and early twentieth centuries', in Jane Caplan and John Torpey, eds, *Documenting Individual Identity*, Princeton: Princeton University Press.

Rule, James B. (1973) *Private Lives, Public Surveillance*, London: Allen Lane Press.

Salter, Mark (2003) *Rights of Passage: The Passport in International Relations*, Boulder, CO: Lynne Rienner Publishers.

Salter, Mark (2004) 'Passports, mobility and security: How smart can the border be?', *International Studies Perspectives*, 5, 71–91.

Salter, Mark (2008) 'The global airport: Managing speed, time, space and security', in Mark Salter, ed., *Politics at the Airport*, Minneapolis: University of Minnesota Press.

Scott, James (1998) *Seeing Like a State: How Certain Schemes to Improve the Human Condition Have Failed*, New Haven: Yale University Press.

Sengoopta, Chandak (2003) *Imprint of the Raj*, London: Macmillan.

Sengupta, Shuddhabrata (2003) 'Signatures of the Apocalypse', *Mute*, 3 July, available at *www.metamute.org/en/Signatures-of-the-Apocalypse/*, accessed 19 December 2008.

Shearer, David (2004) 'Elements near and alien: Passportization, policing and identity in the Stalinist state 1932–1952', *The Journal of Modern History*, 76, 835–81.

Simmel, Georg (1950) 'The Stranger', in *The Sociology of Georg Simmel*, ed. K.H. Wolff. Glencoe, IL: Free Press.

Singel, Ryan (2008) 'New Real ID rules to shut down nation's airports in May?', *Wired*, 11 January, available at *blog.wired.com/27bstroke6/2008/01/new-real-id-rul.html*, accessed 5 January 2009.

Spencer, Nick (2004) *Asylum and Immigration: A Christian Perspective on a Polarised Debate*, Milton Keynes: Paternoster Press.

Stalder, Felix (2002) 'Failures and successes: Notes on the development of electronic cash', *The Information Society*, 18:3, 209–19.

Stalder, Felix and David Lyon (2003) 'ID cards and social classification', in David Lyon, ed., *Surveillance as Social Sorting: Privacy, Risk and Digital Discrimination*, London and New York: Routledge.

Stanton, Jeffrey M. (2008) 'ICAO and the biometric RFID passport: History and analysis', in Colin J. Bennett and David Lyon, eds, *Playing the Identity Card: Surveillance, Security and Identification in Global Perspective*, London and New York: Routledge.

Staples, William G. (2000) *Everyday Surveillance: Vigilance and Visibility in Postmodern Life*, Lanham, MD: Rowman and Littlefield.

Statewatch (2005) 'EU: Biometrics – from visas to passports to ID cards', available at *www.statewatch.org/news/2005/jul/09eu-passports-id-cards.htm*, accessed 17 December 2008.

Suchman, Lucy (1993) 'Do categories have politics?', *Computer Supported Cooperative Work*, 2:3, 177–90.

Szreter, Simon (2007) 'The right of registration: Development, identity registration, and social security – a historical perspective', *World Development*, 35:1, 67–86.

Taylor, Charles (1994) 'The politics of recognition', in Amy Guttman, ed., *Multiculturalism: Examining the Politics of Recognition*, Princeton: Princeton University Press.

Taylor, John, Miriam Lips and Joe Organ (2007) 'Information-intensive government and the layering and sorting of citizenship', *Public Money and Management*, 27:2, 161–4.

Torpey, John (1998) 'Coming and going: On the state monopolization of the "legitimate means of movement"', *Sociological Theory*, 16:3, 239–59.

Torpey, John (2000) *The Invention of the Passport: Surveillance, Citizenship and the State*, Cambridge and New York: Cambridge University Press.

Torpey, John (2001) 'The Great War and the birth of the modern passport system', in Jane Caplan and John Torpey, eds, *Documenting Individual Identity*, Princeton: Princeton University Press.

Turner, Bryan, ed. (1993) *Citizenship and Social Theory*, London: Sage.

Uvin, Peter (1997) 'Prejudice, crisis and genocide in Rwanda', *African Studies Review*, 40:2, 91–115.

van der Ploeg, Irma (1999) 'The illegal body: "Eurodac" and the politics of biometric identification', *Ethics and Information Technology*, 1:4, 295–302.

van der Ploeg, Irma (2005) *The Machine-Readable Body*, Maastricht: Shaker.

Vila, Pablo (2000) *Crossing Borders, Reinforcing Borders: Social Categories, Metaphors and Narratives on the US–Mexican Frontier*, Austin: University of Texas Press.

Volf, Miroslav (1996) *Exclusion and Embrace: A Theological Exploration of Identity, Otherness and Reconciliation*, Nashville, TN: Abingdon.

Webb, Maureen (2007) *The Illusion of Security: Global Surveillance and Democracy in a Post-9/11 Era*, San Francisco: City Lights.

Weizman, Eyal (2007) *The Hollow Land: Israel's Architecture of Occupation*, London: Verso.

Wickins, Jeremy (2007) 'The ethics of biometrics: The risk of social exclusion from the widespread use of electronic identification', *Science and Engineering Ethics*, 13, 45–54.

Wilson, Dean (2006) 'Biometrics, borders and the ideal suspect', in Sharon Pickering and Leanne Weber, eds, *Borders, Mobility and Technologies of Control*, Berlin: Springer-Verlag.

Wilson, Dean (2008) 'Australian biometrics and global surveillance', *International Criminal Justice Review*, 17:3, 207–19.

Winner, Langdon (2002) 'Complexity, trust and terror', *Tech Knowledge Revue*, 3:1, available at *www.netfuture.org/2002/Oct2202_137.html*, accessed 23 December 2008.

Wright, David, Serge Gutwirth, Michael Friedewald, Elena Vildjiounaite and Yves Punie, eds (2007) *Safeguards in a World of Ambient Intelligence*, New York: Springer.

Zedner, Lucia (2003) 'Too much security?', *International Journal of the Sociology of Law*, 31, 155–84.

Zedner, Lucia (2007) 'Fixing the future? The precautionary principle as security technology', paper presented at Technologies of In/Security, Oslo University, April.

Zedner, Lucia (2008) 'Epilogue: The inescapable insecurity of security technologies?', in Katja Frank Aas, Helene Oppen Gundhus and

Heidi Mork Lomell, eds, *Technologies of InSecurity: The Surveillance of Everyday Life*, New York and London: Routledge.

Zureik, Elia (2001) 'Constructing Palestine through surveillance practices', *British Journal of Middle Eastern Studies*, 8:2, 205–8.

Zureik, Elia, Lynda Harling-Stalker, Emily Smith, David Lyon and Yolande E. Chan (forthcoming) *Privacy and Surveillance: International Survey*, Montreal and Kingston: McGill-Queen's University Press.

Zureik, Elia with K. Hindle (2004) 'Governance, security and technology: The case of biometrics', *Studies in Political Economy*, 73, 113–37.

Zureik, Elia and M. Salter (eds) (2005) *Global Surveillance and Policing: Borders, Security and Identity*, Cullompton, UK: Willan.

Zureik, Elia with Emily Smith, Lynda Harling-Stalker and Shannon Yurke (2006) 'International surveillance and privacy opinion research', The Surveillance Project, Queen's University, Kingston, Ontario, 13 November, *www.surveillanceproject.org/research/intl_survey/*, accessed 31 December 2008.

Index

Access Card, Australia 58–9,
    149
active vs consumer citizenship
    140
actuarial justice 102
Africa
    colonial countries 29
    ID card systems 63
Agamben, G. 14, 92
airport security 89, 91, 96, 106, 112,
    116
'ambient intelligence' (AmI) *see*
    ubiquitous computing
Amoore, Louise 73–4, 90, 91–2
Angola 63
Argentina 31, 32
Asher, Hank 76
asylum seekers 115–16, 144–5
Australia, Access Card 58–9, 149
authentication/verification 78–9,
    94, 103, 111, 114–15

Backhouse, James 84
Bauman, Zygmunt 1, 2, 13, 25,

    88–9, 126, 140, 141,
    147–8
Belgium
    e-ID Card 10, 58
    Rwanda 29–30, 47
benefit/welfare claimants 48–9,
    50–1, 54, 122
Bertillon, Alphonse 31
Bigo, Didier 54, 147
    and Guild, Elspeth 143
biometrics 53, 78–9, 110–13, 143
    civil liberties critique of 117–18,
        119
    companies 117–18, 119
    culture of 123–7
    marginalized/ethnic groups
        120–2, 145–6
    radio frequency identification
        (RFID)-enabled passports
        96–7, 102–3
    and related surveillance
        technologies 127–9
    as solution to identification
        problems 113–19

tolerance ranges for identification
115–17
'triple deficit' of 118
biopower 77, 107, 123–4
Blair, Tony 59, 81, 140
Blunkett, David 119, 144–5
'bodily integrity' 124
body
in surveillance assemblage 97–8
see also biometrics
borders 142, 146
airport security 89, 91, 96, 106,
112, 116
and globalization 89, 90, 98
US–Canada 3–4, 57, 150
Bowker, Geoffrey and Star, Susan
Leigh 39, 120
Breckenridge, Keith 87
Brill, Steven 72–3
British colonies 21, 28–9, 29, 31,
35–6
Brown, Gordon 84
business practices 52–3
see also card cartel (oligopoly)

Canada 3–4, 49, 112–13, 150
identity theft and interoperability
95
'Maple Leaf' card 145
'permanent resident' status
66–7
'Security and Prosperity
Partnership' 91
Social Insurance Card 36
Canada–US border 3–4, 57, 150
Caplan, Jane 21
card cartel (oligopoly) 63–5
controlling the means of
identification 69–71
multi-purpose IDs 141–2
politics of 71–2
procurements 71–6
protocols 71–2, 74–5, 76–9
technologies 64, 65, 74–5, 76–9

technology corporations 68–9,
72–6
theoretical perspectives 65–9,
79–82
CCTV (closed-circuit television) 60
Ceyhan, Ayse 5, 13
China 89, 142
Chinese Exclusion Act (1882), US
31
Citizen Identification Act (1943),
US 32
citizenship
challenges for 131–5
development of modern 135–8
and globalization 138, 139–42,
145
historical perspective 24–5
IDs and prospects for 148–51
rights and obligations 46–9, 67,
82, 131, 132
social sorting 41, 43–6, 49–55,
142–8
'citizenship data' 6–7
civil liberties
critique of biometrics 117–18,
119
opposition to ID cards 59–60, 96,
151
Total Information Awareness
(TIA) scheme 100
vs national security 147
civil society 152–3
Clarke, Roger 50
closed-circuit television (CCTV) 60
Cole, Simon 31, 32
Colley, Linda 35–6
colonialism 21, 23, 27–30, 35–6
'internal colonialism' 26
consumerism 73–4, 81, 106–7,
139–40
'core identity' 9, 10, 12
credit cards 36, 51–2, 56, 128, 139
crime control
DNA databases 127–8

crime control (*cont.*)
  historical perspective 30–3
  ID checks 85–6
  see also fingerprinting; terrorism
'cyber-citizenship' 133–4

dactyloscopy 32
  see also fingerprinting
Dandeker, Christopher 33
data-input errors 51
data protection laws 96, 98
data sharing 100–1, 149
'dataveillance' 50–1, 55–6
Delanty, Gerard 138
Deleuze, Gilles 77, 107, 154
democracy 138, 150–1
  and civil society 152–3
democratic participation 141, 150
'disappearing bodies' 125
discipline and control 77, 89–90,
  93–4, 107, 120
'disembodied' information 124–5
DNA databases 127–8
drivers' licences 48
  enhanced 3–4, 49, 56, 133, 134,
  150

e-Government 46, 71, 78, 81, 86,
  92, 134
e-ID Card, Belgium 10, 58
East Germany/German Democratic
  Republic 26, 85
elasticity of screening processes 89
Ellison, Larry 64, 72
Enhanced Border Security and Visa
  Entry Reform Act (2002), US
  97, 112
errors 51, 115–16
ethnicity
  Rwanda 29–30, 47
  see also immigration;
    marginalized/vulnerable groups
European Union (EU) 96, 98–9,
  101–2, 117, 118, 139–40

Eurodac system 120–1
Schengen visa policies 143–4
exclusion 146–7
  marginalized groups 53–4, 105,
  132, 140
  vs inclusive model of citizenship
  141, 147

facial recognition systems (FRSs)
  111–12, 116–17
Federal Bureau of Investigation
  (FBI), US 110–11, 114, 116
fingerprinting
  digitalized 111–12, 114
  Eurodac system 120–1
  historical perspective 21, 28–9,
  31–3
  misidentification errors 115–16
Finland 6
Food and Drug Administration
  (FDA), US 127
Foucault, Michel 20, 77, 107, 123,
  154
France 149
  historical perspective 21, 25, 36
French Canada 23
function creep 36, 59

Galloway, Alexander 77–8, 93, 94,
  107
Gandy, Oscar 51, 55, 105, 106–7
Garcelon, Marc 26, 27
Garland, David 141
Gates, Kelly 133
genetic data 127–8
German Democratic Republic/East
  Germany 26, 85
Germany 25, 36, 47
globalization 7, 8
  and borders 89, 90
  and citizenship 138, 139–42, 145
  of surveillance 54–5, 97–8
  see also interoperability; screens/
    screening

Goddard, Acting Lord Chief Justice
19
Goffman, Erving 9
governing by identification 90–2,
105, 106–7, 111–12, 142
Groebner, Valentin 19, 138
Gypsies 20

Haggerty, Kevin and Ericson,
Richard 55, 97–8, 125
Haque, Azizul, 29
Hayles, Katherine 124–5
health cards 36
healthcare and genetic data 128
Heidegger, Martin 13, 79–80
Henry, Edward, 29
Herschel, Sir William 28–9
Higgs, Edward 24
historical perspective 19–22
colonialism 21, 23, 27–30,
35–6
continuity and change 35–6
crime control 30–3
legibility of citizens 22–7
slave pass system 19–20, 27–8
war-time 33–5, 39, 73, 99
Home Affairs Identification System
(HANIS), South Africa 87
Hood, Leroy 128
human rights *see* civil liberties; rights
and obligations of citizens
Hungary 132

IBM (International Business
Machines) 25, 32, 47, 73–4
ID cards (inc. national systems)
contemporary 2–6
definition and types 6–8
identity and identification 8–15
and Other 11–12, 13–15
and registry databases 42–6
see also biometrics; card cartel
(oligopoly); citizenship;
interoperability; screens/

screening; sorting systems;
specific countries
Identity Cards Act (2006), UK
10–11
identity theft 51–2, 64, 95–6,
119
immigration 99–100
asylum seekers 115–16, 144–5
and citizenship 145
historical perspective 24, 31–2
radio frequency identification
(RFID) 91
and terrorism 40, 84, 100–1
inclusive vs exclusive models of
citizenship 141, 147
India 21, 28–9, 31
Indian Telegraph Act (1885) 29
'interim form' of citizenship 145
'internal colonialism' 26
internal passports 25–7, 69
International Biometric Industry
Association 117
International Civil Aviation
Organization (ICAO) 54–5,
90, 92, 95, 96–7, 102, 103,
112
internet
access and denial 139, 146–7
see also interoperability; screens/
screening
interoperability 87, 90, 95–8, 144
cases 101–3
contexts 98–101
and national security 94–5
Interpol 84, 86, 99
Introna, Lucas 116, 117
Isin, Engin 136
and Turner, Bryan 145
Israel, ID cards 46, 132

Japan 58, 135, 145
Juki-Net/Juki-Card 49, 149

Kaldor, Mary 60

LaserCard 44, 52–3, 63
Latour, Bruno 77
legibility 22–7, 46–9, 82
Lessig, Lawrence 31, 77, 94
Levinas, Emmanuel 13–14
liquidity 88–90, 107
Lodge, Juliet 118

machine-readable travel documents
        (MRTDs) 95, 96, 112
Malaysia 49, 135, 139
'Maple Leaf' card, Canada 145
marginalized/vulnerable groups 39,
        40, 61, 82, 138
    biometric identification 120–2,
        145–6
    exclusion 53–4, 105, 132, 140
    facial recognition systems (FRSs)
        116–17
    Other 11–12, 13–15, 142–3,
        147–8, 153
    power relations 153–4
    see also ethnicity
Marks & Spencer 73–4
Marshall, T.H. 24–5, 136, 141
Marx, Gary 10
    and Reichman, Nancy 51
Marx, Karl 69
Matrix identification technology 76
Mexico 43, 91,
    knowledge of surveillance
        technologies 105
    RFID implants in 128
Microsoft 78, 98–9
military service and citizenship 34, 39
misidentification risks 91–2, 115–17
Muller, Benjamin 132
multi-purpose IDs 141–2

'national citizenship' 136, 139
national ID cards *see* biometrics;
        card cartel (oligopoly);
        citizenship; ID cards
        (inc. national systems);

interoperability; screens/
        screening; sorting systems;
        specific countries
'national' identity 14
national registry databases 7, 42–6
national security
    argument for ID cards 56–7, 58,
        60, 64
    and interoperability 94–5
    see also terrorism
Nazi regime 25, 47
Nigeria 63
NO2ID campaign, UK 151
Noiriel, Gérard 25

O'Harrow, Robert 75, 76
O'Neil, Patrick 118, 119
oligopoly *see* card cartel
Other 11–12, 13–15, 142–3, 147–8,
        153
    see also ethnicity; immigration;
        marginalized/vulnerable groups
outsourced services 52–3
    see also card cartel (oligopoly)

Palestine 132
'panoptic sort' 51, 105, 106
panopticon 77, 93–4
passenger name record (PNR) 96
passports 2–3, 4, 23, 67–8, 69, 99
    internal 25–7, 69
    machine-readable travel
        documents (MRTDs) 95, 96,
        112
    radio frequency identification
        (RFID)-enabled biometric
        96–7, 102–3
    vs ID cards 70
political issues 57–61, 71–2, 120, 152
political vs consumer citizenship 140
Portugal 9, 36
Poster, Mark 107
power relations 120, 153–4
PricewaterhouseCoopers 73, 74

privacy issues 91, 150
  see also civil liberties
protocols
  card cartel 71–2, 74–5, 76–9
  screening 92–5, 104, 105, 106–7

Quebec 132

Raab, Charles 10–11
radio frequency identification
    (RFID) 91, 150
  -enabled biometric passports
    96–7, 102–3
  implants 127, 128–9
Real ID Act/system, US 3–4, 75–6,
    133, 149
remote control 143–4
resistance
  to national ID cards 3–4, 149
  to ubiquitous computing 107
  see also civil liberties
Ricoeur, Paul 126
rights and obligations of citizens
    46–9, 67, 82, 131, 132
Rose, Nikolas 5, 67, 68, 69, 71
Rule, James 56
Russia and Soviet Bloc countries
    26–7, 85
Rwanda 29–30, 47

Salter, Mark 99, 106, 107
Schengen visa policies, EU 143–4
Schütz, Alfred 14
Scott, James 23, 36, 70
screens/screening 85–6
  governing by identification 90–2,
    105, 106–7, 111–12, 142
  identification protocols 92–5,
    104, 105, 106–7
  liquidity and identification 88–90,
    107
  triage 106–7
  ubiquitous computing 92–3, 95,
    103–5

  see also interoperability
'securitized' identity 67–8, 69, 71–2,
    97, 154
'Security and Prosperity Partnership'
    91
'self-attesting body' 126
Sengupta, Shuddhabrata 29
Simmel, Georg 30
slave pass system, US 19–20, 27–8
Slovenia 131, 132
social aspects of identification 66, 67
social insurance cards 36
'social sorting' 41, 43–6, 49–55,
    142–8
'solidarity' aspect of citizenship 141
sorting systems 39–41
  panoptic 51, 105, 106
  politics of 57–61
  social 41, 43–6, 49–55, 142–8
  surveillant 55–7
South Africa
  apartheid era 25–6
  Home Affairs Identification
    System (HANIS) 87
Soviet Bloc countries 26–7, 85
Suchman, Lucy 120
surveillance
  global assemblage 97–8
  and identification 5–6, 11–12,
    137
  panopticon 77, 93–4
surveillant sorting 55–7
Swire, Peter 63
Szreter, Simon 132

Talon (US Department of Defense
    database) 40
Taylor, Charles 14
Taylor, John, Lips, Miriam and
    Organ, Joe 48
technologies 5, 7–8, 13, 40
  see also biometrics; card cartel
    (oligopoly); interoperability;
    screens/screening

terrorism 54, 58, 92, 133
   9/11 and aftermath 64, 75–6, 80,
      95, 97, 100, 104, 106, 112, 134
   and immigration 40, 84, 100–1
   and risk perception 118–19
   see also national security
Torpey, John 23, 67–8, 69–70
travel 22
Trends in Biometrics report 117–18

ubiquitous computing 92–3, 95,
      103–5, 107, 146
United Kingdom (UK)
   benefit claimants 48–9
   British colonies 21, 28–9, 29, 31,
      35–6
   closed-circuit television (CCTV)
      60
   data sharing 100–1
   early criminal identification 31
   'essential nationhood' and threats
      35–6
   ID cards 34–5, 40, 51–2, 58, 59,
      74, 80–1, 101–2, 112, 140,
      141, 144–5, 150, 151
   Identity Cards Act (2006) 10–11,
      95
   and Interpol database 84
   National DNA Database 127–8
   National Register, development
      of 34–5
   NO2ID campaign 151
   online services 48
United States (US)
   Chinese Exclusion Act (1882)
      31
   Citizen Identification Act (1943)
      32
   data sharing 100
   early crime control 30, 31
   Enhanced Border Security and
      Visa Entry Reform Act (2002)
      97, 112

enhanced drivers' licence 3–4, 49,
      56, 133
Federal Bureau of Investigation
      (FBI) 110–11, 114, 116
Food and Drug Administration
      (FDA) 127
immigration 24, 31–2
and International Civil Aviation
      Organization (ICAO) 96–7,
      112
national ID card system software
      64, 72
radio frequency identification
      (RFID)-enabled biometric
      passports 96–7, 102–3
Real ID Act/system 3–4, 75–6,
      133, 149
'Security and Prosperity
      Partnership' 91
slave pass system 19–20, 27–8
Talon (Department of Defense
      database) 40
United States (US)–Canada border
      3–4, 57, 150

van der Ploeg, Irma 110, 124, 125,
      146
verification/authentication 78–9,
      94, 103, 111, 114–15
Verified Identity Pass Inc. (VIP)
      72–3
Volf, Miroslav 12
Vucetich, Juan 32
vulnerable groups *see* marginalized/
      vulnerable groups

war-time 33–5, 39, 73, 99
Weber, Max 69
welfare state and citizenship 136–7,
      141
welfare/benefit claimants 48–9,
      50–1, 54, 122
Wilson, Dean 78–9